OF SCHOOL
AND WOMEN

D.S. MARQUIS

This book is a work of narrative nonfiction.
Names and identifying details have been changed.

Published by BookLocker.com, Inc., Trenton, Georgia
2021

Printed on acid-free paper.

Library of Congress Cataloging in Publication Data
Marquis, D.S.
Of School and Women by D.S. Marquis
Library of Congress Control Number: 2021911090

Cover design by D.S. Marquis
Cover photographs © Author Collection

**For information regarding this book,
please email the author at:**
ofschoolandwomenauthor@gmail.com

Or, visit:
dsmarquisamericanauthor.com

DEDICATION

This book is dedicated to my friends and loved ones who lived in Tallahassee during 1985-1987. And to all hardcore people with strong work ethics, who lived life without cell phones, the internet, computers, and social media. And to anyone, who has ever worked persistently toward a goal and re-invented themself.

AND ESPECIALLY TO:

My Beloved Family

My BFF

Editor Michael Denneny

Professor Rod Kessler

FOREWORD

Of School and Women is a work of narrative nonfiction. Names and details have been changed to protect everyone's privacy. Most events in the story are true. In some instances, the personal experiences of more than one person have been blended into one character in the story. This was done to drive the plot and create suspense.

Chapter 1

From her two-room apartment at Alumni Village, Lynette couldn't see the campus, but she could picture it. The university was out there, she knew, beyond the projects and tenements that crowded her brick strip of off-campus housing. The big quad bordered by streets dotted with palm, magnolia, and cypress trees draped with Spanish moss, the immense football stadium looming in the distance, and the quiet pathways, where students strolled along with their book bags. Would she find friends now that she was on her own? Would she find a job that would provide enough money to pay bills? Would someone like her fit in here? What would these spoiled college coeds think if they knew about the places she had been? The things she had done.

She managed to keep the past hidden from her folks. She wondered if there were any other fresh young coeds who'd been punched by the likes of Papa Joe. Or who'd bunked with an ex-con and ex-hooker. When it came to a wet T-shirt contest and burlesque dancing at the club, she knew her way around, but how would school go for her now? Academic achievement came easy at community college. A three-point-eight grade point average, while earning her Associate's Degree, was proof of that. But was the reckless lifestyle behind her?

The whistling of the tea kettle and a knock at the door interrupted her thoughts. "Just a minute," she yelled, while shutting off the burner on the stove. She ran toward the door, flipped on the exterior light, and peered through the peephole. "Who is it?" Lynette yelled through the closed door.

"It's John, I live up the street." The voice was muffled.

Lynette opened the door as wide as the chain lock would allow. The eyes staring back at her from the smooth, youthful face of the well-built man, were not smiling.

"Hi, I was wonderin' if maybe I could borrow your basketball?" he asked.

Lynette glanced in the direction of her basketball under the plant stand, and then back at the stranger, and lied. "It's almost flat, and besides it's my boyfriend's, so I really can't loan it out. Sorry," she said. "Listen I have to go, it's nice to meet you." More lies. Then she quickly closed the door and turned the deadbolt. Without hesitation, she reached for the cord of the curtains, jerking them closed. Her mind raced with questions. Who the hell wants to play basketball with me? I'm short and I'm white. Who plays basketball at this time of night? Did he see the basketball through the window? What did he do, climb over the bushes and press his face against the glass to see in? How else did he know there was a basketball in here? Lynette had the creeps. And this was all too familiar. She saw the seven-digit number scratched on the scrap of paper laying on the table. She picked up the phone receiver from its cradle and dialed. After four rings, the machine answered. "Hello, this is Warren Jones. Leave your name and number at the tone, and I will return the call."

"Hey Warren, it's Lynette next door. I know we just met, and it's late, but I saw your light on when I came in a little while ago, and, a-a-h, I'm kinda worried about a prowler. Please, call me back as soon as possible. My number is 644-2567." Lynette hung up the phone and returned to the kitchen cabinets to take out a mug. Minutes later, she was relieved to hear the phone ring.

"Hello," said Lynette.

"Hi, it's Warren."

"Thanks for calling back, I was wondering if you've noticed anyone hanging around here looking in the windows?"

"No, why?"

"I feel like I'm being stalked."

"What's going on?"

"Some strange guy just knocked at my door and asked to borrow a basketball. It's just too weird." Calming down slightly from the sound of a familiar voice, Lynette was hoping she was overreacting.

"Well, call me anytime. I'll be home all night. If I notice anyone, I'll let you know. Alright?" Warren sounded reassuring.

"Ok, thanks."

"Bye," said Warren.

"Bye," said Lynette. She hung up the phone.

She wanted to pour the hot water in her cup, but instead she listened to the little voice in her head that told her to secure the apartment. She thought of the bedroom window and slipped toward the doorway, where she detected the wide opened curtains. To decrease being visible by anyone who might be outside, she edged herself along the wall in the darkness of the bedroom. The bricks were cold and rough against her hand and they brushed at her shirt. At arms-length now, from the window frame, she reached out and clutched the draw string of the drapes. Before pulling them closed, looking out, from the edge of the window, she spotted a figure of someone crouching in the shadows behind the line of hedges. The outline of a person's head was certain. From that position there was a perfect view of her bedroom. *Shit, it's him. He's out there.* She jerked the cord, turned, then bounded through the doorway toward the phone in the kitchen and dialed nine-one-one, "My name is Lynette Autry, there's a peeping Tom at Three Two Seven Pennell Circle, Apartment number one."

"Are you inside your home or outside?" the woman's voice asked from the other end of the phone.

"Inside," said Lynette.

"Ok, good, I am sending an officer to you," said the woman. "Are your doors and windows locked?"

"Yes."

"Ok, great. The officer should be there within ten minutes. Is there anything else you can tell me about the suspect?"

"Umm," Lynette swallowed. "He's tall, young, clean-shaven. His hair's shaved short. He's wearing black track pants with white stripes and a matching jacket. He's black."

"Do you want me to stay on the line with you?"

"No, I'm ok, I'm going to call my neighbor again and see if he can see anything out his window."

"Lynette, what apartment is your neighbor in?"

"He's in Apartment two."

"Ok, I'm going to hang up now," said the phone dispatcher.

"Ok, thanks." Lynette pressed the dial tone button and made another call.

"Warren, it's me, can you stay on the phone with me until the cops get here?"

"You called the police?"

"Yeah, the guy's behind the building, I saw him creeping around the bushes."

"Don't worry. He probably just wants to watch you."

"Right. I'm totally freaking out." Another knock came. "Oh My God, there's someone at the door. Hold on." She set the phone receiver on the table, and stealthily she moved to the door and looked through the peephole. *Fuck, it's him again.* Lynette responded with silence.

"I found a basketball. Do you want to come out and play with me?" asked the stranger outside.

Lynette remained quiet. She tiptoed across the room, picked up the phone receiver from the kitchen table, leaned against the wall, and whispered, "It's him again. Go outside and distract him."

"I'm not going out there," said Warren. "Hold on. Let me see if I can see him. I'll be right back."

"Don't hang up," said Lynette.

"I won't."

Lynette could hear Warren set his phone receiver on a hard surface. Her breathing and her heart beating seemed too loud. She stared at the front door making sure that the knob didn't move. To free her hands, she held the receiver between her chin, and her shoulder. Then she slowly opened the kitchen drawer. She reached in and clasped hold of the wooden handle of a steak knife.

"Lynette, you still there?"

"Yeah, did you see him?"

"Yup he's out there. He's still standing near your door. He's holding a ball under his arm, looking out at the street. And, um, he's big."

What she heard next made her feel paralyzed. "He just knocked again."

"Is your door locked?" asked Warren.

"Of course, it's locked. I got the chain on too. Go look out your window again and see what he's doing now."

"Ok, hold on." Warren set down the phone again. Lynette waited in dread. Then she could hear Warren fumbling with the phone. "The cops are here," he said. "They're getting out of the car now."

"Thank God, alright, thanks. I'll call you later." Lynette hung up, set the knife on the table, and darted to the door to look through the peephole in time to see the officer lift his fist to knock.

"Leon County Police," said the officer.

Lynette removed the chain, unlatched the deadbolt, and opened the door. "Hi, I'm Lynette the one who called about a peeping tom." She recapped the story. She gestured toward her basketball.

"Ma'am, have you seen the guy before?" asked the officer. He shifted his weight to one leg.

"No, just tonight."

"We are patrolling the area now. Are you alright?"

"Yes, now that you're here."

"You're not the first to report incidents of this nature. Other residents have seen someone looking in windows around the property." He used his thumb and forefinger to pinch a small notebook from the front pocket of his uniform. Before he could write anything, the radio on the officer's belt blared.

"Suspect apprehended at radio station parking lot." The officer returned the notebook to his pocket, and now held the walkie-talkie to his mouth.

"This is Nelson, I'm at apartment one, copy," He paused, now looking at Lynette. Radio static filled the air. "Ma'am, we got him."

"Thank you, Officer."

"Good work, calling when you did. Call us if you need anything else. My name is Officer Nelson."

"I will. Thanks again."

"Goodnight, Ma'am."

"Goodnight." Lynette closed and locked the door. She exhaled gustily, then turned to see the phone on the wall. After dialing Warren's number again, she spoke before he could say hello, "Hey, they got him."

"It'll be hard to sleep tonight," said Warren.

Lynette agreed. "Thanks again for everything. Goodnight." She hung up the phone, then turned around to switch on the stove burner to make the cup of tea she tried to make earlier. She realized she was exhausted. Dampness lingered from days of rain. She kicked off her shoes. The tile floor was cold. She crossed the room to turn on the small thirteen-inch television.

"We are live from the Orange Bowl in Miami Florida. The Dolphins and New England Patriots meet in a key AFC match up. On the line tonight, with a win, they will take their first divisional title since nineteen seventy-eight. As for the Dolphins, a win tonight and a win next week against Buffalo, and they are assured the AFC title. The Orange Bowl here in Miami is alive with anticipation! The Patriots tonight are pinning their hopes for a divisional title in the strong arm of Tony Eason. With fine running from Craig James, Tony Collins, Eason can look deep to a pair of wide receivers that can burn you from any spot on the field. There's Irving Fryar. Then there's this veteran, Stanley Morgan."

Lynette was fantasizing about her boyfriend, Claude. He would be watching the game in Destin. The television flickered light around the little living room where Lynette now sat on the green vinyl love seat.

"This ABC sports exclusive is brought to you by Lite Beer from Miller. Everything you ever wanted from a beer and less. By Chevrolet, who invites you to live the style and performance of Chevrolet in eighty-six, by Handicam, the astonishingly simple new Sony Handicam. All the excitement of video movies by Sony in the palm of your hands. And by IBM."

She stared at the screen, waiting for the whistle of the tea kettle to summons her back to the stove.

"Hello again, everyone, I am Frank Gifford, along with my colleagues O.J. Simpson and Joe Namath and all of our guys behind our ABC scene. We are delighted to have you with us tonight. We think we could have a real stunner for you. Two football teams within the same division, the AFC. They are two hot football teams."

The soothing sound of the whistle came. Lynette poured hot water into her mug, then dropped in a tea bag. She reached for the tag hanging on a string. On it a quote, *Fresh starts and change go hand in hand*. She smiled to herself. "Nice," she said. Then her head turned to the T.V.

"They have been battling all season. The New England Patriots with a win tonight can clinch this division. They have won eight of their last nine games. They lost the other game in overtime to the Jets."

Realizing the drink was too hot to drink, she reached into her only kitchen drawer, clutched a spoon and began stirring.

"Meanwhile, the Miami Dolphins were defeated November the third, by this New England team. They have won five in a row. But there is something called the jinx over New England. That little black cloud. Remember the little character called little Abner?"

She dropped the spoon into the sink, carried her cup to the desk to the right of the T.V., setting it down next to a cardboard box and a Corona typewriter.

"Every time the New England Patriots come to the Orange Bowl, they go away with a loss. The last time they won here was in nineteen sixty-six, ladies and gentlemen. They have lost seventeen consecutive games here at the Orange Bowl. The players..."

She stepped over to the T.V. set and reached over to shut it off. The room fell silent. The last unpacked box called for attention. She lifted out pencils, pens, paper, paper clips, white out, boxes of typewriter ribbon and correction tape and filled her desk drawers. Stopping occasionally to sip at her tea, she held her paint brushes, and file folders before organizing them neatly. When the box was empty, she carried it over near the front door and set it on the floor. After sipping the last of her tea and putting the cup in the sink, she shut off the desk light. "I've had it," she mumbled.

Her break from worry came when she began her nightly routine. After brushing and flossing her teeth, she stood looking in the mirror, unbuttoning her blouse, until it slipped from her shoulders. She hung it on the doorknob, then did the same with her lacy beige wire bra. She reached her arms around the back of her waist and unzipped her skirt, which dropped and met a kick to the corner of the room. As did the bikini panties. She glanced at her ivory skin, full breasts, and thin waist. She smiled, admiring her straight teeth inside her sharply etched natural lips. "Damn, I'm good looking," she said.

After a shower, her body welcomed a warm flannel nightgown and a triple blanketed double bed. She switched off the lamp, and felt fear climb into bed with her. Lying on her back under the covers, she realized she was living alone in her own apartment for the first time in her life. Sure, she had been on her own since eighteen, but she had always shared an apartment with someone. Someone who was trouble. Her peeping tom was not her old roommate's thieving pal, Papa Joe. She had no black eye, and the only one who had held a knife in their hand tonight had been her. So, she doffed her cloak of trepidation and opted for consoling nostalgia. She reminisced on her decision to move back home with her mom and stepdad for six months. She was glad for the time with them and all their help on move day.

* * *

"This place sure is dingy," said Lynette's mother. She'd been scrubbing the bathroom tub, but had stopped now, and was holding a filthy sponge in her hand. Lynette's mother looked at the sponge and shook her head.

"Yeah, I need a bug man too," said Lynette. She swept a cockroach into a dustpan. The front door burst open and a man came in, red-faced and out of breath. In his hand, Lynette saw a bottle.

"Didn't you see me flashing my lights? I had to pee so bad, I ended up going in my Pepsi bottle," said Daddy. He rushed through the doorway into the bedroom. He glared at Lynette. "Mmm, Mmm, Mmm, Eva Maria."

Lynette learned years ago that expression meant that this daddy, mother's husband-number-three, her step-dad-number-two, was really irritated. The first time he had said it was during dinner one night when he announced that he couldn't believe he'd married someone who smoked and had a kid. He went on further to add that he swore he'd never marry someone who had been divorced either. And back then he shook his head, and said "Mmm, Mmm, Mmm, Eva Maria" just like he did now.

"Where's Momma?" asked Daddy. Lynette pointed to the bathroom door, which was open. He stepped through the doorway. "Hi, Momma," He bent and kissed her on the head. She was sitting on the edge of the tub rinsing out a bucket. "Don't look, Momma," Daddy emptied the Pepsi bottle into the toilet and then slosh went the water. Momma laughed.

"Oh, come here," said Momma. "Let me give you a hug to make you feel better." Momma stood up stretching her arms out in front her body. Daddy returned her affection and wrapped his arms around his wife.

"We're making good progress. Don't you think?" Momma asked.

"The bathroom looks good," Daddy praised and then asked, "What can I do to help?"

"Here," Momma passed him a box from the floor. "Take this out of here."

Stepping out of the bathroom, with an empty box in hand, Daddy stopped at the bureau, where Lynette stood unzipping a duffle bag.

"The weather forecast calls for sun tomorrow, but it will be cold tonight, thirty-five degrees, so wear your long johns, daughter." Daddy dropped the box he had been holding. "When is the power scheduled to be turned on?"

"Tuesday, I think, four days without hot water." Lynette held socks in her hand.

"Maybe you can run an extension cord from your neighbor's apartment so you can have a light in here?"

"What am I supposed to say? Hi, I'm Lynette. I just wanted to know if you could give me some free electricity." She opened a drawer and threw in a handful of t-shirts. "Oh, that sounds lovely."

"Oh, come on, it won't be that bad," said Daddy. "It's better than being in the dark half the week." He was flattening the box.

Lynette knew he was probably right, and she sighed. "Ok, I'm going," she said. She stepped out of the bedroom and took the few steps through the living area to the front door, opened it and stepped out into the pouring rain, walked twenty feet past the rhododendron bushes and the sliding glass door that offered a full view of her kitchenette, then to the neighbor's apartment door and knocked. When the door opened, Lynette saw a clean shaven, wavy blonde haired, petit man.

"Hi, I'm your new neighbor, Lynette Autry." She reached out for a handshake.

"I'm Warren Jones, Nice to meet you," he said. "Lousy weather for moving. What are you studying?"

"Right now, how to survive without electricity." Lynette glanced at the extension cord in her hand. "My power won't be on for a couple of days, the hurricane and all, has the Tallahassee Utilities company back logged with work orders. Any chance, I could run this from your unit so I can at least have a lamp on?" She lifted the extension cord in her hands to show it to him.

Warren's eyes widened, he shrugged his shoulders, "Sure, why not." He reached out for the plug and the cord Lynette passed him and plugged it into an outlet just inside his door.

Lynette noticed his deep pock-marked face and thought about how severe the acne must have been. "Thanks so much. I owe you." She smiled and looked down at the muddy, wet ground, where she would have to trail the cord.

"No problem, welcome to the neighborhood," said Warren. He bent to slide the cord under the door. "Hang on a minute, I'll give you my phone number in case you need anything else." He opened the door. "Come on in," said Warren. Lynette could see the apartment was the same floor plan as her own, galley to the right, green vinyl loveseat and desk to the left, bedroom straight ahead. She watched him grab a notebook and a pen from his loveseat, where lined up against it were framed splatter paintings. After scratching down his phone number, he tore out the sheet of paper. Lynette reached out to accept it.

"I'm heading out now, so I'll see you later." Warren grabbed his keys off the loveseat and stuffed them into the front pocket of his jeans.

"Thanks again, Bye," said Lynette. The door of apartment two shut with a thump.

Lynette ran the orange extension cord behind the bushes flush against the building and carried the remaining coil of cord into apartment number one, where Daddy was searching through a toolbox on the floor. He looked up to see Lynette stepping toward a lamp. Her long ash blonde hair and flannel shirt were soaked now.

"Well?" he asked.

"Well," Lynette answered, "Now I know my new neighbor, Warren." She plugged the wicker lamp cord into the extension cord. And when the bulb lit up, she announced triumphantly, "And the Lord said, let there be light. And there was light!"

"Aha, I'm so glad that worked out," said Daddy.

Momma came in the room. "Me too."

Lynette was now taking off her wet shirt and hanging it on the kitchen chair to dry. The box marked, *KITCHEN*, sat on the floor waiting. She squatted to open it, then began stocking the old rusty metal kitchen cabinet sink combo with cereal, tea, and peanut butter.

"Single life isn't complete without these," said Lynette. She held a pack of Ramen noodles in one hand and a package of Oreos in the other. She looked over her shoulder at Daddy. "Thanks for the care package, it will come in handy. And thanks for the good idea about the neighbor's electricity."

"You're welcome," said Daddy. He hugged Lynette with one arm while holding a basketball under his other arm. "At least you didn't move in before Governor Graham lifted the state of emergency. I heard on the radio, that there were still some places without power from Hurricane Kate." He moved near the window, where he bent down to place the ball under a plant stand. "Extensive damage to the campus too. City-wide curfew is finally lifted, though." He picked up a long board and carried it across the room. "Momma," he yelled, "I'm almost done with the bookshelf." He set the board on top of two cinder blocks.

"Ok, well, the bed is made," said Momma. She was sitting on the bed, taking a break.

Daddy looked out the window at the diminishing daylight. "Well, I don't want to drive home in the dark. Let's finish up and go grub. Things look pretty good around here. Good job, Momma."

"Alright," said Momma. "I just want to hang the candle sconces. Can you get the hammer?"

Daddy went right to work. He took two long screws from the toolbox and met Momma at the brick work around the front door. After Daddy drove the screws into the cement between the bricks, Momma hung the sconces. "There! Looks very pretty!" said Momma. "What do you think, Lynette?"

Lynette had been spraying cleaner in the sink, and she turned around to see. "I love it," she said.

"I saw a Captain Dee's on the way in. It's about five minutes from here," said Daddy. He pulled on his coat, while Momma was heading for the front door. "Lynette, you can follow us there, and then we'll say goodbye from the restaurant."

Lynette tossed the last of the crumpled newspaper that she had been picking up off the floor, into a box. "Alright, I'm ready." She grabbed her flannel shirt, and her purse. Daddy held open the door. "You know, daughter, it could be good for you to have a guard dog.

Maybe Momma could bring Tashi here on her next visit. He's going to miss you."

* * *

Remembering the drive home from Captain Dee's that night, Lynette realized that her apartment was in the heart of a poor black neighborhood. Looking out the car window, she had seen the dilapidated porches, houses with hardly any paint left on them, and litter in between the weeds of front yards of Levy Avenue. She had lived in worse neighborhoods, and being broke, she thought, isn't illegal. Lying in bed now, she pondered the correlation between poverty and crime. She wondered if peeping tom lived on Levy Avenue.

She remembered how the rain poured down while she had groped through her purse for the front door key the first night that she came home to the apartment alone. Boxes, Windex, bleach, sponges, and rags were scattered throughout the apartment. Dishes were piled on the kitchen table. The tile floor was cold. The smell of floor wax and bleach tainted the air. No hot water. Carrying the lamp to the bathroom doorway dragging the slack extension cord behind. Taking a cold shower. Had the guy been watching her that night too?

She rolled on her side and reached into the nightstand to comfort herself with pink plastic rosary beads. They had been a part of her life since birth. She carefully wrapped the beads around her left hand and gently placed her thumb on the crucifix, where she rubbed the crusty glue that held the cracked cross together. As a young girl, she used to wonder if God was angry when the cross had split.

The Rosary, prayer endorsed by the Catholic Church, came from the Latin word, Rosarium, meaning crown of roses. The beads that the church meant for counting prayers, Lynette ritualized in a personal way. Her beads triggered memories of comfort and hopes for the future. They were her conduit from past to present. A symbol of faith. Her first memory of kneeling to pray was at age four. Her grand-mère by her side, discovering the mysteries of the clicking beads, Lynette had felt the pull of blind faith. Tonight, she prayed the *Hail Mary* and *Our Father*, and blessed all her loved ones, and thanked God for the good. Then she analyzed the day's evil.

"God bless the man, who was arrested. May he do better," whispered Lynette in the dark. Her right hand touched her forehead, her chest's center, then her chest's left and chest's right. She could hear the rain beginning to fall. The droplets tapping on the window made for a lullaby. Her eyes closed. She faded, and soon slept, eventually arriving at the deep REM sleep she had read about in her psychology books.

* * *

Which is worse, job hunting or working? Lynette had driven up and down the streets downtown, uptown, all over town all day filling out employment applications. Now on South Adams Street, she decided that the answer to that question was job hunting. Today was the worst. The morning had begun with a cold shower in chilly December weather. Now the sun was setting, and still no job. She could hear her mother's voice. "Don't come home from job hunting until you've got an offer. Even if it's not the job you want, the important thing is to secure income. You can always look for a better position later." And Lynette held herself to that standard. The downtown clock chimed four, and still no W-4 Form had been signed. A woodpecker was striking a tree trunk. He flew off when he heard the rustle of Lynette dropping onto a bench nearby. She sighed. Newspaper in one hand, pen in the other, Lynette reviewed the classified ads of the Tallahassee Democrat. Her expression was a mix of intent, and desperation, when the man in the blue suit jacket approached.

"Had any luck yet?"

Lynette looked up from the newspaper. "Not yet," she said. "And how did you know I'm in the market for a job? Is it the blue dress, the heels, the trench coat, or this?" She waved the classified ads, with the circle around the ad that read, *Wait Staff wanted: The Brass Rail, 228 South Adams St. Apply in person.*

"I'm a smart guy. And I'm the assistant manager of the Governor's Suite. I might have a position that could interest you. The name's Mike." His hand met Lynette's in a handshake. "And yours?"

"Lynette, nice to meet you."

"Do you have time to meet my boss at the restaurant?" asked Mike.

"That'd be great," said Lynette.

"Ok, see that door" he was now pointing toward an unmarked glass door. "That's the side entrance. Follow me," Lynette stood and walked alongside Mike. The sound of her heels snapped the pavement.

"Tell me something about your work experience."

"Well, I'm a transfer student at FSU and I've got six years of restaurant and bar experience." Lynette was hopeful that maybe Mike was her ticket home from the job hunt. Eagerly, keeping up his pace despite her tired feet, she now stood in front of the glass double doors, watching him jiggle his key in the lock. The door opened and Mike guided the way to an atrium decorated with two brass storks standing on the floor in the corner and a brass bonsai tree sculpture hanging on the wall. Lynette, now trying to appear graceful, followed Mike up a narrow staircase that wound around to the second floor. At the top, there was an open door at the end of the hall. "Looks like Mr. Reed is in. Mike gestured for Lynette to step ahead. "After you." Walking a few steps more, a man's voice drifted out the door.

"Alright, but don't let it happen again, because, heads will roll."

Lynette had reached the doorway and was now looking at the face of Mr. Reed, looking at her. His eyes were tightening. "I've got someone here, so later."

Precisely after the handset of the phone hit the receiver, Mike seized his opening. "Mr. Reed, this is Lynette, and she's interested in waitressing or bartending."

"Hello, Mr. Reed, it's nice to meet you." Lynette flashed a smile and turned her head toward Mike. "Thanks for all your help."

"Please sit down." Mr. Reed motioned toward a chair across from his desk, then glanced back at Mike. "Let me know when that shipment comes in tonight, will you?"

"Will do," said Mike.

"That'll be all," said Mr. Reed.

Lynette dropped into the seat in front of the desk, waved to Mike and watched him turn and leave.

"Tell me about yourself," said Mr. Reed.

"Well, I'm enrolled for winter semester at FSU. Classes begin the first week of January. I'm working my way through school and I need to work thirty to forty hours a week. I've been in the restaurant and bar business for six years now, and I've tended bar in the dingiest to the finest places. My first barmaid job was at a little dive in Colorado. I worked there while food waitressing at a Mexican restaurant. When my manager got tired of me working two jobs, he decided to train me behind the bar. After that, I moved to Destin, Florida, where I worked at a beach resort and a poolside Tiki Hut, which brings me to the present."

"Well, I've got nothing to offer you right at the present time, but there are a couple of waiters graduating this semester, who will be quitting in two weeks. I don't want to hire anyone until after the holidays, so call me in January and I'll have a job for you."

"Thank you very much for your time, Mr. Reed." Lynette stood to shake his hand. The phone rang, and Mr. Reed answered it.

"Yes, I'll speak to him. Stewart, did you get my message?" Lynette spoke in a whisper. "I'll call you in January." Mr. Reed responded with a nod. Lynette led herself out of the office and out of the restaurant.

Outside now, preparing for more pavement pounding, she sat at the bench where she had met Mike. She realized that her next stop was across the street. Grateful, she traipsed in that direction. Now standing at the door, in green and gold stenciled letters, Lynette read, "The Brass Rail open 5-10 pm." It was only four thirty and the joint wasn't open yet. Through paned glass, she could see the cooks were busy setting up the kitchen for dinner. She tried waving her hand, but that did not catch anyone's attention. She decided to walk back to her car, when she noticed a metal door to the left of the glass door facing east. The door was ajar. Lynette was not going to pass up the opportunity. It might lead to the Brass Rail. She felt the warm breath of conditioned air blow gently from inside the building, and she was about to grab the knob, when the overweight chef she had waved at through the glass, was walking toward her. "We don't open until five," he said. A cigarette protruded from the side of his mouth.

"I'm interested in applying for a waitress job."

"Alright." The chef stepped outside, now holding a match to his cigarette. "The guy to see is Tony. Come back at six, that's when he gets here."

"I'm Lynette." Her hand outstretched, she shook hands with the chef. A plume of smoke swirled above his head.

"The name's Jim."

"Jim, do you have an application I can fill out?"

"Sure, come on in and I'll see if I can find one." He took a final puff of his cigarette, threw it down, and stepped on it. Lynette followed him into the dining room, where they approached a buxom woman wearing an apron and holding a handful of silverware.

"Karen," said Chef Jim. "This is Lynette. She needs an application." Karen's eyes narrowed.

"Have you waitressed before?" asked Karen.

Lynette began the well-rehearsed interview spiel she had given Mr. Reed no more than twenty minutes earlier. All the while, she was walking behind Karen until they reached the hostess stand, where Karen rustled through its insides until she found an application that she extended in Lynette's direction. "Come back after six and I'll tell Tony you'll be here."

"Thanks a lot, I hear The Brown Derby is hiring, so I'm going to head over there and then I'll be back. Hope you make lots of money tonight."

Lynette was about to turn and head for the door, when she heard Karen, "Yeah, me too. Gotta make rent."

Steadily, Lynette trekked over the red cobble-stoned sidewalks back to her car. Keeping her heels from getting caught in between the bricks, she silently played a child's game at high stress times like these. "If you step on a crack, you'll break your mother's back." As a child she remembered being genuinely worried she might be home one day, when her mother walked in from work complaining of back pains. Lynette was always worried about something. In the big Winnie the Pooh book of life, she could relate to Piglet. Her cold exterior was a front a lot of the time, but deep down she knew she was more sensitive than most. When she read J.D. Salinger's, *The Catcher and the Rye*, she wondered if she was as sensitive as Holden Caulfield before his nervous breakdown. He had worried about the ducks in Central Park. *Where do they sleep at night and where do they go when it's cold?* She was sensitive now.

In the parking lot, she saw a grey bearded man walking toward her. Over his left shoulder he carried a black trash bag filled with what appeared to be aluminum cans. The filthy blue nylon jacket he wore flapped open. He glanced at Lynette with weary eyes, "Do you have a quarter?" he asked.

Lynette's response was to dig out three dimes and seven pennies from her pocketbook. When she dropped the coins in his hand, he smelled of a mixture of tobacco, ancient body odor, and alcohol. He tipped his torn stained beret, smiled, and said, "Thank ya, Ma'am."

Lynette was about to turn the corner, when she looked back at the old man, now bent over the trash receptacle foraging for more cans. She wondered where he would sleep tonight.

In her Toyota, she considered her job possibilities. Working at the Governor's Suite, the hours would be great for study time, but terrible for the bank account. All the job possibilities so far, assumed that if a college student wanted work, it had nothing to do with being self-sufficient. Lynette needed full time work to support herself, not just mad money for the weekend or Spring Break fun in Ft. Lauderdale.

She was determined. She searched her car floor for the Tallahassee map Claude had bought when they visited the city for the Tina Turner concert. She found the map and carefully traced out directions to the Brown Derby. She pulled the Toyota Corona out of the parking lot and onto Adams Street, turned right on Park, and left on Monroe. Almost missing the final turn, the tires screeched, when the car veered into the mall parking lot.

After carelessly driving the wrong way in the lot, she parked the car, brushed her hair, refreshed her lipstick, and stepped out into the evening air. Pen in hand, she entered The Brown Derby. The dining room was large. Near the hostess stand, the Christmas tree blocked the view of the main dining room. Soon, a hostess directed Lynette toward the back of the restaurant to a private dining area, where Lynette rushed through the application and waited for the manager.

The interview was over in a flash and the balding supervisor hired her that night with a start date of tomorrow's lunch shift. She had succeeded in landing a job. It would have been time to go home if it was the best job she could find. However, she decided to return to The Brass Rail, where there was potential for working dinner shifts in a much plusher place. Nights meant better money in the restaurant business. Bigger dinner tabs meant bigger tips.

She pulled her car into the utilities company parking lot. Parked now, sitting in her car, she grabbed a pen from the passenger seat, and on the dashboard, she filled out another application.

Inside the Brass Rail, a crowd was shuffling in for dinner. Lynette noticed the chef talking with a man, who was adjusting his necktie. He wore big black horned rim glasses. A second later, Karen appeared through a door that concealed a dark, musky stairwell. It looked like a perfect prohibition raid escape route. Lynette's eyes locked with Karen's and they stepped toward one another. The man with the glasses trailed beside her.

"Hi, forgive me I cannot remember your name," said Karen.

"Lynette Autry."

"Tony, Lynette's here to apply for a job. I told her you'd be here after six." Karen caught a glimpse of her wristwatch. "And here she is, eleven minutes past."

"Hello Lynette, I'm Tony Ruccolo. He reached out to shake hands. "I'm the assistant manager of The Brass Rail, Tuto Bene's, Andrew's Second Act, and Maxin's."

"A pleasure to meet you, Mr. Ruccolo," said Lynette.

"Let's go upstairs and we can talk." Tony gestured the way. Lynette tracked behind. The hall ended abruptly with another door ahead of them, revealing a carpeted stairwell. A waiter stopped to let them pass by. "Lenny! That case of Johnny Walker Black just came in. It's inside the door at the loading dock. Please bring it up to the bar."

Lenny nodded. "OK," he said, now hurrying down the stairs with a full tray of dishes hoisted on top of his shoulder. Lynette figured she must have looked perplexed, because Tony seemed to offer an answer to the question that was in her mind.

"The kitchen is downstairs. Maxin's Lounge is upstairs," said Tony.

As they climbed, slow jazz music poured over them. At the top of the stairs, the lounge was dark, with a sunken dance floor. The booths all around the main floor were raised up a step. A waitress wearing a black skirt, bow tie and black fish net stockings was lighting candles. A five-piece band played on stage, and sensual vocals came from a plump African goddess with corn rowed hair. Her song ended with a note of such strong primordial passion that the bartender, who had been counting money, looked up from the cash register. Lynette's soul drifted on the last note of the tune until the room fell silent. The goddess stepped off the stage and walked toward Lynette and Tony. The clicking beads in her hair broke the silence.

"Sound check is all good, we'll be back before eight," said the goddess.

"OK," said Tony. He walked toward the bar and interrupted the bartender's cash count. "Mary, any coffee? Lynette, would you like anything?"

"No thank you," said Lynette. She really could have used some, but she was proud of the fact that she never accepted anything on an interview no matter how informal.

The bartender set a napkin and a cup and saucer on the bar. "Thanks, Mary," said Tony. He added cream and sugar to his cup, and then carried it to a nearby table, where he and Lynette sat down.

"Here's my application," said Lynette, now handing over the document.

Tony began scanning it right away. "So, it looks like you've worked the front of the house and the back. Bartending, waitressing, busing, aerobic teaching, nurse's assistant, and preschool teaching. I like it," said Tony. He took hold of his cup. "What is your school schedule going to be like?" His mouth on the rim, he sipped his coffee and looked over at Lynette. His expression was thoughtful.

"I plan on school during the day and work at night." Lynette tucked her hair behind her ear.

"At this time of the year someone always quits, besides, legislature will be in session soon, so this place will be busy. As far as a bartender position is concerned, there are none. My bartenders have been with me for years and I'm not anticipating any resignations right now." Tony pushed his black rimmed eyeglasses closer to his face. "Call me in a few days and check in. I'll definitely have something for you."

"Alright, I'll call you on Thursday," said Lynette. "Should I wait until after six?"

"That would be fine." Tony stood and reached out his hand. Lynette willingly accepted his invitation to shake on it.

"Thanks for meeting with me, Tony." Lynette swung her head from side to side. "What is the best way out of here?" asked Lynette. Tony smiled and turned his head in the direction of the stairs.

"Bye, now."

During the chilly walk back to the car, Lynette smiled to herself. She would be starting her new waitress job in the morning. And she had landed two possible backup positions. She was planning to celebrate over a grilled cheese sandwich and shrimp flavored Ramen noodles as soon as she reached her apartment.

* * *

Lynette stood at her small kitchen table waiting for the coffee to drip. She emptied a pile of bills and coins from the apron pocket, still tied around her waist. Tips were fair for a weeknight, but would she make enough to pay February's rent? She was grateful that the apartment had electricity and she had work. Lynette's time serving Grogs and Prime Rib at the Brown Derby was winding down. She had only been there two weeks, when Tony called with a start date at the Brass Rail. She couldn't wait to get out of the Derby. She had enough of the short lunch hours, white trash, weak tips, and conversations in the wait station about spouse abuse and drug abuse. It was depressing. She realized she was the only college student working day shift. One waitress had come to work with bruises on her arm and face. Lynette wondered about the bruises she couldn't see under the uniform. At least she hadn't gone hungry at the Derby, and she earned enough cash to cover January's rent. She was allowed any one meal at no cost from the lunch menu per shift and each of those meals she devoured during the two short weeks of employment. "Work in a restaurant, Lynette, and you'll never go hungry," her mother had always told her. She untied her waitress apron, turned and threw it on the kitchen table. Then she pulled out a chair and sat down. Courses would begin in a week. Life in Tallahassee was taking form. Lynette's thoughts were diverted when she heard a knock at the door.

"Who in God's name is that?" Lynette murmured to herself, remembering the basketball saga, as she stood on her sore feet and stepped to the door to look through the peephole. "Who is it?"

"It's little ole me!" The voice coming through the door was familiar. "Open up, it's cold."

"Oh, Sweetie, what are you doing here?" Lynette unlocked the chain, then the dead bolt, and swung open the door. The draft of wintry air blew in. "Welcome to my house," Lynette gestured for the man and his duffle bag to come in, quickly closing and locking the deadbolt and chain lock behind him. Now spinning around, she could see his bag and Tallahassee Democrat Newspaper had fallen to the floor. His hands were outstretched in an invitation, and she rushed to him.

"It's so good to see your face," Lynette was drawing back now to admire his thin frame, blue eyes and wavy dark hair. "What a wonderful surprise, what did I ever do to deserve this?" Their lips met for a kiss.

Looking into Lynette's eyes, Claude whispered, "You deserve everything you want, Babe. Do you want me?"

Lynette broke the embrace, to pull him to the green vinyl love seat to sit. "So how did you get here? I thought your car was dead."

"I rented a car. And during the whole trip, all I did was think about my lady," he stroked Lynnette's cheek and moved a hair out of her face. Lynette snuggled against him, her head on his shoulder.

"I'm quitting my job, and I'm moving to Tallahassee to be with my lassie." Lynette's eyes widened. "There's no point in me staying in Destin when you're here. I've already lived two weeks without you, and I can't take anymore," said Claude. He was looking down at her face and lovingly stroking her hair. "I'm flying up to Boston to see my parents for the holidays; then I'll pick up my last Sandestin paycheck and move in with my dream girl until I find a job, if that's ok with you?" Claude reached for Lynette's hand. "I know you don't want us to live together, but you can't keep me from moving into the same city."

Lynette's response was to kiss his nose, his cheek and then his lips until she had him melting under her spell.

"You sure do taste good." Claude licked his lips, smiling and sighing now. "Mmm Mmm, Lynette."

"I'll taste even better after I brush my teeth." Lynette stood, then led him by the hand into the bedroom, where he sat down on the bed. Claude's eyes settled on a stuffed Koala bear on the pillow. There was an Australian Flag hanging from a ribbon on the bear's neck. Claude grabbed it and wound up the lever in his back. The Australian "Waltzing Matilda" tune chimed from the little bear. Lynette was now watching him from the bathroom doorway.

"So, this is my humble home for a while," she said with a mouth full of toothpaste. "What do ya think?"

"What are you keeping this around for?" Claude's eyes narrowed with disgust. "So, you can dream of Travis? I'll bet he gave this to you." A trombone sounded off in Lynette's head. She still often thought about Travis. Claude spoke with resentment. "You'll live with him, but you won't live with me."

"I've already been that route." Lynette was now raising her blouse over her head. "I'm not living with another man again unless I'm married to him." The blouse fell to the floor. Claude's eyes now on her, she promenaded toward the bed, where she stood to unzip her khaki skirt and let it drop to the floor. She had his full attention now. Taking the bear out of his hands, and climbing on top of him, she spoke softly, "Kiss me."

"You sexy thing." Claude shed his jealousy. Overcome and ready for I-miss-you sex, they enjoyed each other. And the next morning, Claude put his plan in motion: He returned to Destin and quit his job. Since his car was dead and had been impounded from the spot, where it had broken down, he decided to cut that as a loss. He didn't have the money to fix it anyway, especially after buying his plane ticket home for Christmas. What he knew was that he had to move forward, hire an attorney and get himself out of debt. He and his ex-old lady had dealt and snorted a lot of cocaine. They maxed out all their credit cards. They spent all their money living the life of Riley in Pensacola. How he allowed that to go on for eight years, he still had no answer. Would he be able to start clean? He knew it would be a struggle. He was determined to get his life in order. Would he ever feel good enough for Lynette? It hadn't occurred to him that he needed to feel good enough for himself, first.

Chapter 2

Dawn rose through the windows at one fifty-seven Crenshaw Court in Alumni Village. Two people were laying in a double bed. One asleep, the other was staring at the phone on the nightstand. The young woman rolled over to look at the sleeping figure in the bed next to her. She saw the deep lines in Mami's face. *I put them there*, she thought. How could I be twenty-three years old, and already divorced twice? I'll never forgive myself for dragging mi padres through living hell. Her brown eyes were buried now in a wincing face. Her body flinching, her memories erupting. The crowbar hitting the motorcycle again and again. The rapid upsurge of anger now exploding inside her. The needles in the trash can, the large skillet in her hands being hurled through the air, the weight of the toilet seat coming down on her head and falling around her neck, and waking up to the sterile smell of the hospital. Her heartrate was now well above normal and she was panting. Her hand was full of sweat, when Mami reached over to hold it.

"Maria, it's ok, baby, it's ok," Mami was cradling her daughter's face. "You are in Tallahassee today, safe, y comenzando nuevo."

Maria was sobbing violently, her hands clutched at her mother's arm. "Let it out, baby. Let it out," said Mami.

And Maria's cry out loud ended when she bellowed a declaration, "I'll get my education here at FSU. I'll be a doctor and I won't be held down anymore." Exhausted but quiet now, she drew back from Mami and rolled on her back. "I love you, Mami."

"I love you too, Maria."

"I told you to call me Marie."

"Ok, I love you, Marie. ¿Tienes tiempo?"

Marie reached for a watch lying next the phone. She was putting it on her wrist, when before she could say it was just about eight o'clock, the phone rang. Marie answered, "Hola, Papi." The conversation began with the weather.

As the murmur of the telephone conversation continued, Mami sat up and stepped toward the suitcase laying open on the dresser. Pulling out some clothes, she draped them over her arm and noticed stacked on the floor in the closet the cardboard boxes requiring her attention. "Dios Mío," she mumbled. She shook her head, then stepped to the bathroom. Minutes later, she was dressed and unpacking a box of books.

"Mami, Papi wants to talk to you." Mami looked up from the heavy textbook entitled Nursing Pharmacology that she was shelving and nodded. Marie lay down the phone receiver to take her turn in the bathroom.

Under the sink were boxes filled with bottles and tubes of Estee Lauder products. A handbag hung from the doorknob. Marie reached for the bag and pulled out a prescription bottle. After taking out a pill, she popped it in her mouth, all the while grabbing with her free hand an open can of diet Coke on the edge of the sink. She chased it down with the few sips of flat soda. Then began moving creams and serums and cosmetics from the box on the floor to the medicine cabinet. One jar she opened. Dabbing her pinky finger in it, she rubbed the cream under her round brown eyes. With another jar, she did the same, applying it in long strokes to the smooth brown skin on her face and neck. From a small zipper bag full of lipstick, she chose her favorite. The tube read, "Carnal" and she applied it to her glamorous lips. Glancing at her reflection in the mirror, she turned away unsatisfied and gave her attention to the box. Stooping once more, she lifted out the final item, a stethoscope, which she draped over the towel rack. She grasped the empty box in one hand and her handbag in the other. When she stepped into the bedroom, Mami was hanging up the phone. "Only one more trip! And we will be done moving me in," said Marie.

"Dios Mío! Marie, do you have any more of those wake-me-up pills?" Marie tossed the empty box in the closet and sat down next to

Mami on the bed, where she rummaged through her handbag and pulled out a hairbrush.

"I don't know why you want to go back to school," said Mami. She held a tissue to her face and was blowing her nose. "You are a nurse, isn't that enough? You had a good job at the hospital. When I was in Cuba," said Mami, who was just getting started before she was interrupted.

"I'm not working in medicine to marry a Doctor. I want to be a doctor," said Marie. She stood up and stomped out of the room. Mami followed her and sat at the kitchen table fumbling with a tangled necklace. "Here, Mami." Marie set the glass of water and a Benzedrine on the table. Watching her swallow, Marie thought about how only just a few days before, she had lifted the meds from the hospital.

"I can't believe I quit smoking. If only I had waited until this move was over. I sure could use a good *Salem One Hundred* about now. As soon as I dress, let's leave, so we can beat the lunch hour traffic out of town. You remember how awful it was driving down Apalachicola Street last night when we came in. And it's cold in the evening around here. This weather may be the only thing that will keep me from getting A's in school."

Mami was closing her suitcase. Marie dressed herself in a pair of sweatpants, and a t-shirt tied at the waist. Then the two women walked out the door and down the stairs. Their heads tingling as the amphetamines began to take effect. Chatting about threatening looking clouds above, the women failed to notice the boughs of moon loblolly pines, dogwoods, loquats, and Japanese maples waving farewell. The trees were donning their best moss drapery too. Some were whispering plans to make shady tunnels along the road out of town.

Marie stood on scattered pine needles on the pavement, while unlocking the door of her nineteen eighty-four maroon Chevy Impala. A bushy tailed squirrel, munching a crabapple, under a canopy of pines, watched as Marie loaded a suitcase into the trunk and climbed into the driver's seat. Frost on the windshield reminded Marie that she wasn't in Miami anymore. She switched on the defroster and sat rubbing her hands together when Mami got in chattering about whether Papi found the beans and rice in the refrigerator. Marie thought about her parakeet. Papi had called him a squawking little nuisance and threatened to toss him out. She would feel better once she got her feathered friend to Tallahassee. Now headed East on I-10, Mami lay back on the head rest.

"Let's stop to get a bite to eat once we turn on I-75," she said.

"Ok, we'll stop around Lake City," said Marie. She turned the tuning knob on the radio and landed on one of Mami's favorites, *La Bamba*. While Mami hummed along, Marie drifted off into her past during the miles toward South Florida. She did that a lot lately. She remembered how both her ex-husbands had drained the life from the pores of her soul. Sucking her dry of any purpose that was her own. Her second divorce had been final for about a year. Why she had married him in the first place, she didn't know. He was handsome enough, and his little son was sweet enough. How did she get from coffee in bed and picnics in the park, to destroying his motorcycle with a crowbar? She wondered if she would ever forget that awful day. She could still see the look on her stepson's face when she had told him goodbye.

Surely, life in a new town would help her move forward. Wouldn't the new surroundings wash away all the old anxiety? She had made it as a nurse, but would she be able to make it in the pre-med program? She imagined herself competing with all the male students and how she would show them up. She'd be living on her own now. Her attorney had made sure of that. With marriage behind her, what could stop her from being successfully independent? And a capable student?

She looked at the odometer, and noted that she had driven sixty-seven miles, when Mami said, "Oh, Marie, you always do things the hard way. Whatever you are looking for, I hope you find it, my hita."

"Things will be different, Mami. I'm going to do what el abogado helped me to realize I've always wanted, to be a doctor."

"How long do you think it will take you? Papi and I need to make plans for sending out graduation invitations. The program shouldn't be too bad," said Mami. "you are already in the medical field."

"Si, Mami." Marie told her mother what she knew she wanted to hear.

"I'll be worried about you in this city all by yourself. You don't know a soul. Who will fix your car if it breaks down?"

"No te preocupes. I will be fine," said Marie. The truth was, that she wasn't certain of the truth. She just wanted her parents to be proud of her. Not wanting to talk anymore, Marie turned the knobs on the radio until a news broadcast filled the car. "According to the *Orlando Sentinel News* this week, The Florida Bankers Association launched a campaign to halt the laundering of cash by drug dealers. William Sutton, President of the trade group, said federal officials estimate illicit drug money passing through Florida is valued at $80 billion. Much of it is laundered through banks, thrifts and brokerages, Sutton said. The FBA distributed kits to help employees identify techniques used by drug dealers to hide the source of their cash. And now for…"

"Hey look, we're in Lake City," said Marie. She was oblivious about the state-of-affairs in Florida. She fastened her eyes to the road, tuned out the news from the radio and drove her car down the ramp of Exit four thirty-five.

* * *

On the pallet on the living room floor, Marie didn't sleep well. The furnished apartment had a double bed, but she often didn't use it for fear of getting so comfortable that she wouldn't wake up on time. Her brain just wouldn't shut off at night. While studying Microbiology, Zoology, and Chemistry, it usually wasn't before four in the morning that the amphetamines wore off. This morning was no different. Just before eight in the morning, she threw off her blanket and stood up. Still wearing the sweats from the day before, her first thought was that rent was late. She wished she could have accepted the hospital shift offered to her for today, but she couldn't miss class again. After a cup of expresso, she would have to get back the money she had loaned out.

That morning, anger escalating, her palms sweaty, Marie stood outside and lifted her fist to knock on her neighbor's door. "Kerry! Answer this damn door! It's Marie." She knocked again. "I know you are in there. Your fucken stereo is so loud, the Pope can hear it in Rome. Kerry!"

The door chain jingled. A chubby short haired black woman swung the door open.

"What's up?"

"My Penney's statement came in the mail yesterday. How many uniforms did you buy? Every single one in the store?" Marie's words were now mowing Kerry down. "You charged over a hundred dollars."

"Hey, take it easy; I only bought one," said Kerry. "What in the hell you be talking about?"

"It's only been three weeks since you borrowed my card. You can't forget how much you spent that easy." Marie unfolded a paper she had been holding. "Look at this statement." There were line items highlighted in yellow. "You still haven't given me any money. Come on, you have gotten at least one paycheck by now."

"Marie, I'll pay you tomorrow. I gets my check tomorrow." Kerry slammed the door and turned up *King of Rock*, a RUN DMC rap song. The lyrics spewed out an open window.

Marie turned and ducked into her own apartment to phone J.C. Penney Company. After a short wait on hold, she finally got to explain that there were charges on her card that she did not make. When she didn't get the response she wanted, she asked for the woman's supervisor, who said that she might be able to have the charges billed on a separate account, if the charging party would be willing to fill out a charge application. Satisfied with that idea, Marie finished the call with a polite thank you and bye.

Then she turned to her parakeet. "Buenos Dias, Henrique," she said. She uncovered and opened the cage. Henrique blinked his tiny eyes and puffed up his blue chest feathers. The bird hopped to the open door.

"Hola," said Henrique. He fluttered and landed on the back of the kitchen chair. Marie tossed a cardboard cylinder onto the floor. Henrique, now curious, fluttered over to explore it with his beak. Marie smiled and watched him climb on and perform a bird version of a log roll. She left him to play, while she filled his food and water dish. "Pretty Boy," said Marie.

"Pretty Boy," said Henrique.

Marie tied back her long brown hair and slid on her sneakers. Then she bent so Henrique could board her finger once more. She swept him up to her shoulder, where his beak nibbled at her ear lobe. "No, no," said Marie.

"No, no," said Henrique.

"Oh, mi amor, I can always count on you to make me feel better. I love you Henrique." Marie slid a monitory finger under Henrique's toes and lifted his little striped head to her lips for a kiss. "Now, back to your swing." Gently, she settled him inside his cage and closed the door.

Outside now in the fresh January air, under the loblolly pines, Marie jogged around Alumni Village. She smiled when she saw the red flash of two cardinals swoop by her one behind the other. She watched as they disappeared in the tree branches. At the playground, a mother pushed her child on a swing. Marie could see her breath in the air. *Damn, it's cold,* she thought. She was glad to be wearing gloves. In a better frame of mind, she returned to the stairs of her red brick two story building, out of breath, ready for a shower.

* * *

Marie arrived at the Fisher Lecture Hall wearing a sweater, carrying her maroon knapsack. "Good Morning, Desmond. Hola, Maggie!" she said. "How are you today?"

Two custodians looked up from their chores. "I can't complain, because Maggie here does enough for the both of us," said Desmond.

He stopped pushing his broom and propped himself on the handle. "She just needs her vacation, and I hope the Lord intervenes in the mean times, so she be in better spirits when she gets back." Desmond tipped his cap and resumed his sweeping.

Maggie scowled at Desmond, and shook her head, then looked to Marie. "I got something for you, my friend." Maggie had been cleaning the window, and she was now tossing a spray bottle and a towel into a cart. She led Marie southeast of Fisher Lecture Hall to the maintenance complex. In the bowels of the building, they stopped in front of a mop and broom closet, where two other custodians were huddled drinking coffee from Styrofoam cups. Marie waited in the hall, while Maggie went inside a closet. She wasn't gone long enough to be missed, when she returned smiling with a mouth full of decayed teeth. "This, I find for you." Maggie handed Marie a satin garnet jacket. On the front were the words, *Florida State Seminoles* embroidered in gold. On the back was an embroidery of a big Seminole Indian head.

"Mucho Gracious! Maggie. This coat is just what I need. It's so cold here." Marie hugged Maggie and kissed her on the cheek.

She slipped into the jacket, crossed campus, and strutted into the Lecture Hall. She took her seat next to a blonde-haired young man in the front row. His face was splattered with freckles. His eyes widened with unspoken infatuation.

"Hola, Flynn! How are you feeling today?" asked Marie.

"The beans on the salad bar tasted funny last night. Perhaps I had a touch of food poisoning, that's what my Aunt said." Flynn smiled meagerly. "Sometimes I wished I could live in the dorm, but she needs me to help out at the house."

"She's lucky to have you. I'm glad you are feeling better," said Marie. "Are you studying at the law library tonight?"

"I have Zoology class," said Flynn. "I can pick you up after that, if you want?"

"Ok, I'm going to the Novena at the Co-Cathedral at six. I'll be ready to go by seven." Marie was now unzipping her knapsack along with other students in the lecture hall.

The sounds of books slamming on desks, and pages turning filled the room. The doctor approached his podium. Voices hushed. "Tuesday, we discussed the DNA molecular structure of the guppies; today we'll take a look at the hybrid theories." Marie's attention was floating out of the classroom, until she saw Flynn writing in his notebook. She leaned her face toward his notes. Flynn saw this and accommodated her by sliding his notebook closer, inviting her to copy them. And this is how it went for the whole class period.

When the lecture ended, Marie reminded Flynn not to forget his bottle of water, before hugging him goodbye.

"Adios, Marie," said Flynn.

"Adios," said Marie. She turned on her heel and walked across campus to Wendy's Restaurant. She wrapped her new jacket tightly against her body and zipped it to the top. At Wendy's feeling lightheaded from hunger, she took a seat, where she had a good view of the parking lot. When she saw the blue Volkswagen car pull in, she stayed seated, head down, staring at the hybrid notes she did not understand. A dark-haired man wearing a black wool zip neck sweater pushed open the glass doors and a cold wind whirled about the warm corner, where Marie sat. She looked up, pretending to be surprised.

"Hola, Seniorita. I hope you haven't been waiting long. I apologize for my tardiness, but I had to stop by the Johnson building to pick up my test results," said Lamont. "So how is your Physiology class?" He set his book bag on the seat of the booth.

"Bien," said Marie. "How did you do on your exam?" She noticed the five o'clock shadow on his chin.

"I got a ninety without a curve, and with the curve I made a ninety-seven. I had the second highest score in the class. Some guy who already took half the course last year got the highest score," said Lamont. He sat down across from her and reached for the pencil he had behind his ear. "Last year, he dropped out to recover from a bad car accident."

"What happened?"

"I don't know exactly. But the guy will probably make for a confident attorney one day." He was reaching around his body for his wallet. "I wish I could be more like him."

"Hey, what is this? You are excellent at what you do." Marie put the book she had been reading into her bag. "Twenty-five years old and already graduating from law school this year. That is more than my ex-husbands will do in a lifetime."

"Well, what would you like to eat?" asked Lamont. He was holding the cash he had taken from his wallet and was now headed for the cashier. "Tengo hambre."

"I think I'll have a potato bar and a diet Pepsi."

Lamont ordered for himself and then for Marie. She could feel him reveling in her company, wanting their relationship to be more.

"Are you sure you don't want anything else?" asked Lamont.

"Sí, estoy seguro." Marie returned to the booth in the corner, close to the salad bar and potato fixings. Lamont set a tray of food and drinks on the table. He passed Marie a plate with a potato. She noticed his clean fingernails. "Mi Mami will be visiting when it gets warmer. I'm bringing her to classes with me. I keep telling her she has to watch out that she doesn't get atrophy of the brain."

"You better go dress your potato," said Lamont.

Obeying, Marie stood, and carried the plate to the salad bar. She turned and noticed Lamont watching her. She piled her potato with cauliflower, broccoli, green beans, beets, cottage cheese, and mushrooms. She hurried back to her seat. Her stomach now growling.

"How's your burger?" asked Marie.

"It's fine," said Lamont. He wiped his face with a napkin. "So, your mom, is she driving or flying up?"

"She'll ride up with my father." Marie paused to cut her potato. "Would you like to meet my mother?"

Lamont swallowed. "Sure, any reason I shouldn't want to meet her?"

"Well, no. De Nada, right?"

"I suppose. What do I have to worry about?" Lamont dipped his last French fry in some catsup. "You're just another Cuban with polyester pants and ruby red lips." He set a corporate law textbook on the table.

Marie followed suit and took out a book. Reading and eating, and all the while peeking over at Lamont, comparing herself with him. Marie thought now about how little experience he had with women, and how he was just as Cuban as she was. Unlike her, he was wealthy. Lamont's Dad was a successful architect, and his mother was an RN at one of the finest and most well-known hospitals in Miami, *Baptist and Holy Cross*. Marie figured that was why he was somehow attracted to her. She was a nurse like his mother. Marie's thoughts were intruded on by Lamont's voice.

"It's two o'clock," said Lamont. "I've got a two thirty class."

Marie watched him while he packed his book and carried the empty plates and cups to the trash can. He now stood near her smiling. "Thank you for your company. I'll call you."

"I appreciate the lunch." Marie closed her book. She stood to collect her bag and watched Lamont through the window climbing into his car. She looked at her watch to confirm it was an hour before her next class. Then she walked toward the glass door and tried to pull the door that read *PUSH*.

While she walked toward campus, she thought about how her schedule was spread out on Tuesdays and Thursdays. This pissed her off, but the class times she had wanted on registration day, had been filled. It was always like that for new students. The already enrolled students had priority over the new entries. Marie hadn't worked for three weeks, so she thought she had better phone the nurse pool at the hospital. She stopped at a pay phone in front of the Strozier Library, where the sweeping limbs of the great southern live oak tree were on guard duty. After dropping a quarter in the coin slot, she dialed the phone.

"Hello, Mrs. Langston, this is Marie, Marie Martinez. I was wondering if you had any work for me." Mrs. Langston put her on hold. Marie looked up at the library stairs and recognized a thin man waving at her. He was wearing a knitted beanie hat and outdated bellbottomed pants. She waved back.

"Marie, how about working for me tonight, we need someone in ICU, graveyard shift." said Mrs. Langston. "Be here at ten thirty to spend some time with the charge nurse."

"I will. I'll be there at ten. Thank you, and you have a great day!" Marie hung the receiver in the cradle with a bang. The man in bell bottoms stood in front of her now.

"Hi! Vahid. And how are you today?" Marie glanced at his wedding ring.

"Better now that I've seen you," said Vahid. He reached out for a hug.

"How's your wife?" asked Marie. She accepted his hug. "I was just talking about you with Lamont. He tells me he made a great score on the taxes' exam. How did you do?"

"I passed, and that is all I shall tell you. So where are you off to, my pretty lady?" Vahid flashed a smile from thick lips. "I see you are wearing a little school spirit!"

"You know what? This morning, I was just walking into the Fisher lecture hall when one of the custodians called me over to the maintenance building and told me she had a prize for me." Marie felt Vahid's bubble eyes on her, sizing her up. "I almost died when she showed me this jacket. I'm so grateful. I love it."

"You still didn't answer my question," said Vahid. "Where are you off to?"

"Well, to be honest I just found out I'm going to work tonight and I'm on my way to my three o'clock class," said Marie. "Why don't you come with me and we'll chit chat until it starts." Marie brushed a lock of hair out of her face.

"Yes, I will walk with you," said Vahid. They strolled under the canopy of trees. And when they passed under the yellow belly of the sapsucker, who had been enjoying the syrup from the sweet tapered acorn in his beak, the bird took flight with such a flurry that Vahid ducked to avoid a collision.

"Dios Mío, there's poop on your sleeve," said Marie.

"Where?" Vahid's eyes surveyed his right shirt sleeve. Marie pointed it out on his left sleeve. He swung his head around and could now see the poop. "Ah, this is a good omen."

"Here," Marie held a tissue in her hand and reached toward the sleeve to wipe it down. "Let me help you."

Vahid took a step back and held up his hands in front of his chest. "No, no, no. Not until after I play poker tonight."

"Ok, Vahid." Marie's eyes opened wide. She put the tissue in her pants pocket. "You're leaving that bird shit on your sleeve?"

"Yes, it is lucky," said Vahid.

Marie was looking straight ahead now, trying not to look at the poop.

"So, what sort of law do you plan to go into, Vahid?"

"Immigration law, I hope. My parents are still in my country, in Jammu. I wish to bring them to the U.S." His bubbly eyes blinked. "They have never met my children."

"Well, here's my stop," said Marie. Then she hurried toward the Dittmer Building.

* * *

Class went by quickly and Marie was already in her car driving down Stadium Drive when a beige Toyota cut her off at a stop light. She felt rage pulsing up, triggering her to roll down the car window and crane her neck out. "Qué Diablos!" yelled Marie. "Damn, mucho frio." She rolled the window up and drove down Lake Bradford

Road. Minutes later, she was unlocking the door of her apartment. She heard Henrique whistling and looked to his cage, where he perched on his swing.

"Hola!" Marie spoke softly. Henrique cocked his head.

"Hola!" said the parakeet.

"Did you miss me?" She touched Henrique's long splotched gray and turquoise tail through the bars, opened the cage door and lifted him to her shoulder. She grabbed the phone from the cradle on the wall, then pressed the buttons on the receiver. She listened to the ring followed by the incoming voice message.

"Hi this is Flynn. Leave a number and I'll call you right back."

"Hi, it's Marie, I'm working tonight at eleven, so I can't study with you at the law library. Maybe I'll see you at church. Bye." Henrique was twisting to groom himself. Marie hung up the phone, waiting for him to finish and then swept her finger underneath the tiny bird's toes. "Te quiero and Buenos noche, Henrique." She kissed his black and white feathered head before safely returning him to the cage.

After a grooming of her own, Marie stood naked now at the ironing board, pressing her nurse's uniform, all the while remembering her last shift at the hospital at the Intensive Care Unit with a patient who almost died from a drug overdose. He had AIDS. *Fucken AIDS*, she thought, it had transformed the hospital. A fatal disorder of the immune system and no cure in sight. It flooded the hospital with despair and death. Marie, heavy with the gravity of it all, set down the iron and flipped the white dress over, rubbing the material with her hands to smooth it out. She didn't notice the open curtain on her bedroom window, when her pinky finger touched the sole plate. "Ouch", she shouted, jerking her hand away, now raising it up to take a closer look. Popping the finger in her mouth to sooth the burn, she used her free hand to stroke the dress with the iron a few more times, before resting it on its heel and bending to unplug it from the outlet.

Hurrying, she grabbed the dress off the board, and moved to the bed, where she had earlier laid out her white tights, nursing cap, handbag, and white shoes. She glanced at the clock, and realized time was running short. And while humming along with the Lionel Richie tune, *Say You, Say Me*, she dressed. Then she switched off the radio before she had a chance to hear the wide strides of a jogger pounding against the grassy ground outside her window.

After swallowing a Bene, and checking her appearance in the full-length mirror, she tied her thick brown hair in an up-do. Then reaching behind her head with a bobby pin, she pinned down her nursing cap. Satisfied now, she grabbed her handbag, and white sweater, then stepped outside into the sharp night air. Instantly, she was aware of the moon. Pausing to stare at it, she noticed its plump round face shining down, making Alumni Village look like somewhere else. *The emergency room will be wild tonight*, she thought.

* * *

Nine hours later, the morning was colder than the morning before. The windshield of her Chevy was covered in frost. How could this be Florida? thought Marie. Before complaining, she felt the adrenaline still running through her from her hospital shift. Saving people's lives was like that for her, a real rush. While she drove west on Apalachee Parkway, she reflected on her night. Would she ever learn not to take the patients home with her?

As usual the hospital had been short staffed. Around midnight a man had been admitted with a travelling blood clot. It was a matter of time before he would have a stroke or a massive coronary attack. The charge nurse yelled "Code 3". The patient's chest heaving, face distorted, heart in cardiac arrest, the ER team began CPR. After the chest thrusts, the breath of resuscitation, thrusts, breath, thrusts, breath, thrusts, Mr. Hearth returned to the land of the living.

In the ICU, before Marie signed out to go home, she bid a farewell to Mr. Hearth.

"It's you. Thanks for what you did. Can I take you out to dinner when I get out of here?" Mr. Hearth, now conscious, was weak but managed to muster up a smile.

"I don't know if your heart could stand it, or your wife." She smiled back at him, and now averted her eyes to the IV bag and the connected tubing. "Get some rest. I'm going home. Katie will be your nurse for the day."

Now behind the wheel, it was close to nine in the morning. She turned the car onto Levy Avenue, and thought about stopping to pick up cigarettes, but denied the impulse remembering the Norman Vincent Peale's philosophy that she forced herself to memorize. *Two words: deny yourself, are important to self-control. Self-denial in the present to gain benefits in the future is the hallmark of a rational human being.*

A rational human being, Marie dwelled on the last line as she pulled into her parking place on Crenshaw Drive. How could she be rational when it came to Kerry? She reached for her purse, desperately searched for her make up bag, and found her rationale, Benzedrine. Looking at the bottle, she decided not to take one. After all, she was still pumped from the happenings at the hospital. Through the windshield, she could see Kerry's apartment, next door from her own, and then the mania rose-up, transforming her into a Ms. Hyde. Marie, winded from running up the stairs, she banged on the apartment door. The door opened a crack. Marie tore in. "Kerry, do you have my money?"

"Not yet," said Kerry.

Like lava from a live volcano, Marie continued badgering the woman behind the door, "God damn it, how can you be so ungrateful? I saved your ass last month." Marie swung her handbag against the door, and then used her other hand to push the door open, accidently knocking Kerry off balance, and onto the floor. Kerry stood up and ran to her telephone. Marie stayed at the doorway. "You know, you better call the ambulance not the police, because you're leaving this apartment on a stretcher, unless you give me my money."

"Marie, you go crazy, calm down, man! You're messing with me. Take it easy." Kerry raised her hands out in front of her, palms motioning downward. "I'll get your money to you. Something came up. My car broke down on the way to work yesterday. It cost me a hundred bucks to fix it."

Marie heard a car coming. She glanced at a sedan pulling into a parking space next to her car. This signaled a phony calm over the scene. The driver's side door opened, a man, wearing a blue uniform, got out and walked in the direction of the building. "Good morning, ladies," he called out.

"Good mornin'," shouted Kerry from her doorway.

"I received a call about loud yelling and banging," said the FSU campus police. He was now climbing the stairs. Marie spun around in time to see him reach the top. The lines on his face and sagging jowls suggested he was a no-nonsense sort of guy.

"What seems to be the problem?"

"Officer, sir, I'm only here trying to get the money that Kerry borrowed from me over thirty days ago," said Marie. She reached up to straighten her nurse's cap. "I apologize for any disturbance to the neighborhood and my neighbor, sir."

"Ladies, let me make something clear. I don't want to make life difficult for either one of you, but this is the second time this week, I've come out to this building for a disturbing the peace call." The officer lifted his hands to his waist. "If you choose to continue this sort of behavior, which makes life difficult for me, I have no choice but to hand you both over to the police. Are we good?"

Marie could see he was serious, and she nodded. "Yes sir." Glancing in Kerry's direction, she beckoned her to say something.

"Yes sir," said Kerry.

The officer turned and was now walking toward the stairs. Another man, wearing a tool belt appeared from the side of the building, on the lawn. Marie stepped to the railing and waved at him.

"Good Morning, James." She twirled her hair in her fingers.

"Hi Marie," James was climbing the stairs now. He cradled a box in his arm.

"I still have a leaky faucet in the bathroom."

"Your faucet is on the work order list," said James. He stopped in front of Kerry's place, where she stood in the doorway. "Hi Kerry. You two aren't arguing again, are you?"

"We are just fine," said Marie, before Kerry could open her mouth. "Just a little passionate Cuban discussion."

"You better work things out rationally before the real cops show up at the door. You don't want to have a record that will prevent you from seeking a job in the field you are studying, whatever that happens to be." James set the box down in front of the apartment, two doors down. "I've seen cops make it impossible for people to get a job anywhere at all," said James. He put a screwdriver to a porch light fixture and under a knitted brow, he winked in Marie's direction.

"Kerry, just pay me back when you can. I really need the cash." Marie figured she better cut her losses.

"I will," said Kerry. "I'm getting some loan money soon, and I can pay you then." The door closed.

Marie noticed the campus police car was still in the parking lot. And she saw the officer climbing out of the vehicle. He waved at Marie. "Young lady," he said.

"Yes, Sir." Marie looked down at him from the balcony.

"Can you come downstairs for a minute?" asked the officer. "I'd like to talk to you."

"Ok," said Marie now climbing down the stairs, from where she could see the officer's forehead was creased.

"Don't make things difficult," he said. "You know Kerry's already on academic probation, she has a history."

"I know. She told me." Marie actually felt sorry for her. "And she told me she might be getting evicted."

"About your money, I overheard, and I doubt you'll ever see it again." He picked up a cola can from the ground and tossed it in the barrel nearby. "I'm going to tell you what my dad once told me, and I'm telling you this, because I don't want to see you get in trouble. When you loan money, don't expect to get it back."

"I'll remember that, and thanks."

Minutes later, Marie was inside her apartment listening to a slew of voicemails, while Henrique played with a string of wooden beads.

"Hola, Marie. Lamont, here. Just called to ask if you'd be interested in dinner tonight at Ruby Tuesdays. You can reach me at home around four. Have a good day. "

"B-E-E-E-E-P!"

"Hi, Marie. This is Flynn. I thought maybe that since, well, since we didn't get to study last night, you would want to study today sometime. Call me. Adios, Amiga."

"B-E-E-E-E-P!"

"This is Jan with the Greenwood Trust Company. I am calling for Marie Martinez. We still haven't received your January VISA payment. It is important that you contact me at 1-800-662-3330."

"B-E-E-E-E-P!"

The machine rewound itself. Marie's exhaustion felt heavy on her. She grabbed a Butterfinger candy bar and sat on the floor with Henrique. Maybe the officer was right. She decided she wouldn't worry about the money Kerry owed her anymore. After finishing her chocolate, she would tuck in her parakeet, shower, dress, and attend Chemistry class.

Chapter 3

Lynette wasn't sure why, but after Christmas she found herself living with Claude. The contingency was that it was temporary until he found work. In a whirl, over her recent move, two new jobs, and anticipation and registration into college life, Lynette had no time for reflection until now. Should she question the morality or implications of the living arrangement? Was the company necessary in her life for survival? After all, grilled cheese sandwiches wouldn't warm a bed at night. Was she destined to be with Claude? Or were they both each other's rebounds refusing to see the foul?

In late January, Lynette was relieved when Claude landed a manager's position at Wendy's fast-food restaurant on Thomasville Road, in the Northeast quadrant of the city, about a half an hour from Lynette's apartment. Despite Claude's pleading to continue living together, she pushed him to look for a place on the opposite side of town in order to be close to work.

"What is that smell?" Lynette stood waving a can of Lysol.

"I don't know. Did you burn something?" asked Claude. Trying to avoid the mist, he stepped out of the room.

"No," said Lynette. She sat down in the kitchen chair and began counting tip money. She could hear running water coming from the bathroom. Her face winced. She could still smell something. She grabbed the Lysol and followed the smell to the bathroom. Claude was sitting on the edge of the tub.

"What are you doing?" asked Lynette.

"Washing my feet," he said.

"Wait a minute." She picked up his work shoes from the floor. Sniffing them, she spouted a laugh. "It's your damn feet. All this time I been thinking there was some dead mouse in the closet or something and it's your feet. You knew!"

"Well, I didn't want you to leave me because I had stinky feet." Claude laughed nervously. He held a bar a soap in his hand and was holding his feet under the running water.

"Déjà vu." Lynette remembered her folks.

"What's a déjà vu?" Claude hung the washcloth he had been using on the rack in the shower.

"Your stinky feet. My mom and my second father went through this with his feet." Lynette saw Claude staring back at her smiling shyly. "Too funny."

"What? He had stinky feet too," said Claude. "I'm so glad, I'm not alone." He swung his legs around to the towel on the floor. Lynette sprayed his shoes with Lysol. Then pitched them into a corner.

"I'm gonna make a dropped egg on toast," said Lynette. "you want one?"

"No, I've been looking at food all day." Claude walked through the bedroom and into the living area, where he sat on the loveseat, and slipped his feet into clean socks. Lynette stood at the sink, filling a pan with water.

"So, how was the Rail today?" asked Claude.

"For a Sunday brunch, it was slow." She was dropping the bread into the toaster, when she looked up to see Claude toss a plastic bag on the table. "I'm gonna look for a bartender position," said Lynette.

"Bartending, huh." Claude was now reaching into his pocket.

"I need to make more money." She turned the stove burner on high. Claude sprinkled weed into a rolling paper.

"Hanging around guys all day at a bar." Claude's insecurity reared its ugly head. "I don't like it." The ends of the joint were between his index fingers and thumbs. He tightened the roll looking intently at Lynette. A glass in hand, she stepped to the table and poured a cranberry juice. She met his stare and watched him licking the rolling paper.

"It's bad enough, I have to worry about college guys." He stood up, grabbing the lighter from the table. "I just love you, Lynette

Autry." Her eyes met his. A line appeared between his brows. He bent to kiss Lynette on the head, before stepping away.

"I love you too," she said.

Claude opened the front door, lit up the joint, and took a hit. "Ya know, I'll be looking at a couple apartments tomorrow." He blew smoke out the door. "Unless you've changed your mind, and I can stay here." He stood taking another drag, and another, the THC taking affect, he was smiling now. Lynette turned to blow a kiss his direction, before dropping an egg into the boiling water.

"It's getting chilly out," said Claude. Taking a final drag, feeling as though that was enough, he snuffed out the joint on the brick wall outside the door, and moved inside, closing the door behind him. "You know I could help with the bills and if I stay here you won't have to work." He sat now on the loveseat reaching for the newspaper.

Lynette ignored his futile attempt at changing her mind. "There's a position open at the airport lounge, I'll be going to apply for it tomorrow after classes." She spooned her egg on the toast she had been buttering and sat down to enjoy her meal.

* * *

Lynette parked her beige Corona on West Pensacola Street. After dropping coins in the parking meter, she walked east, slowly, pausing at the corner to check her campus map, making sure she was going the right direction to the fine arts building. When she looked up, the

Fraternity House, Delta Tau Delta, stood on the corner. A colony of voices filled the air with loud cheer. Lynette continued north on Copeland Street, begrudging the Sorority Houses, Kappa Delta and Delta Gamma, whose porches and front lawns, were an overflowing sea of companionable students. She remembered how during the admission process she had been wait listed for the Broadcasting program, and without question, consented to the back seat offer of the English Education program, because getting out of the restaurant and bar business took precedent over career choice. It never occurred to Lynette to apply to more than one school, so that she would have a better chance of getting into a Broadcasting program. For Lynette, settling and being practical was a way of life. She accepted the English Education program on the premise that it was better than nothing. FSU called Lynette, at twenty-two years old, an older than average undergraduate, and with that label came qualification to live at Alumni Village. That's what all tenants were called on the ninety-acre compound of eight hundred apartments spread through ninety-six buildings. Older than average undergraduates. The rent was affordable. Lynette thought often how fortunate she was to have a monthly rent payment of one hundred and twenty-five dollars. When she reached Alpha Phi, she was glad to cross West Call Street, to the doorway of the Fine Arts Building, where she didn't have to be reminded that she was an older than average undergraduate, who wasn't getting a free college ride on the back of a happy family.

Once inside, she found herself for the first time in a huge lecture hall. A beautiful tan blonde stood down the front, wearing a wide serpentine gold chain around her neck, made noticeable by her open collared blouse with shoulder pads. She had a voice like a weather girl. She must be in the Broadcasting program, thought Lynette, now taking her seat in the back for Meteorology one-oh-one. A girl seated to Lynette's left pushed a stack of papers her way. She had big hair that smelled of hairspray. Lynette looked at the stack, took a stapled packet, and passed the rest to the hand on the right. After tossing her packet on the tabletop, Lynette bent in the isle looking through her book bag for a pen and folder full of paper.

Until the teacher spoke, she kept her head down, scanning the syllabus. *Atmosphere, Weather, Climate, Hazards, and Energy,* were the first topics listed. Her mind wandered again, this time about how being a student was easy. She was glad to be sitting down. Her feet were still tired from the eight-hour waitress shift the day before. She slouched in her chair and managed to elevate her legs, by placing her feet on the seat in front of her. The lecture droned on. Intently listening, Lynette wrote notes like a dog. When class ended, she saw other students chattering and smiling, but Lynette was too tired for small talk. She was still hunting for the perfect job.

Outside, she rushed to her car, climbed in, pulled out of the metered space, and drove south on Woodward Avenue, west on Gaines Street, passing Doak Campbell Stadium. On Lake Bradford Road, she glanced at the clock on her dashboard, and turned west on

Levy, then onto Pennell Circle, where she jerked the car to a halt in the parking lot of Alumni Village. She tore into her apartment to change for the job hunt. She kicked off her sneakers, wiggled out of her jeans and ripped off her New Orleans t-shirt. "Red, I'll wear red," she said aloud to herself. After ripping garb from her closet, she tossed everything on the bed and dressed. Then back in the car in a flash, map in hand, she plotted the way to another potential employer. "Ok, looks like it's right on Lake Bradford Road to West Orange and down Capital Circle to the airport," said Lynette, talking to herself again. "About five miles."

Through the automatic doors, Lynette stepped into the airport terminal. She could hear the heels of her red shoes, tapping the floor and someone repeating the words "Shoe-shine" in a salesman pitch. Passing the Avis counter on her left, the agent's red uniform reminded Lynette she too was wearing red. She was glad she had chosen the pencil skirt with a slit in the back. Ahead, Lynette saw the sign that read, *Lounge*. Pausing, she looked around for a ladies' room, and found one just behind her. Slipping in for one final primp, she applied some red lipstick adjusted the red beads that dangled over her white blouse with the buttons down the back. She untangled a hair from her red earring, and took a deep breath, before stepping back into the terminal.

Her stroll had intent. She pulled open the Lounge door. Straight ahead, she could see the bar, overlooking the tarmac. A Piedmont jet sat behind the long wall of glass, which was parallel with the long bar and its long line of black leather barstools. To the right were three stools facing left and behind them in the corner, a juke box which sat beneath a television bolted to the wall. It was a clear day, and the sunlight slatted in through the blinds hanging at half-mast. The lounge was empty except for three men on barstools, all seated alone with a couple of empty stools between them. On the left end, behind the bar, there was a short young woman with long blonde hair trailing down her shoulders, wearing a girly head band. Lynette made her way through the cluster of round tables and chairs. Close enough now, Lynette, could see the bartender's pudgy face.

"Hi, what can I get ya?" said the short bartender. She was removing yellow rubber gloves from her hands.

"I'm here to apply for the bartending job."

"Oh, that's great. Hi, my name's Becky."

"Hi, I'm Lynette Autry."

"Have you filled out an application yet?"

"No, this is my first time here."

"Well, let's get you one then. Follow me." Becky stepped out from behind the bar.

Lynette followed behind, passing through the doors on the left side of the bar, which brought them to the cafeteria, and a food line. Becky waved at the young skinny guy in an apron, and a white paper cap at the register. Lynette smiled in his direction. In the kitchen, fried chicken sat in metal baskets over hot oil. Prep tables were filled with fruit and vegetables. And across from a walk-in cooler, near the exit door, was the doorway to an office, where Becky turned and entered. Inside the small office, a woman's thin frail face with big eyes looked up from the paper she had been reading.

"Hey, Jan," said Becky. "This is Lynette, she's here for the bartending job, Lynette, this is Jan. Ok, I gotta go, I got customers." Becky disappeared out the door.

"Hello," said Jan.

"Hi, nice to meet you," said Lynette.

Jan lay her paper on the desk and raised a cigarette to her mouth. She held it there, acridly smoldering around her frizzy grey hair, while she swiveled in the chair to a file drawer, from where she promptly pulled an application. She took a final puff, before pressing it into the ashtray. "Fill this out in the dining room and then bring it back to me." Jan handed off the application. Her voice was hoarse, "Do you need a pen?"

"No, thanks, I've got one," said Lynette.

Moments later, Lynette reappeared in the cafeteria, where she dropped in a seat at small table against the wall, and began scratching down her memorized contact information, work history, job references, hours available to work, social security number, and birth date. After signing and dating the bottom of the back side, she rose from her seat to pass once again through the cafeteria and the kitchen. The sound of her high heels tapping on the kitchen tile, called attention from the eyes of the kitchen staff. When she returned to Jan's cluttered, smoky office, she noticed a chair had been cleared. "Knock, Knock, Jan, I'm all done with the application."

"That was fast, come on in and sit down." Jan's eyes were on the chair, where Lynette took her seat, crossed legged, pushing the application across the desk. "Let's have a look," said Jan. She grasped the employment application, her eyes scanning the front side, then resting on the back side. "You have lots of experience. So, why do you want to work here?"

"I prefer bartending over food waitressing, and the airport is close to my apartment. It only took me ten minutes to get here." Lynette was giving her best elevator pitch. "I just moved here last month and I'm working my way through college. Right now, I have classes Monday, Wednesday, and Friday mornings and I'm available any other time."

"When could you start?"

"I'll need to give a notice to my current employer, when do you need me?"

"Now, actually. We just lost a bartender."

"Well, I could talk to my boss at the Rail and let him know I'm leaving, if you're saying I'm hired. I like to give notice."

"Ok." Jan's attention shifted to someone outside the office. "Oh, Hi, Larry."

Lynette turned to see a corpulent balding man stepping through the door. He wore a button-down short sleeved white shirt, necktie, and a smile. He locked eyes with Lynette.

"Well, Hello," said Larry.

"Hello," said Lynette. She smiled back at him and caught a whiff of his cologne.

"Lynette, meet Larry, our manager of Jerry's Caterers. Larry, this is Lynette Autry," said Jan. "She's applying for bartender."

Lynette stood up and met Larry with a handshake. "Nice to meet you."

"The pleasure is all mine," said Larry. "Did you fill out an application?"

"I got it here," said Jan passing it to him. He reached out for it with his left hand. Lynette noticed his gold chain bracelet and wedding band.

"Let's go to the dining room and talk for a few minutes." Lynette stood. "Ladies first," said Larry. He motioned for her to go ahead of him. They settled at a table.

"Jerry's Caterer's runs the lounge and the cafeteria at the airport," said Larry. "Our kitchen also prepares and stocks the aircraft galleys with the meals and snacks and drinks for all the flights for Piedmont, Atlantic Southeast, and Oceanair airlines, ASA, Federal Express, etc. Well, you get the point." Larry was now scanning her application. "Experience looks great. Are you working now?"

"I've been waitressing at the Brass Rail for a couple of weeks, but like I told Jan, I prefer bartending, and the airport is closer to my apartment. I'm working my way through school."

"Let me check your references and you can call me later this evening or tomorrow morning."

"I will. Thanks so much for meeting with me, Larry."

"No, thank you for coming in." Larry stood now, smiling, and Lynette did the same. He reached out for a handshake. "Well, I gotta get to work. Bye now."

"I'll call you. Bye-bye." Lynette sauntered back into the lounge, where she could see Becky was now loading glasses from a table onto a tray.

"Hey, how'd it go?" asked Becky.

"Larry's checking my references and he told me to call him tomorrow. My fingers are crossed," said Lynette. She really had a good feeling about getting the job, but it would sound pretentious if she said so.

"Well, good luck." Becky carried the tray toward the bar.

"Thanks, Becky, Bye." Lynette made her way through the tables and chairs of the lounge and pushed open the glass door. In the terminal, she reflected on Larry's smile and handshake. She figured she had the job at hello. And the next day she learned that she was right.

* * *

"I got a job at the airport lounge," said Lynette. Her arms were around Claude's waist. "I'll be telling the Rail tonight that tomorrow will be my last shift there."

"Oh Yeah, well, despite that I want to stay right here with you," Claude hugged her close, "I put a deposit on an apartment this morning."

"When are you moving in?"

"I'll miss you." Claude spoke softly. "Are you sure you don't want to come with me?"

"You know I'm not living in sin anymore."

"Yeah, I know." Claude broke the hug to dig in his jacket pocket for his cigarettes. "I'll probably pack up and start sleeping over there tomorrow. It's across the street from work, so it'll make things easy, no car and all." He pinched a cigarette from his pack and stepped toward Lynette, who was now sitting at the desk. "Let's not talk about my moving out anymore, the New England Patriots are going to the Super Bowl. I just want to bask in football happiness. Now kiss me." Claude leaned in for a kiss. Lynette lifted her face and returned the smooch.

"I gotta head to work," said Claude. "I'll be home around midnight."

"Ok, I'll be heading out to work shortly, too. See you later." The door closed with a thud. Lynette felt time moving forward.

Outside, Claude zipped his jacket, and lit his cigarette. Then staring upward at the line of pine trees, he thought maybe Lynette would miss him so much when he moved out that she'd beg him to come back. He was thirty-one, and he felt old. Would his luck hold out with Lynette until he got his shit together? He took a drag from his cigarette and watched the smoke leaving his mouth. He stepped over to his rental car, and took one more drag from his cigarette, before tossing it to the ground and stepping on it. He climbed into the driver's seat and road toward Levy Avenue, clinging to his denial.

* * *

Claude sat at the end of the Tallahassee Municipal Airport bar, his back against the cafeteria doorway, his eyes on the Super Bowl game on television. The New England Patriots were playing the Chicago Bears. He had been stirring the ice cubes in his glass, but had stopped now, to lick the rum from his finger and stare at the bartender. "Claude plus Lynette, it has such a ring to it," he said. "Mmm, you are so beautiful."

"Do you want another Bacardi and Coke, Claude?" asked Lynette. She capped his ashtray full of Winston butts with a clean ash tray, and skillfully replaced the dirty with the clean. She winked at him and dumped the ashtray in the trash behind the bar.

"No," he said. "I'll nurse this one at least until second quarter. Thanks though, Good looking!" He pointed now in the direction of a stocky looking guy with wavy black hair approaching the bar. "You just got a customer."

Lynette turned, grabbed a napkin, and set it down in front of the man, who had taken a seat on a stool at the center of the bar. "Hello, sir, what can I get for ya?"

"How about an Absolute martini with an extra olive," said the man. He spoke with a British accent.

"Absolutely," said Lynette. She flashed a smile and stepped toward the mixing station.

"Is this the super bowl?" The man's eyes were on the television.

"Sure is," said Claude.

"Claude, what's the score?" asked Lynette. She was adding a dash of dry vermouth to the shaker full of ice and vodka. Claude chuckled like Peewee Herman and pointed to the TV screen.

"There's the score now," said Claude. The man with the accent, along with the rest of the men at the bar turned their heads to see.

Lynette hurried out from behind the bar to bus tables. She went into a trance, a safe place where her mind could try to illuminate dark places. Loading her tray with dirty glasses, she pondered whether she would always be reminded of her old boyfriend, Travis, when she heard a British accent. And would Claude's cigarettes and his love of football always remind her of her mother's second husband? Would every boyfriend just be a search for the permanent father she never had? A longing for lost time and experience? Would she merely be spending the rest of her life trying to fill the gap? Her biological father had been a loud, flashy musician, so she was told. She had never seen him in anything but a suit and tie during dinners out that usually ended in a pub crawl. Sure, he had taken her shopping a couple of times, dropped off a bicycle once, and had picked her up occasionally at her grandmother's house when the two did play father and daughter, but she longed to see him fixing her bicycle, or eating a simple chicken and potato dinner at the table, like the ones she shared with her stepdad-number-one, the second of mom's three husbands, whom she hadn't seen for years, either. *Oh, Mom's three husbands,* she thought, *My three dads.* None of whom were around much during Lynette's high school years. Middle school years, though, there was one memory that stood out. It was something stepdad-number-one had once said, *One day Lynette, you are going to be beating the guys off with a stick.* Right now, she knew he'd been right. Missing what she had missed was part of who she was now, but she smiled to herself, savoring this recollection. Suddenly, trance time was broken with the roar of a DC-9 that taxied into a nearby gate. Then the man with the accent spoke, snapping her mind back to the present.

"So, you must be new here."

"As a matter of fact, I am," said Lynette. She loaded glasses under the bar near the sink filled with soap. "I just started working here last week, and my first training session was with Lou, whose place I'm taking. She's moving to Paris with her French speaking husband. I think he has a job lined up as an interpreter. I guess they don't do too much hiring here at Jerry's Caterer's, since the airport is relatively small. I really lucked out," said Lynette.

"Yep, Lou has been here for a few years, I believe. She's full of beans, that one. How about Lori, is she still with Federal Express? She and Lou go way back," The man said.

"I don't know about Lori. Like I said, I've only been here for a week."

"What brings you to Tallahassee?" he asked.

"School," said Lynette. In her hand was a grimy towel. She threw it in a bin under the sink. "I'm Lynette, by the way."

"I'm Stewart." He took his wallet from his back pocket and tossed it on the bar. "How do you like working here?"

"I like it better than waitressing. Much better. I figure it's a lot easier telling a bad joke, pouring a beer and making a five-dollar tip than it is serving five people salads, dinner, drinks and deserts and making the same five-dollar tip." Lynette glanced at Claude, who was motioning her over. She lifted her chin in his direction. "Excuse me, Stewart." Lynette walked to the end of the bar where Claude sat.

"You ready for another?" asked Lynette.

"You're getting pretty friendly down there with him," said Claude. He spoke softly not wanting anyone to hear him.

"Just doing my job, dear, fraternizing." She poured him another drink and was about to check on two old ladies at a table when Claude interrupted.

"Hey, where's my lemon twist?"

"Sorry, sir." Lynette played as she reached in her garnish tray and rubbed the rim of his cocktail with a lemon twist. A tall thin man entered and sat down in the bar stool next to Claude. His face was mottled with blemishes of some kind, cyst-like severe acne and scars.

His nose was crooked, like it had been broken in the past. "Hi, Cameron, is it a Budweiser?" Lynette hoped.

"Hey, how'd you know? How's it going? Watching the super bowl, huh? Carol never let us watch sports around here, I like you already," said Cameron.

"Would you believe, an airport regular?" said Lynette. She directed the comment to Stewart, who sat close to the draft beer tap, where she now stood pouring Cameron's Bud.

"Hey, Stewart, how's it hanging?" said Cameron.

"Pretty tight, how about you, mate?"

"You two know each other," spurted Lynette. She set the beer on a napkin in front of Cameron.

"Hey, don't forget my employee discount." Cameron was ignoring her comment.

"Never, Cameron," she grabbed a small stack of napkins, placing them on a tray, she looked at the two men sitting side by side, "This is my boyfriend, Claude."

"Yah, I kinda figured by the way he was slobbberin'. Just kiddin', man." Cameron lifted his glass to sip the foam off the top of his beer. "I've been known to drop my share of cheap shots."

Lynette was walking outside the bar, passing the men from behind, when she heard Claude defend his ego.

"Don't worry about it, man. You're slobbering and you don't even go out with her."

Two old ladies paid with a fifty-dollar bill. "I'll be right back," said Lynette. "I'll get some change next door." She dashed toward the restaurant through the side door. Cameron picked up his beer, then moved to a seat next to Stewart. The two of them leaned in close and talked softly.

Lynette reappeared, carrying a wad of small bills. She handed the change to the ladies, who had already stood up to collect their bags and purses. "Have a great trip," said Lynette. She snuck up behind Claude to kiss him on the cheek.

"Very nice," he said. He stood up and hugged her. "It's half time, I'm gonna head home to watch the rest of the game." He reached in his back pocket and pulled out a ten and left it on the bar. "I'll see you tonight."

Lynette picked up his cash, then watched him walk through the menagerie of tables and chairs toward the lounge exit, where he turned around and blew her a kiss. Lynette raised up her hand, pretended to catch it and plant it on her cheek.

Now with Claude gone, it was back to work. Lynette scanned everyone's glasses. Noting that they were all full, she turned her back to the customers to open the cash register drawer. She took her hand full of ones and fives, re-counted, organizing the cash in the trays. For an instant, the cable TV service ceased. There was quiet for a few seconds. Just long enough for Lynette to look at the blip on the TV screen, and overhear Cameron talking to Stewart in almost a whisper. "Nice haul. Live Oak, usual time." Then the TV abruptly came on.

Nice haul. Haul of what? Lynette couldn't imagine two more unlikely people being acquainted with each other. She would have to mull that over. Her thought was broken when Stewart's voice cut in.

"Well, Lynette, how much do I owe you, I drink these bloody things all the time and I still don't know how much you charge for them."

"Just for you, three dollars and fifty cents," said Lynette.

"Here you go, sweetheart." He handed her a ten-dollar bill. "Keep the change," said Stewart. He glanced over at Cameron. "Good seeing you again, mate. As they say in the airport lounges, I've got a plane to catch, bye!" He collected his brief case and overcoat, then sauntered toward the lounge door.

"Guess he liked you." Cameron watched Lynette scoop up Stewart's empty glass and cash. "Don't expect that kinda tip from me."

"I'll expect more from you, since you're a regular." She turned to ring up accrued drink orders. Cameron looked down to where Claude had been seated.

"Hey, what happened to your boyfriend?"

"Halftime, he went home to finish watching the game," said Lynette. A rush of people shuffled into the bar. She now understood why Larry scheduled both a bartender and a cocktail waitress for each shift. When Peg had called in sick, Lynette was glad and figured she could have all the tips for herself. The four other bartenders she worked with during the past week kept insisting that the bar could really get swamped, but she hadn't seen it until this moment. Suddenly drinkers were surrounding her. Many were interested in the super bowl. During the fourth quarter, even airport employees hid in the corners of the lounge drinking Coca colas.

When the highball glasses were used up Lynette resorted to serving mixed drinks in wine glasses. The trash receptacles overflowed with Styrofoam plates from the restaurant, and cigarette ashes flew all over every time Lynette walked by the trash. Tables were sticky with grenadine spilled from Shirley Temples. There were no more lemon twists and lime squeezes. An old man with glasses and a grey beard got a scotch on the rocks, but he had ordered a Jack Daniels on the rocks. The lady who ordered the Roy Rogers for her son, got a Shirley Temple. Six people under age popped in and tried to order drinks. A big lady in a green and white striped jump suit wanted to order dinner with her margarita. Then Lynette looked up and saw Cameron pouring beers for people at the bar. What would Larry think, if he saw this situation? Lynette really didn't want to find out, so she acted quickly, while standing on a chair, she spoke in a loud voice.

"Ladies and Gentlemen," Lynette announced. "Let me have your attention. There will be no more table service because we're short staffed. If anyone needs another drink, please come up to the bar. Thank you for your cooperation." Lynette jumped from the chair and ran behind the bar. She was finally gaining some control over the mob, when the whole bunch stood up to pay their tabs. They were all in a hurry and had planes to catch. After what seemed a long stint at the cash register, Lynette saw the crowd depart as quickly as they had arrived.

"Thanks so much for pouring those beers for me, Cameron. I was really in the weeds. No wonder I was supposed to have a waitress on tonight," said Lynette. "I don't know what I would have done without you." She took a deep breath and hopped from table to table to push in chairs and add empty glasses to the tray in her hand. "Well, I survived, even though this place looks like a scene from a natural disaster. Everyone was fairly patient, except that nasty chick in the blue dress." Lynette brought the full tray of dirty glasses up to the bar and unloaded them, then trudged back out to collect more. "I totally went out of my way and told her that since she had to wait so long for her Hennessey, that it was on the house. The bitch didn't even leave a tip." Cameron had been washing glasses, and he stopped now, to pour a drink of water. Lynette returned with the tray filled with dirty ashtrays. She stood over the trash, dumping cigarette butts.

"Here, take a minute," said Cameron. "I poured this for you." He set a glass of water on the bar.

She gratefully gulped it down, grabbed a clean towel and a spray bottle of cleaner. Then headed out to clean up the final remains from the mob.

"I hate that when the planes are delayed," said Cameron. He was back on his bar stool now swallowing the last of his beer. Lynette had been wiping down a table, when she glanced up and saw his empty glass.

"Cameron, why don't you pour yourself a beer on Larry for all your help."

"You know, Lynette, I really think I'm gonna like you." He carried his glass behind the bar to the tap and reached for the Budweiser draft handle.

* * *

Dillan worked late that evening at the Tallahassee Municipal Airport. Two belt loaders needed repair just before the end of his shift and an aircraft, waiting to be sold, still needed to be run. At four in the morning, it had been twenty-six degrees Fahrenheit when he had changed a tire on a commuter plane headed to the Turks and Caicos. Then there was the de-icing of the Federal Express jet and the flight delays due to the record low temperatures. He had hoped to leave work in time to stop at the lounge and get a beer before heading home. At the bar earlier, he had seen the new bartender. In his mind, he could still hear her voice. He liked the brightness and mindfulness in it. Now, in the maintenance shop, cleaning up, he recollected his stop at the bar earlier that day.

* * *

"Hey Dillan," said Becky. "Have you met Lynette? She just started working a couple of weeks ago."

"Hello," said Dillan.

"Good to meet you," said Lynette. She had been squeezing lime wedges into drinks on a tray, when Dillan had noticed her long-painted fingernails, and her lowcut collared button-down tan shirt. The top three buttons undone, enough to make a man not be able to look away. Her body looked hard, like she worked out. Dillan remembered the shoulder pads in her shirt, it wasn't that, it was her biceps. He had seen them flexing while she carried the tray loaded up with full glasses.

"Can I get you a beer, Dillan?" said Becky. The sound of her voice had snapped his attention toward the upturned bottle of gin that she was pouring in high ball glasses.

"No, I'm working, just grabbing some lunch to bring back to the shop," said Dillan. "Thought I could catch the space shuttle launch. It's supposed to launch at around two-thirty. That's if they don't cancel, it's already been delayed as it is." Dillan's almond shaped hazel eyes scanned the lounge. "Man, You guys are busy."

"Yah, Legislative Session. They meet in January and February this year, it's an even year. Next year it will be an odd year so they will meet in March and April. It'll be standing room only at peak hour with full flights coming and going for the whole session," said Becky.

"I'm glad," said Lynette. "I need the money, gotta pay tuition. And I'm glad I'm finally down to one job, I just did a two week overlap with the Brass Rail, where I worked before here finishing out my two weeks' notice."

"Oh, you'll make some money today," said Becky. "I made three hundred in tips yesterday, and you'll probably do the same tonight. Legislature time is our bread and butter."

A college girl, Dillan liked that idea. He had watched as Lynette made her way through the crowd carrying the tray of drinks to a table in the corner. With her back to him he had followed the outline of her body in the tight pin striped tan slacks she wore. Careful not to appear like a perv, he had looked back at the television, just in time to hear CNN Live T.V. "T Minus 21 seconds, T Minus 15 seconds, Solid Rocket Booster Engine Gimbal now under way."

Dillan had noticed the folks seated at the bar looking at the television. "T Minus 10, 9, 8, 7, 6, 5," said the T.V. announcer. People in the lounge counted along with the voice. "We have main engine start." And that's when the whole room had roared, the people at the tables, the people standing, the people running in from the restaurant had counted along with the television. "4,3,2,1 and lift off, lift off of the twenty-fifth space shuttle mission." Dillan threw his hands in the air. The lounge had been filled with clapping and war whoops. Everyone's eyes watched the Challenger on the screen. "And it has cleared the tower," said the announcer. Everyone saw it shooting through a clear blue sky, with the orange and yellow flickering of fire behind it, the white trails of smoke dividing into two and suddenly the shuttle was gone, and there was dead silence in the airport lounge, and on the television. "It looks like a couple of the solid rocket boosters ahh blew away from the side of the shuttle in an explosion," said the announcer. Mission Control Silence. "Flight controllers here are looking carefully at the situation. Obviously, a major malfunction." More silence. Then the announcer said what Dillan already knew. "We have the report from the flight dynamics officer that the vehicle has exploded."

Dillan stood silent with the crowd, his eyes watery, his hands clutching the Styrofoam containers that were lunch for him and his boss. He bowed his head and shook it. Slowly voices had begun again with words of regret, disbelief, sorrow, shock.

"Oh Man, there's nothing left of it or them," said Lynette. She had been holding a bar rag in her hand, and she tossed it on her tray.

"That's unbelievable," said a stranger at the bar stool next to Dillan.

"How sad," said Becky. She bent to grab more glasses to set for another drink order.

Dillan had felt so disconcerted the second he had seen the explosion. "They should have cancelled," said Dillan. He remembered the sound of his own solemn voice.

Hours later at the aircraft maintenance shop, standing at the sink, feeling the warm water and rough lava soap washing away the day's work from his hands, Dillan regarded the healing cut on his thumb knuckle and then scrutinized the sky through the window. He thought about the shuttle crash and all seven crew members just gone. *They should have cancelled. They should have cancelled,* he thought. How many times had he confronted pilots, pissing them off when he grounded flights? He couldn't count. But what he knew, was that no plane would ever crash because his hands had been on it. The sheet metal, and their wings, were smooth and alive in his hands. Their hydraulics, electronics and fluids had a pulse. Their engines had respiration. And temperature conditions needed to be conducive for flying that space shuttle. Given miniscule doubt of the conditions for flight or conditions of the aircraft, the flight on his watch would get cancelled without a second thought about having to reschedule.

His mind turned to the view outside, the deep looming blue gray clouds emerging in the west covering what might have been a beautiful sunset. He shut the faucet water, and ripped paper towels from a roll. While drying his hands, he understood the sound of thunder and stepped toward the open shop door in anticipation of lightning. A second passed and the fork of light spread. The storm clouds swarmed like a governed crowd instructed to corrupt the airspace. Dillan hoped for a short-lived fast-moving storm that might be over before the next flight was due to land. The wind blustered, causing the paper towel in his hand to flap. Then something unexpected happened. Two planes burst through the rapidly growing dark side of the sky. They were flying in formation for a split second before one began a deep descent. Dillan recalled the extent of rapid decompression from flying jump seat many times in A-4's. The other plane ascended. Moments later, Dillan could see that the descending aircraft was a C-130. The pilot was performing a steep approach landing. Suspiciously, he cocked his head, listened with a trained and passionate ear to the familiar sound from his past, Lockheed Hercules engines. One of the engines on the approaching aircraft was shut down. The other plane turned and headed south. Immediately, he was taken back to 1977, the year he was in boot camp. But what were two C-130's doing at this airport?

A mixture of rain and hail cascaded, just as Bryan Smith, the airport Assistant Manager, briskly entered the air freight building, cutting through the connecting doors to the shop.

"Dillan, a military plane has landed here for some emergency maintenance. All the guys from General Aviation have gone home. Where's your boss?"

"He's gone home too," replied Dillan. He threw a paper towel into the can nearby. "I, ah could go talk to the pilots if you want. I used to work on those planes in the Marine Corp."

"Sure, I'll escort you," said Smith.

Both men walked with purpose to the large intimidating aircraft that looked so out of place at the small airport. The storm had moved out as fast as it had moved in leaving behind cold air. Three guards, armed with M-16 rifles and 9-millimeter pistols, in full blue and white uniforms stood around the plane. The guard at the bottom of the stairs approached the airport crew.

"Mr. Johnson, this is one of our contract maintenance personnel," said Smith. "Dillan Maccaw."

"What seems to be the problem?" asked Dillan. He stood at attention.

"A low oil pressure light on the port engine, we shut the engine down before we lost all the oil pressure," said the Captain.

"Well, I'll need a work-stand to open the cowling," said Dillan. "I'll be right back." He disappeared into the air freight building thinking how unique an opportunity it was to be working on a cargo plane again. When he returned pushing the work-stand, Dillan scanned the port side of the aircraft. Pointing his eagle like nose upward, he noticed there was a port navigation light out. He climbed the stand up to the engine, lifted the upper cowling, shined a flashlight with the hand inscription, "High-speed", and then released the latches to the lower cowling. He spied something shining inside. The light revealed a badge. Dillan reached for it, placing the find in his shirt pocket. Then he focused his attention on the Sich D-27 prop fan engine. Only a few minutes later, he descended the work-stand and reported to the pilot that he had discovered the loose line on the oil tank. Dillan knew it would take twenty minutes to tighten the line and run the engine for a leak check, but the process seemed to take longer because not once did the nearest guard stand at ease. Dillan descended the work-stand.

"The plane needs oil servicing, and a new navigation light." Dillan pointed toward the dead bulb.

"I thought it would," said the flight engineer. He was bent lacing his shoe. A small package slipped out from his shirt pocket. Dillan shined his flashlight on the ground, and there the contraband lie, a package of Joya De Nicaragua cigars.

"Oh, thank you," said the flight engineer while he reached out to retrieve the smokes.

"We've got mobile-2 here, which is what this plane requires," said Dillan. "The bulb, I don't know if we have it in stock. I'll check." Dillan trotted across the tarmac toward his truck. He reached into his pocket to get his keys and felt the badge. He pulled out both, opened the palm of his hand and glancing at the card, he read, *Juan Jose Diaz, Howard Air Force Base*. He put the badge in his pants pocket, put the truck in reverse and drove around the maintenance shop. He first searched through his bulb supply to no avail. The navigation light would have to wait. Then he walked around back to his oil supply area and found the tank of mobile-2 oil and hoisted it on the four-wheel truck. His movements had purpose and despite the enormous weight, his strides were quick. He wheeled the tank to the bed of his pick-up, where he effortlessly lifted it aboard. He headed for the giant craft, replenished the oil supply, tightened the lines, and once again spoke to the pilot on the tarmac.

"Well, Captain, except for the navigation light, she's ready to fly." He reached the end of the stairs and pulled the maintenance stand clear from the aircraft wing. "You better get that light fixed at your next stop. Get the logbook, and I'll sign this off."

"Will do." The captain turned and climbed the starboard stairs set. As was customary for mechanics to do, Dillan followed inside the hold, while the pilot, copilot and flight engineer climbed the hold stairs leading to the cockpit. The armed guards followed behind Dillan and the three of them stood near the tactical military-camo netting that hung in the hold, creating a foyer between the cargo area and the cockpit. Dillan could see the stacks of wooden crates behind the net.

"You wait, I'll bring the book down," insisted the Captain. A guard hastened to the bottom of the stairs. Dillan uneasily followed the Captain's orders as the third guard assumed a position by the open door. The flight engineer poked his head out the cockpit door and spoke to break the heavy importunate air.

"Where did you learn your way around these planes so well?" asked the flight engineer.

"In the Marines," said Dillan. "I mostly worked on A-4's."

"Where were you stationed?"

"I did boot camp out in San Diego and served my first duty in Yuma, Arizona at the Marine Corp Air Station."

"Yeah, I spent some time in Phoenix."

The Captain interrupted and climbed down with the logbook. "Here, quickly log and sign off the maintenance."

Dillan complied and the flight engineer appeared at the cockpit door and set something on the stair landing. "Here is an address, where your company can send us an invoice," he said.

The captain reached up and grabbed the card and handed it to Dillan. Then he signaled to the guards that it was time to go. He surprised Dillan with a handshake and a thanks.

Dillan could sense the guards cautiously watching as he dismounted the stairs. Once Dillan's feet were on the tarmac, he turned and watched the stairs retract into the plane and the door slam shut. Jumping into action, he hurried to the front of the plane and waited for all the engines to start. After pointing toward the taxi way, he saluted. The pilot returned the salute, and the plane taxied toward the runway. He stood now, looking up at the dark night sky, no moon, but clear. Good sky for a take-off, he thought. He fastened his eyes to the plane taxiing toward the runway. Bryan walked up beside him.

"Nice work, man." Bryan spoke loudly from behind, over the roar of the engines.

"All in a day's work. Look." Dillan was staring in anticipation at the C-130 as it reached the runway. Full of reverence, he listened as the engines spooled up, watching the aircraft accelerating, lifting its nose, and taking flight. "There it goes. Perfect sky for flying." He listened to the roar. He watched, until the plane disappeared from his sight. Long enough so that Bryan had grown restless.

"Alright, Dillan, I'm heading in. See you tomorrow." Bryan turned and was returning to the terminal.

"Yup, see you tomorrow." Dillan rubbed his brow on his sleeve. His hands, he wiped on his coveralls and then checked his pockets for keys, when he felt the badge in his pants pocket. Quickly, he turned, jogging toward Bryan, badge in hand. "I meant to give this to the pilot." Bryan turned around. With an outstretched arm, palm open, Dillan showed what he was telling. "Maybe you can mail this out," he said. He handed off the badge.

"What is it?"

"Some mechanic's badge."

"Where'd you get it?"

"Found it inside that C-130. The mechanic must have lost it while he was crawling around in there. It's from Howard Military Base."

"Where's that?"

"In Panama."

Bryan attempted to read it. "Too dark out here."

"Well, that guy's badge is a long way from home," said Dillan. "Go in your office, turn on the lights and read it."

"Yeah. I suppose so."

"I'm going home to have a beer." Dillan turned to walk toward the shop.

Chapter 4

Sunday morning, the prominent student center chapel on the hill overlooking the University mesmerized Marie. For her it was a place of power whenever she drove past it. And today, the Co-Cathedral of St. Thomas More was obscured with a thick fog that surrounded it like an envelope. Marie was the letter, waiting for a delivery into some new world. She parked her Chevy Impala in the last metered space of a long line of cars on Tennessee Street. Wearing peach slacks and a white sweater, she climbed from the driver's seat, then lifted her right wrist to her face. "Nine-oh-five, good," Marie thought. "Only five minutes late." She spied the parking meter and checked her handbag for spare change. No luck. "Aw, fuck it," she mumbled under her breath. Through the car windshield, she glanced at the two crumpled parking tickets on the passenger seat and thought, What's one more?

She ran, keys jingling in her left hand, up the stairs to the concrete walk, which led her closer to the brick and stucco old Spanish styled cathedral with the side steeple. As she passed the shrubbery bed, she didn't notice an earthworm had just reached up from the top of his burrow and was now visiting the surface. Under the cover of a palm leaf, the worm hunted for nourishment. Marie's eyes tracked the seven tall columns of stained glass over the entrance of three doors, where she entered through the center door of God's house. Satan was watching for lost souls to slip through the cracks, when a robin landed in the shrubbery bed and began tugging on the worm. Marie was inside now, standing in reverence, looking down the aisle at the large crucifix above the altar. Stepping quietly, she scanned the T-shaped chapel for an empty pew seat. Out of breath, Marie took a seat in the front row and waited for enlightenment.

The Catholic priest, a Father Juan was announcing the reading of a chapter from Luke, and the congregation was making the motions for "In our minds, on our lips, in our hearts." Marie looked on with fondness and a longing to be a part of this response to the worship.

A long shag hair style, deep set eyes, and charismatic smile, made Father Juan gently handsome. Marie thought he had a face like an angel at the altar, as pure as the sheep and as paternal as the shepherd. In his purple Advent robe, beneath which he wore a black sweater and black pants, which brought out his dark features in an alluring, titillating way, Father Juan spoke of trust in his sermon. He preached about relationship, friendship, love, and the Love of Christ. He analyzed the love of mankind in the Widow's offering from Mark, Chapter twelve, verses 41-44. "Who gave more? he asked, "The rich men, who gave out of their wealth, or the widow, who gave out of her poverty?"

Marie contemplated the question, her eyes cast down briefly. She felt an awesome attraction to this man of the cloth, who she could swear had several times during the sermon, looked her in the eye.

"Equivalent to only a fraction of a penny, the widow, put in everything. She gave all she had to live on," said Father Juan, who definitely did look her in the eye. Marie understood it to be an invitation. "So, as you go about your mornings today," The priest glanced Marie's way again. "Give Christ all you have, as the widow did, and you shall reap the harvest of all of God's joy and love and hope. And this is the word of the Lord."

"Thanks be to God," said the congregation.

Marie lost herself in the Eucharist. "And when the supper was ended, he took the cup and he broke the bread, and said, "This is the body of Christ, and blood of the new and everlasting covenant, which shall be given up for you."

During the communion procession, Marie looked on as the first three kneelers said, "Amen" after receiving a wafer. The first man opened his hands to receive the bread, and a second one, his mouth, the third, her hands. *Which was correct?* she wondered, then took a chance. Like an actress, she tilted back her head, closed her eyes, and felt the warmth of Father Juan's presence hovering above her as he placed a wafer onto her dry tongue.

"The body of Christ," Father Juan echoed.

"Amen," said Marie. The purple robe brushed her through the railing of the altar. Rising to return to her seat, she forgot to make the sign of the cross, but did kneel as the congregation did kneel. Heads bowed, all but one, Marie's, whose face couldn't turn away from Father Juan.

"And the Lord be with you."

"And also, with you," said the congregation.

"May He lift up the light of his countenance upon you and grant you eternal peace. Mass is ended. You may go in peace and wait for the joyful coming of the Lord." Father Juan dismounted the altar stairs. He floated down the aisle by the pew, where Marie sat.

The congregation began the processional behind him toward the door. Marie remained seated at her pew, taken in by the beauty of the church's architecture and artwork. Columns of stained glass lined the elevation of each wall. Lantern shaped lite fixtures dangled from the cathedral ceiling. The combined columns of stained glass behind her depicted a hallowed Jesus, wearing a red and gold robe. In Jesus' left hand he held a staff with a cross on top. The church was quiet now, and Father Juan was returning toward the altar. He now stood at the podium. Marie watched him shuffling papers. She broke the silence with talk.

"You know, I just really loved your sermon," said Marie. She sidestepped out of the pew. "To tell you the truth, I haven't been to church in a while, and something just told me to come this morning. This chapel is so beautiful. I just had to stay and admire it a little bit. You know what I mean?" She smiled then boldly climbed the stairs to inspect the Eucharist table.

"Hi, I'm Father Juan, and you are?"

"Marie Martinez."

"Will you be joining us again?" asked Father Juan. He closed the Bible on the podium.

"Well, you know how us college students are." She thought about how she had failed her last Microbiology exam. "We just might have to find some time to say a little prayer every now and then, especially around test time."

"I'm a college student at FSU, myself," he said. Keeping an appropriate distance, he joined Marie at the table.

"That's very interesting that you are a student." She turned her attention to a gold box, "What's this?" she asked. Her voice was childlike.

"It's a relic of a saint, and so is this one over here." Father Juan gestured to the back wall. "The statue is a relic of St. Felicity and the box is a relic of St. Felix." Marie could see Father Juan's face brightening, and she felt that all too familiar power struggle of the flesh challenging her.

"Would you be interested in joining the church?" asked Father.

"Yes, as a matter of fact, I was just thinking about asking you about it," said Marie.

"Why don't you follow me to the office, and we can talk more about it."

"Sure." Marie followed him out through the doors of divine mercy. She had an eleven o'clock class, but if she hurried, she could still make it on time. After all, how long could this talk take?

Moments later, Marie sat in the parish office decorated in contemporary art. It was posh for a priest, yet warm like a home. Red curtains framed the window to the left of where Marie sat, and above Father Juan's desk was an art print of a celestial ocean view and sunset with the sun's rays parting the clouds. A dark shag carpeted the floor. The desk was made of mahogany wood, matching the file cabinet under the window. To the left of the doorway, there was a loaded bookshelf. If not for the crucifix above the door with the blood dripping from Jesus' extremities, the room could have passed for any business office. Standing near the mahogany coat rack in the corner by the window, Father Juan unzipped his purple robe and carelessly hung it alongside his street coat. Then he sighed and turned to close the office door. He opened cabinets on a console, where he switched on the power to a stereo. The sound of George Winston's piano music rushed into the room like water over a dry riverbed.

"Ok, here we are," said Father Juan. He closed a manilla folder that had been open on the desk. Leaning forward in his chair, smiling he was checking his calendar, when a small knock sounded from the door. "Come in," the priest called out. A young brunette girl, wearing jeans and a white sweatshirt bearing FSU across her generous bosom peeked in the door cradling a Bible.

"Hello, Ivonne," said Father Juan. "Come in and have a seat."

"I'm here for a ten thirty appointment," said Ivonne.

"Hi," said Marie. She smiled in Ivonne's direction. Father Juan returned his attention to his calendar.

"Marie," he said. His deep-set eyes now gleaming in her direction. "Let's make an appointment for Saturday, say right after evening Mass?"

"Ok," said Marie. She watched Father Juan reaching into the desk drawer.

"Here, I have some rosary beads for you," he said. Marie moved close to the desk. Father Juan reached out and pressed a pouch of black beads into her open hand.

"I'll see you about five o'clock on Saturday then," said Marie. She gathered her handbag from the chair and left the office. Ten minutes later outside the church, she could still feel the warmth of his hand on the pouch she squeezed in her palm.

* * *

Saturday afternoon at St. Thomas' Co-Cathedral was full of the spiritual revelation that the change of season can bring. A new world, a new outlook, a new dimension where the old burden that once gnawed at the soul is lifted, then replaced by another. Marie's mother, who had been Spain born and raised under the strict rule of the Pope stood revering the cathedral.

"Dios Mío," she said. "This is a beautiful church."

"Mira, Mami, Si, it is," said Marie. "Look at the way the sun is shining through the stain glass windows." She led her mother to the front pew. "This is where I always sit."

Father Juan entered wearing his purple Lenten robe. The altar boy followed behind with the cross on a pole. A guitar player sang and played the Old Rugged Cross in the background. The priest mounted the altar, turning to face the congregation.

"Good afternoon."

"Good afternoon, Father," the congregation answered.

"The Lord be with you."

"And also, with you."

"God damned, he's good looking," Marie whispered to her mother in Spanish.

"Marie, he's a priest," said Mami. She spoke to scold. "Suficiente."

"He's a man first, still a man," said Marie. Her mouth was smacking chewing gum. Marie couldn't stop thinking about the appointment, when she would be alone with him.

An hour later, when Mass had ended, Marie and her mother followed the congregation out the front doors of the church, where Marie introduced her mother to Father Juan.

"Is our meeting still on?"

"Wouldn't think of missing it." Father Juan looked at his watch. "Would you mind if we begin a bit early?"

"The sooner, the better, they say," said Marie.

Marie's mother seemed preoccupied with the splendor of the architecture and the memories it conjured up within her. She turned her face to Father Juan.

"This is a beautiful church," said Mami. "And a beautiful Mass."

"Mrs. Martinez would you like to join us upstairs?" Father Juan held his hands behind his back.

"No, I think I'll wait here and light a candle for my mother, Ok?"

"That will be fine, it was a pleasure to meet you. God Bless you, Mrs. Martinez."

"Thank you, good to meet you too. And God Bless you too, Father."

Mrs. Martinez was kneeling at the bench near St Mary's statue when Marie and Father Juan turned to leave the sanctuary. Marie glanced over her shoulder and saw the smoke from the match her mother had used to light the candle swirling up in the sunlight.

At the parish office, Father Juan removed his robe as he had done before, flinging it on the mahogany coat rack, revealing the black jeans and FSU sweater underneath.

"Please sit down," said Father Juan. He took his place behind the desk.

"Well, now that your catechism classes are underway, and you're attending novenas, how do you feel about membership?" his deep dark expectant eyes looked up from a paper he held in his hands.

"I'm interested in learning more about it," said Marie.

"Were you baptized?"

"Yes, but my family didn't go to church. They worked long hours. And my father doesn't talk about it, but I feel like he must have seen God on that raft out at sea, when he escaped Cuba. God's the only way he and his cousin could have washed up alive on the beach in Miami. And let me tell you something. When my mother would ask my father to take me to church, my father always said, 'Life will bring her to her knees.'"

"Do you believe in confession, Marie?"

"No."

"No, what do you mean no?" asked Father Juan. "You must believe in confession."

"You know that John Chapter fourteen, Verse six says that the one way to the Father is through Jesus Christ," said Marie. "I really believe that. I mean I don't need a messenger between me and him."

"Well, let's do it this way. You tell me about your life and don't think of me as a priest, instead think of me as your friend."

"I was born in Connecticut, and later lived in Portland, Oregon for a few years. Then my father got a job as a custodian in Miami. I lived there until I moved here six months ago."

"Go on."

"I'm twenty-three years old, and I have been married and divorced twice."

"Did you marry in a church?"

"Yes. God, you should have seen our wedding, over three hundred guests. My father got a loan for ten thousand dollars to pay for that wedding. When I got divorced, he was grey. Really grey. Let me show you a photo of him." Marie opened her wallet and was searching for a picture of the man who she both admired and resented more than anything.

"See that gray streak, I put it there." Marie shoved the picture across the desk in front of Father Juan. He bent his neck to study the photo.

"You look like him." Father Juan handed back the photo.

"I've heard that before." Marie fumbled through her purse again.

"So, tell me about your marriage."

"He was older than I was, me seventeen and him, twenty-three. To me he was gorgeous, romantic. He proposed to me in this exotic restaurant over champagne. The one caret diamond ring was in the bottom of my champagne glass. You wouldn't believe our honeymoon, a cruise to the Bahamas, we spent the whole five days locked in our cabin. He used to lay in bed and say, 'This is an adult playground. Anytime you want me, you just ask me. No matter where I am, call, and even if I'm really not in the mood, I'll please you. And from you, he'd say, I'll expect the same. We sky dived on our honeymoon. God, did I think that I loved him."

"What went wrong?"

"Everything. He wasn't coming home at night. When he would, he was so drunk and high that he would just pass out. One day I found a syringe in the trash in the bathroom, so when he came home one afternoon, I put it on the table to confront him about it. I was so angry. We were yelling, it got louder and louder, until he shook me real hard and slammed me against the wall. I was cooking, pinto beans in a crock pot, when I grabbed the whole thing and threw it at him. That scarred his chest." Marie's eyes begin to well up with tears from all the remembering.

"Then what happened?"

"I remember running to the bathroom screaming 'I hate you' I said it over and over. He chased me and I tore off my diamond ring, then flushed it down the toilet. I remember his eyes. They bugged out of his head. He went wild, and I remember thinking,' What is he going to do? Try to take the toilet apart to find the ring?' I saw the toilet seat ripped from the tank and he struck me. Eight hours later, my girlfriend found me lying unconscious on the bathroom floor in a puddle of blood with the toilet seat around my neck."

"Oh my God, it's a wonder you're not dead."

Marie bowed her head looking down at the floor. "And you know what? Henrique was there, in the bathroom with me, perched on the sink." She shook her head, "Henrique," The corners of her mouth turning up slightly, she lifted her face. "He's my bird friend. I saw my girlfriend, and I saw Henrique."

"Where did he go? Your husband?"

"He says he went to a friend's place and didn't think I was hurt that bad. I was in the hospital with bandages around my head for six weeks. I filed for a divorce as soon as I got out."

"Did you and your family press charges?"

"No, I loved him." Marie began to cry. Father Juan pushed the box of tissue across the desk, and she gladly accepted. Wiping her tears, blowing her nose, blotting her mascara, Marie was flooded with memories, like a hurricane going round and round with the eye in the middle not knowing when it would pass. Hurricane Marie hit Port Juan. She expelled all her pain, all her heart, sharing and baring her soul. Her mind, every single memory she could think was flapping. How she came to move to Tallahassee. How much she loved and missed her late Grandmother, the date of her birthday. How she felt betrayed by her second husband, and how he had forced himself on her and she had destroyed his motorcycle with a crowbar. She told him about her possible eating disorder and her parents' secrets. The stuff that had been buried deep down. Deep like the tick that has been burrowed in so long that the skin grows over it. So deep that only the surgery of Father Juan could have removed it.

"I have memories of being fondled by my father's friend. He would tell me that my parents would be so ashamed if they found out and that I should keep it secret, to keep them from killing themselves over it. I could never tell anyone. I see his face above me, and we were always at a party. My mother and father were in the other room, I could hear them talking. They must have thought I was playing with my cousins. I hate them for not stopping him. I hate them for not knowing. God, I hate myself for letting this happen."

Then in a long overdue catharsis, Marie rose from her seat and threw the chair over onto the floor. Her chest heaving, she ran to the window, her hands clutching the windowsill, she leaned into it, head bowed and pressing on the glass of the window. Father Juan stood and pressed a Kleenex in her hand. He touched her shoulder gently.

"It wasn't your fault. Everything will be Ok."

Marie inhaled and let out final wail of pain. Her face wrenched with anxiety. Somewhere, in her secret rain of tears a light of truth was shining on the child that had been lost in years past. The storm was subsiding, and the child was inhaling the fresh air of innocence. Exhausted, Marie turned to Father Juan, who escorted her empathetically back to her chair, that lay turned over on the floor. He picked it up, motioned for her to sit, reached for her hands, and holding them both in his, he knelt in front of her, bowed his head and said, "Let's pray."

When prayers were ended, she remembered her mother was waiting for her in the sanctuary.

* * *

Headed North on Stadium Drive, the Chevy Impala turned left onto Varsity Drive, right on West Pensacola Street and veered into a metered space on Woodward Ave. Marie opened the car door, stepped out, ignored the parking meter, and walked toward Learning Way, turning into the Mendenhall Building. When she reached the hallway leading to class, she saw near the door of the lecture hall, a thin blonde headed young man smiling in her direction. Marie recognized his pointy chin, and freckles.

"Hey, you sure are cutting it close," he said.

Marie looked at her watch, "Hey, Flynn. What do you mean close? I still have one minute." She reached out for a single arm hug. Her other arm was holding a spiral notebook. "Come on." Her arm on his shoulder, they walked into class to take seats in the front row.

"Did you do the reading last night?" asked Flynn. He was now bent over his book bag removing a textbook and a binder.

"I worked last night," said Marie." She opened the spiral notebook she had been carrying. "Can I borrow a pen?"

"Well, the chapters are so thick with vocabulary." Flynn reached into a zipper pouch on top of his bag and pulled out two pens, handing one to Marie. "I read it twice."

"If you took notes, I'd love a copy of them." Marie smiled and accepted the pen. The truth was that for two hours she had tried to do the reading. Like always she didn't come close to finishing and what she did read, she didn't understand. She highlighted every single word she read, but that made no difference. She had to rely on her ambition, gift of gab, sex appeal, and attaching herself to people in the right places. This is how she had maneuvered her way through nursing school, and she would have to lean on Flynn in the pre-med program.

The Professor stepped up to the podium, and began," I have graded your tests. When I call your name, please pick up your exam. And while you are waiting for your name to be called, please answer the three questions on the overhead projector for a discussion. These essay questions came directly from this test and only three people got these questions right."

Marie did what she always did, copied the questions down in her notebook. Flynn did what he always did and wrote down all the answers.

"Marie Martinez," called the professor. Marie stood up, side stepping to the end of her row of seats. She headed toward the front to pick up her test paper. She flipped over the first page, reviewing her test while walking back toward her seat.

"Flynn McCartan," called the professor.

She saw Flynn standing, now sidestepping to the end of the row, choosing to exit the row of seats from the left. Marie edged her way through the row and shrunk into her seat. She sucked in a deep breath, blinked her eyes, and was about to flip to the last page, when she looked up to see Flynn returning to sit beside her.

"How'd you do?" she asked.

"I haven't opened it yet?" He lifted the first page. Marie returned her gaze to the bottom of the last page of her test. She sighed and was relieved that she had passed. "With the curve, I made a sixty-eight," said Marie. She spoke softly. "How 'bout you?"

"With the curve, one hundred and eight." Flynn slid his test paper into the pocket of his binder.

After the lecture, Marie copied Flynn's notes over lunch. When she got home, she felt bloated from her four trips to the salad bar. Now in the bathroom of her apartment, looking at her reflection in the mirror with self-loathing, she placed her hands on the sink for balance and knelt in front of the open toilet. She stared at the water. The smell of urine exacerbated the nausea she felt. She shoved her hand in her mouth and thrust her fingers down her throat. She began to gag, cough, heave, and then finally to vomit. Relieved, she closed the toilet lid and flushed. Exhausted, she lay her arms on the lid and plunked her head down. She lingered this way for some time, until the ring of the phone nipped at her. She opened her eyes and stared through the open door, waiting for the answering machine to take the call.

"Hello this is Marie, I cannot take your call right now, please leave a message at the beep." *B-E-E-E-E-P*. "Marie, Mami aqui, Papi and I want to visit. Llámame."

Marie stood up and returned to the bathroom faucet. She splashed water on her face and brushed her teeth. She made her way toward the blinking light of the answering machine on her dresser, then pressed *play*. "Hello, Marie this is Pat Johnson from Tallahassee Memorial, can you work Labor and Delivery tonight at eleven? If so, give me a call by five. *B-E-E-E-E-P.* "Hola, este es Lamont, preguntando si quiere juntos en el estudio de esta noche en la biblioteca de derecho. Dame una llamada." *B-E-E-E-E-P.* "Marie, Mommacita aqui, I miss you. Call me." *B-E-E-E-E-P.* "Hi Marie, it's Juan, about our Bible study tonight, I'm calling to let you know I'll be about a half hour late."

Marie phoned the hospital to line up work. Then she flipped on the stereo loud enough, so she could hear George Michael's new song, *I Want Your Sex,* from inside the shower. She recalled the first time she had heard it. She had been pulling her car around to the rectory after Mass had ended on Sunday. And now while undressing to climb into the shower, she was crooning to the lyrics that were pouring from the radio:

> *There's little things you hide*
> *and little things that you show*
> *I said I won't tease you*
> *Won't tell you no lies*
> *I don't need no Bible*
> *Just look in my eyes.*

The water in the shower now caressing her body, she remembered how she had turned left onto Pope Street, and left on West Virginia Street as if she wasn't in control of where the car was going. That was when she had spotted him walking on the sidewalk.

She had pulled the car close to the curb, jerked it into park, and then leaned across the front seat, and rolled down the passenger side window.

"Hi," said Marie. Her face was bright and breezy.

"Well, hi. What a surprise." said Father Juan. "I have the new catechism books." He bent down to peer into the car. "They just came in."

"Oh, that's great."

"I could go get one for you," said Father Juan. He was still wearing his Cassock shirt and was clutching a Bible in one hand.

"Ok, I'd like that. But before you do, want to grab a bite to eat?" asked Marie.

"Sure."

"I was so hoping to try that Nick's Restaurant on South Monroe."

"I've been wanting to try that place too." Father Juan vigilantly glanced over his left shoulder and then his right.

"I'll drive," said Marie.

"You don't mind?"

"Of course, I mind, I'm in my right mind. And I'm minding my own business. and I have a mind of my own. And you better mind me."

"Ok." Father Juan climbed into the front seat. He pinched the collar of his shirt and was now kneading it between his thumb and forefinger. His Bible lay in his lap. "When we get back, I'll run in the rectory and get the books for you."

"Thank you, that'll be great." Marie heard the passenger door close and she shifted the car into drive.

"Wow, I love the leopard print." Father Juan spurted out.

"You really like it. You don't think it's too much?" asked Marie. She glanced down at her shoes. "Everything matches."

"What else are you wearing that matches?"

"Nothing," said Marie. She saw Father Juan turn away, then heard him taking a deep breath.

"I apologize, I shouldn't have said that. So, how was the hospital this week?"

"Oh, I'm so glad you asked. Last night, we delivered a beautiful baby boy, breech and premature, but he's ok. Then there was a mother and her twins with fevers, and an allergic reaction." Marie paused, gesturing to a pedestrian to cross the road. "And how about you? How was Mass on Saturday? What was the sermon about?"

"The lost art of fasting. I was surprised you weren't there."

"I'm so sorry I missed that sermon. My shift started at four o' clock. But you know what? I believe fasting cleanses the body and detoxifies it."

"I see. It can also strengthen your faith, increase patience and humility." Father Juan gestured with his thumb. "I think that's it on the left."

"Ok."

"Turn here." Father Juan motioned left again.

Marie pulled the car into the parking lot. Father Juan opened the car door first, climbed out and walked around the rear of the vehicle to meet Marie. They walked side by side and Marie felt him brush against her shoulder. She could smell the church on him, incense she thought. Father Juan held the door open, while Marie entered the restaurant. A waitress with menus in her hand approached.

"Two please," said Marie. The waitress led them to a booth near the window.

"Coffee?"

"Yes, two." Said Father Juan. "You did want coffee, didn't you?"

Marie was holding the menu, glancing over the top of it. "I did, thanks, but let me tell you something, I plan to order my own breakfast."

"Mui Bien." Father Juan read his menu now.

Minutes later, the waitress returned with two mugs of coffee that she thumped onto the table. "Are you ready to order?"

Marie met Father Juan's gaze across the table, he lifted one eyebrow. "Yes?"

"Can I get the special with a poached egg instead of fried?" asked Marie.

"Yes." The waitress was writing on her check pad. "And how about you?" She turned her face toward Father Juan.

"The ham and cheese omelet with whole wheat toast for me."

"Ok, then, my name is Mary, if ya'll need anything." Mary collected the menus and dashed off.

"So, do you like Tallahassee?" asked Marie.

"I moved here from New York," said Father Juan. "This is my last semester before major seminary."

"I've been here since June," said Marie. "I'm from Miami. I'm in the pre-med program."

"How do you like it so far?"

"I'm so happy to be here getting my education," said Marie.

"To getting our education then," he said. He raised his coffee mug, then took a sip. Marie did the same.

The water ran all over Marie in the shower now as she remembered how Father Juan had reached his hand, palm open across the table and bowed his head to say a blessing over breakfast. "Pray with me," he had said. Marie had placed her hand in his. She recalled how the heat of him infused itself in her palm. Now wrapping in a towel, in the bathroom, staring at herself in the mirror, an energy ran through her that couldn't be bridled. She couldn't wait to see him again. She stood applying face cream, while she recalled being at the rectory. Juan had to grab that catechism book for her. They both had to use the restroom after the ride back from Nick's Restaurant. He had gone first, while she wandered around the residence, where he slept. She had even snooped inside a closet. Well, that's what you get when you leave the door open, she remembered thinking. It was dark inside, there were lots of boxes, and she had seen a zip lock baggie laying on one of them. *El pasto*? She had wanted to get a closer look, but the sound of the toilet flushing had startled her. She laughed at herself, recalling when Juan had appeared, saying, "Your turn," she had pretended that she was studying a painting of the Last Supper hanging on his wall. And now here she was expecting him to visit for a Bible study

Marie hurried about the apartment. She turned to a big shopping bag on the floor of her bedroom and found a black mini dress. The leopard dress she had worn to breakfast lay neatly folded in the bottom of the bag with the tags pinned on it. She was planning to take it back to the store, along with the black dress, since she couldn't afford to keep them. She slipped into the dress and black shoes. On the kitchen table, she set two cups, cheese, and crackers. Her Bible, which she had jacketed with a handmade quilt and lace book cover, she carried from the bedroom to set it on the end table next to the green vinyl sofa. On the kitchen counter, she lit an evergreen scented candle in a short glass jar. Henrique squawked and flapped his wings when the knock came from the front door. Once inside, Father Juan settled at the kitchen table.

"So, what's it like living in the rectory?" Marie stood at the center of the table. She was pouring expresso into a cup for Juan. His chair back against the wall, he sat cross legged, ankle over knee, opening himself.

"Well, I share the building with Monsignor Murray, and Father Alvarez." He popped a piece of cheese in his mouth. "When guest priests come to town, they stay in the building too."

Marie had claimed her place at the table, and sat now pouring her own expresso.

"What is your major?"

"I'm working on my master's degree in Religion Ethics and Philosophy."

"What classes are you in this semester?"

"Sex, Marriage, and Family in the Bible"

"Oh, really. That's interesting." She was holding her cup with both hands, blowing the steam from the hot liquid.

"And Religion verses Science Conflict and Bible studies of Death and the Afterlife. The Religion Science Conflict course you would think interesting too, especially since you are studying sciences. What do you think about Darwinism and the theory of evolution?"

"What do you mean?"

"Do you think you evolved from the apes?" He held a cracker in his hand.

"Yes."

"What about Genesis? Adam and Eve? Satan?"

"I believe in them too."

"Well, you can't believe both."

"Why would you say that?"

"Because if I didn't, I'd be out of a job, that's why." He uncrossed his leg, and now sat with his legs open, taking up more space than the chair could hold. "My job is to argue that we didn't evolve from apes and to advocate for the theory of creation."

"Ok," said Marie. "That's your job, not mine."

"Hey, are you ready for that Bible reading?" asked Father Juan, now clutching the black leather binding of his Bible.

"Sure." Marie moved through the aroma of the evergreen candle to the sofa. Father Juan followed.

"You have the King James Version, right?"

"Yes," said Marie, pinching the lace on her Bible cover. "It was your recommendation."

"Let's start with Song of Solomon Chapter four, verses one through fifteen." The sound of pages turning filled the air.

"Do you feel comfortable taking turns to read?"

"Si." She poised a yellow high lighter.

"Ok, I'll start." Father Juan read verse one. "Behold, thou art fair, my love; behold, thou art fair; thou hast doves' eyes within thy locks: thy hair is as a flock of goats, that appear from mount Gilead."

"Thy teeth are like a flock of sheep that are even shorn, which came up from the washing; whereof everyone bears twins, and none is barren among them," read Marie.

"Thy lips are like a thread of scarlet, and thy speech is comely: thy temples are like a piece of a pomegranate within thy locks," read Father Juan.

"Thy neck is like the tower of David builded for an armoury, whereon there hang a thousand bucklers, all shields of mighty men," read Marie.

"Thy two breasts are like two young roes that are twins, which feed among the lilies," read Father Juan. He closed his Bible and dropped it on the coffee table. Leaving his intentions there alongside of it.

"I've been thinking about you a lot lately."

"He estado pensando en ti." said Marie.

"You are beautiful, and so passionate about life. Todo el mundo debe decir eso de ti," said Father Juan.

"No sé,"

"I've never met anyone quite like you, Marie."

"I've never met anyone like you, Juan."

"I suppose one could say we are reciprocal souls."

"I don't know that word, how do you say, *reciprocal?*" Marie's attempt at pronouncing it failed.

"It means that we both feel the same way about each other."

"Oh, that's good then."

"Yes. Yes, it is," said Juan. "Marie, take off your glasses. I want to look into your eyes."

Marie set her glasses on the table. She could see his eyes begging her, feel them burning her skin. Her Bible, which now lay shut in her lap, she eased onto the table next to his.

"Would it be alright," said Juan. "if I kiss you?"

Marie nodded, and she felt the heat of his fingers cup her face. She surrendered to the arousal she had felt for months, since that moment he touched her tongue with communion bread. She smiled cunningly, as he leaned in to meet her lips. Her lips willingly parted to taste him. The craving took on a life of its own. His hands ran through her hair. She wrapped a hand around him resting it on his ass, as the other hand landed on his chest, in constant motion toward his waist, where she pulled his shirt tail out of his pants. Her kisses, invasive and relentless. Barely clinging to reason, she gathered her senses enough, to hear him wedge in, "Dios Mío, I'm afraid I can't control myself any longer. Do you need me, like I need you?"

"Si," said Marie. To the sound of her own breathing, she took his hands in hers. "Stand up," she said. Then she knelt beneath him, unfastened, unzipped, and dropped down his slacks. Pushing him until he fell back, sitting bare on the sofa. Her eyes stalking him, she shoved the coffee table away. Her hands on his knees parted his legs. She told him to hold still, while she reached her arms behind her dress, unzipping it, draping one sleeve at a time over each shoulder, until the dress, and her senses, fell to the floor. She paused naked in front of him before kneeling between his legs.

Chapter 5

Lynette couldn't wait to get away for a break. While packing her suitcase she was feeling grateful for her good grades, and for having money for a weekend getaway. The tips at the Airport Lounge had been plentiful and she felt like her money worries were over. This week she had made over five hundred dollars with tips and hourly wage combined. The legislature was in a special preliminary session hashing over the State's education budget, so the bar had been full of drinking politicians all week. What tips they didn't leave, the Medical Association Members who travelled through, did.

"This trip is just what I need to recover from the super bowl," said Claude. "forty-six to ten." He shook his head. "Well, this trip, and the Red Sox going to the World Series. Swane-e-e-e-e-e-e!" sang Claude. He was carrying the last piece of luggage to the Toyota.

"The super bowl was two months ago. You really need to let it go. At least New England made it to the super bowl." Lynette stood at the trunk unzipping her suitcase to add a hairbrush. "Just think about Mickey Mouse."

"I guess we're ready to hit the road," said Claude. He stood behind Lynette, wrapped his arms around her waist, his chin on her shoulder. "Orlando with you is gonna be excellent." When he released his hug, he stepped toward the passenger side door, pretending to trip and fall into the car. Lynette looked on at his Vaudeville stunt. She pressed her lips together and shook her head.

"You're crazy," she said. Claude opened the door and waited for Lynette to climb in, then he leaned into the cab and flashed a smile.

"Crazy about you."

"I know." Lynette returned the smile. "Hey, I'm hungry. Let's stop at Hardees, on the way, and get biscuits."

Claude walked around to the driver's side, slid across the seat and laid a lip lock on Lynette. "What are we waiting for?" He did a Pee Wee Herman imitation, pretending his hand was attacking him, he yelled at it, chuckled and then backed the car out of the parking lot. After a Hardee's stop, the car reached the highway, Claude fired up a doobie. Led Zeppelin's, *Looking in Through the Out Door,* tape blared from the cassette player. Claude was well on his way to oblivion. "After this trip is over, I'm gonna start saving for a car," said Claude. Smoke bellowed from his mouth. When half of the joint was gone, Claude offered Lynette a hit. Lynette's expectation gave way to resignation, the hopeless resignation of co-dependency, disguised as love. She got stoned by association.

"Let me see the map." Lynette jerked down the sun visor and opened the map. "Shit, do I have a buzz. Shouldn't we be picking up the Florida Turnpike pretty soon?" she asked.

"I've got everything under control, dear, just sit back, and enjoy the scenery," said Claude.

"Sure is a gorgeous day. Look," Lynette pointed at the sky out the windshield. "that cloud, what does it look like to you?"

"I don't know, what does it look like to you?"

"A big penis." Lynette was laughing at herself.

"You're so funny."

"Oh, I forgot to tell you I got an eighty-five on my trig test yesterday. Thank God for my tutor."

"You have a tutor?"

"Yah, he works at the tutoring center. He's a grad student."

"What's he teaching you?"

"I just told you, trig."

"Is that all he's teaching you?"

"Don't worry, dear, the only wick dipping in this beaver is yours." Lynette laughed.

"How are you ever going to be a schoolteacher with a mouth like that?" Claude's tone distilled indignation. "Just enjoy the scenery."

Lynette's buzz had been killed. She fell silent. For a little while, the THC had made it easy to forget about who she was when she was with Claude, that someone he wanted her to be, rather than herself. She opted out of the whole change in atmosphere, closed her eyes, and drifted off to nap. When she woke up, the car was at a toll booth on the Florida turnpike. Claude was reaching out the window taking a ticket.

"You sure are pretty when you're asleep."

"I really took a little nap," said Lynette.

"Yep, we should be pulling onto Highway five thirty-five in about an hour. Are you hungry?"

"I could eat, what do you have in mind?"

"First, I need some coffee, and I can eat whatever you want to eat."

"Let's see what signs are ahead," Lynette rolled down her window and felt the wind on her face. "So, did I miss anything?"

"You missed me, didn't you?" A Pee Wee Herman chuckle rolled out of his mouth. Lynette caught sight of a billboard.

"Hey, let's stop at Arby's," said Lynette.

And after roast beef sandwiches, French fries, and pop, they were back on the pike heading south for Disney World's Contemporary Resort Hotel. It was afternoon under the central Florida sun, when Lynette and Claude carried their bags along the sidewalk lined with bright red and yellow chrysanthemums. "Look," said Claude, "Here comes the monorail." They stood watching it zip into the A-Frame building.

"Oh, man, it feels like summer here," said Lynette. "Tanning weather."

At the registration desk, Lynette let Claude handle their reservation mix up, while she wandered the nearby areas of the atrium. Silk trees in pots dotted a sitting area under the monorail platform. Light poles shaped like umbrellas with globes dangling in a circle lit up the green seats-in-a-square underneath. Above it all, the concourse looked like layers of bedrock in the Grand Canyon. Red clay, yellow, and orange. There were shops and restaurants, escalators, and lots of people. Lynette stood staring into the *Concourse Sundries and Spirits* shop, until Claude snuck up behind her.

"Babe, you will never believe what just happened." He paused to put the room keys in his pocket "Our room got upgraded because they gave our reserved room to someone else. We're staying in a suite overlooking the Bay Lake."

"For the same price?" asked Lynette.

"Yup," said Claude.

"No fucken way," said Lynette. "I can't believe it."

"And it comes with a free breakfast via room service. Come on, let's go check it out."

In the room, Lynette set her toiletries on the black granite countertop in the bathroom. She admired her change of clothes in the mirror. She sported a white linen spaghetti strap shorts romper with a powder blue collar and white sandals. She stepped through the room marveling at the décor, making her way onto the balcony, where Claude sat holding a map in one hand, and a cigarette in the other.

"Do I look totally contemporary?" asked Lynette. She spun around and struck a pose with a hand on her hip, her chin up.

"Contemporarily beautiful," said Claude, "Now, come sit with me." He took the final drag from his cigarette and snubbed it out in the ashtray. Lynette sat in his lap, looking out at the lake.

"Ok, I have here the map of the Magic Kingdom." Claude looked at Lynette. "Now, here's what we're gonna do." He pointed at the tiny red cartoon marked Main Street USA.

"Right there, we're going to feed the ducks. Then we're going to Liberty Square, Fantasy Land, and Tomorrow Land. It's going to be so much fun."

"I can't wait, I'll get my camera," said Lynette.

Thirty minutes later near Cinderella's Castle, Lynette saw her chance for the iconic photo she wanted. "There he is Claude, take my picture with Mickey."

Then outside the Hall of Presidents, they shared an ice cream cone. Once inside, they were in awe of just how life-like the wax figures were. "I'm surprised they have President Reagan already," said Claude.

Next, Lynette saw the banner that read, *It's a Small World*. "I went on that ride when I was little girl, when we lived in Los Angeles," she said. "Come on, Claude, let's go on it." On the boat gliding through the singing and dancing children, Lynette felt the warmth of Claude's arm around her and his hand on her shoulder.

Finally, they arrived at Tomorrowland. And after rotating in the theatre of *The Carousel of Progress,* Claude looked at his favorite ride ahead, *Space Mountain.* The rollercoaster ride inside, was dark, fast, and full of flashing lights and loud sounds.

"That was so fun," said Claude. "I wanna do it again."

"Not me," said Lynette. "Did you hear me screaming in there?"

"That was you?"

"Yah, on that last drop, I didn't expect it," said Lynette. "It was freakin' steep."

"That's funny," said Claude. "How about we eat, and then we'll hop the monorail back to the hotel."

"Ok," said Lynette.

"Hey, did you see the guy that was in the Space Mountain line in front of you?" asked Claude. "The old one?"

"The one wearing the mouse ears?"

"Yah! He reminded me of the old manager I had when I first got hired at Sandestin, about a year before you started working. He had a real heavy French accent and at a staff meeting one time, he's telling us how we're supposed to be more dignified when waiting on the customers. So, this is what he does." Claude stopped now and was poising himself directly in front of Lynette. Then he began wildly waving his arms, speaking with vigor and resolve in a French accent.

"And when you are waiting on zee tables, please do not look like you are landing a plane."

Tickled by the performance, Lynette laughed out loud, and stopped to mimic Claude's comical imitation. Claude laughed and pulled her close to his side.

"Not bad," he said. "You're almost as funny as me." He kissed her forehead. "Shall we be off, Madame?"

"We shall, Monsieur."

It was close to midnight when Lynette sat on the balcony wearing a pastel blue satin negligee. She felt the cold ceramic tile under her bare feet. A warm gentle breeze was blowing her hair. Hotel guests could be heard splashing and swimming under the stars. Claude appeared at the doorway smelling clean. He stepped to the railing looking out at the lake.

"This is luxury," he said.

"Yes, it is," she said. "It's been a great day." Lynette joined him at the railing and wrapped her arm around his waist.

"All because I shared it with the most beautiful girl in the world," said Claude. He turned to face her. "You're the best thing that has ever happened to me. Don't ever leave me, Lynette." He wrapped his arms around her and pressed himself against her. He took a deep breath and sighed. "Tomorrow, breakfast in bed, and EPCOT Center, and let's make dinner reservations in Morocco."

"Claude, what was your favorite ride today?" Lynette spoke in a sultry voice, her mouth reaching up to his ear.

"I haven't taken it yet," Claude cupped her chin in his hand and stared deeply into Lynette's soul. "I love you, Lynette." In slow motion he bent to kiss her, and she responded, arching her back and pressing her breasts against his chest.

"Take me on your favorite ride, Claude." She held his hand and led him inside and onto the bed.

* * *

The curtains were open a crack and the light from the streetlamp outside was shining through the condensation on the glass into the bedroom. With Lynette in an aggressive position, Claude climaxed, then lay limp on the mattress.

"I love you," Claude whispered, and like a robot, Lynette responded the same, "I love you too." Claude fell fast asleep. Lynette did not. She was restless. The moon was full, the wind was blowing, and the celestial light was calling her. It was time to detach. That damn crooked penis will probably give me another bladder infection, Lynette thought. Him lying there, smelling like fast food, his greasy shoes, and smelly feet, his desperate need to be only something with me and nothing without me, *I can't stand it*, the little voice in her head said.

That all too familiar feeling of that invisible sign she carried around that said, I won't be here long, reared its head from the nomad that lived in her subconscious, from years of roaming from place to place with her folks until she had some thirty to forty addresses by the time she was eighteen. The spirit in Lynette was constantly in motion and filled with wanderlust. She felt the pull of the earth, and something deep inside her, shouting that it was time to move out, get out. She had outgrown her circumstance and had had enough. She wanted to sail away, fly away. Getting in deeper felt like quicksand, holding her down and she needed to go up and away.

While Claude lay sleeping, Lynette slipped into her sneakers, sweatpants, and a sweatshirt. Then quietly, she leashed up the dog and together, they snuck out from the Alumni Village apartment. Once under the night sky filled with stars, she could sense the blustery air, and the smell of pine. It was a night to moon bathe, and the dancing branches, rustling leaves, and pine needles dropping on her shoulders, were a symphony of change. Lynette and the dog put their noses to the air. They walked to spots on the grounds they hadn't been before. Not once did she think of the peeping tom. So inside herself, so in touch with each gust of wind and the elements and the earth and some rhythmic force in motion, calling her into the night, to search, that when something inside her shifted, under the altar of it all, it was in that moment a drifting seed of a sunder planted itself. And Lynette embraced the chaos it would bring.

A week later, she couldn't believe it had been a year since she had moved to Tallahassee. She sat now on the floor of her apartment. Boxes, bubble wrap, scissors, tape and picture frames were scattered about. Singing along with the radio, to an old Boston tune, *More than a Feelin'*, her mind whirled memories of the face of the man looking out at her from the portraits. Portraits of her and Claude. There was the glass bottomed boat ride at Wakulla Springs, where they had seen the peaceful, grazing manatees. There was the trip to New Orleans to see the Saints play the Giants, the trip to Boston to meet his folks and attend an old friend's wedding, Doug Henning's Magic Show in Pensacola, Disney World, Epcot Center, the dinner cruise in the Gulf with her folks. Then the trip to the photo studio for the portraits. In a state of a total paradox, she was gift wrapping and boxing up framed portraits to be mailed out to friends and family.

On the drive to the post office, windshield wipers swiping, she ran a red light while coming out of the Hardees' drive through window. Trying to stir the sugar in a coffee and keep the packages from falling off the front seat and onto the floor into a banana peel, Lynette thought about how she never really missed Claude when he wasn't around. Contrarily, it was more of a relief that he wasn't around now. She pulled into the post office parking lot, cut the engine, and asked herself, *why am I mailing out these pictures?* The rain pelted against her as she stepped out of the car. She ran into the building trying to shield her packages from getting wet. Once inside the building, all decked out for the holidays with greens, lights, and a small tree in the corner with candy canes hanging from its boughs, she asked herself again the same question, *What the hell am I doing sending this shit out?* Then she relinquished that since they were all packed up and ready for shipping, and that she already held a place in line, she may as well mail them.

After she had done so, she thought some more in the car on the way to her Human Relations class. She had to turn in a paper, on which she had written, *sometimes it's best to break out the social housecleaning broom.* She knew she'd be sweeping Claude with that broom soon enough. In the interim, his long hours at work mitigated her impending dread of the turmoil that she would be causing when she did.

With classes ending, she was glad to have the night off from work to study for finals. She picked up her book, notebook, umbrella, and walked out of the classroom, not speaking a word to anyone. She headed to the door into the hallway, down the stairs, and out into the rain. Cutting across the soggy wet grass, she remembered she had parked on West Jefferson Street. Her sneakers were soaked now, and she was glad to be walking on the sidewalk. Through the rain, her eyes focused on the Chi Omega Sorority House. Lynette had been in high school when women were slaughtered there. She remembered hearing about it on the news and her mom talking about it. She figured Ted Bundy, the serial killer, to be a horrible whack job. Thank God he's in jail. She shuddered, as she passed the house, scanning the area for campus security phone booths, hoping she'd never need them, but marking their locations, just in case. By the time she reached the car, it was pouring, and she was grateful for her umbrella. The thoughts about breaking up with Claude whirled around in her head again. They just wouldn't go away. Sending out the portraits told a lie about what she really felt. Just a few more days until Christmas break and then, she told herself, she would have to act on her thoughts. Christmastime, after all, was a time to take stock.

* * *

The gas gauge was at less than a quarter of a tank. A Sunoco station was just ahead at the intersection of State Road NE 65 and Route 20, in Hosford. Across the street there was a figure of someone dressed in a yellow raincoat, hunching over an army green duffle bag. It was difficult to see if it was a man, woman, or child because the rain was heavy on the windshield and the driver's full bladder held her attention prisoner. The car reared a sharp right to park in front of a gas pump, marked self-serve. When the car door opened, the driver climbed out, then jogged under the protection of the carport into the gas shop. Eyes scanning for a sign that said restroom, they locked on it, and made a mad dash for the toilet. Once mother nature's call was complete, money was exchanged at the cash register, and pumping gas would complete the mission of the stop. Now, standing with her back leaning against the car, the handle of the pump in her right hand, Lynette's eyes caught the figure in yellow she had observed earlier. It was most definitely a man. He was standing close to the road now facing the traffic. She watched him put out his thumb, when there was an oncoming car. The rain had let up a bit, but the sky promised that this was only a break before the next downpour. Lynette shook her head. These were country roads, and in these parts, one had better be prepared to walk, because scoring a ride hitchhiking was highly unlikely.

The clunk of the pump trigger signaled the tank was full, and she hung the nozzle, screwed down the gas cap, and snapped the cover shut. When she turned to reach for the car door, she noticed the hitchhiker crossing the street heading toward the shop. Now that he was closer, she could see he was old and grey, and soaking wet. Lynette climbed behind the wheel, pulled the car around toward the road to continue west. The old man was walking past the driver's side window, and she rolled it down to get his attention.

"Where are you headed?"

"Trying to get as far as Panama City today," said the stranger.

"On Christmas in the rain, huh? I'll give you a ride. You're not going to mug me or anything, are you?" The young woman asked as she sized him up. His face was soft, and he smiled with his eyes. His short grey beard was clean.

"No, no" His head shook while he spoke. "I'd be real grateful for a ride." He glanced downward in humility. He was waiting for an answer.

"Ok, then, get in." The woman leaned over to unlock the passenger door. The stranger picked up his bag and walked around the rear of the car. He opened the passenger door.

"You can put your bag in the back."

"Ok, thank ya." When he opened the back door, he noticed the dog.

"That's Tashi, he's friendly." Lynette was looking into the rear seat. The rusty Llasa apso stood in the seat wagging his tail.

The stranger smiled. "Hello." He looked at the dog, while he dropped his bag on the floor. Tashi climbed over to sniff it.

"All set?"

"Just about," said the stranger. He closed the back door, then leaned in through the front door. "The name's Ben. I didn't catch your name."

"Lynette," she said.

"Lynette, Can I buy you a cup of coffee? I was going in to get one for myself." Ben looked back toward the shop.

"No, thanks. Hey, I'll pull up to the door."

"That'd be fine." Ben dropped into the front seat and waited for Lynette to pull the car around and park.

"Ok, I'll see you in a few minutes." Ben climbed out and Lynette watched him until he was inside the store. She wondered if everything he owned was in that duffle bag in her back seat, and she took how he left it alone with her as a sign that he probably wouldn't mug her.

Tashi climbed over the console into the front seat looking up at Lynette. "You wanna cookie?" Lynette reached into a box of Alpo Snaps. "Sit, Tashi." He sat, and gladly accepted his treat. "Good, good, good." Lynette praised. While chomping and crunching his cookie, he dropped half, which Lynette handed him. Then she peeled back the lid of a Tupperware container of water, offering it up. Tashi nosed it, his long pink tongue lapping up his drink. When he finished, Lynette grabbed a napkin and wiped his beard. After which, she fastened a leash to his collar, and led the dog out of the car to do his business. She had just enough time to return to the car and settle when she saw Ben step out of the store. He held a cup in his hand and pressed a brown bag against his chest with the inside of his arm. He opened the door with his free hand and dropped down into the passenger seat.

"Gee, I didn't mean to be so long," said Ben. He set his cup on the dash." Hell, the coffee was all gone, I had to wait for a new pot." He placed his brown bag on the floor.

Tashi climbed off Lynette's lap and headed for Ben's.

"Off." Lynette pointed toward the rear seats. Tashi turned to obey, until Ben extended affection.

"Well, hello there, Tashi." The old stranger talked gently, while scratching the dog's neck with his free hand. "He's alright," said Ben. Tashi wagged his tail and jumped in his lap, sniffing at his coffee and his beard. Lynette could see him melting under the dog's attention. She figured he likes animals. Another sign she would not be mugged.

"Is the heat too much?" Lynette asked.

"No, the heat's just fine."

"Ok then, we're off." Lynette backed the car out of the space, then drove West on Route 20.

"So where in Panama City do you need to go?"

"Well, I was planning to get to the Salvation Army, if I could. What about you, are you going to Panama City?"

"No, I'm going to Santa Rosa about an hour from Panama City, but I'll take you to the Salvation Army."

"Do you know where it is?"

"Not really, do you?"

"It's right off 98." Ben pulled a folded paper from his jacket pocket. "I got the address right here."

"Ah, we'll find it." Tashi was now lying down in Ben's lap. His head resting on the console.

"So, what is your story? I mean, what brings you to the side of the road on Christmas?"

"You know, I was in the army for over twenty years. I had a wife, kids, all grown now, got a divorce and after, I started travelling." He took a sip of his coffee.

The car in front was moving slowly, Lynette decided to pass. The Toyota swerved.

"Careful." Ben spoke softly.

"Sorry 'bout that," said Lynette. The car was moving steadily now. "I had a boyfriend until I broke up with him the night before last. I left a Dear John letter in a plastic baggie on the windshield of his car."

"Gee, I s'pose you did what you had to do."

"I hope I did the right thing. Hurting people. It's lousy, ya know." Tashi lifted his head, the heater blew his fur around, and he staggered into the back seat. Ben swallowed the last of his coffee and Lynette could see him reaching for the brown bag on the floor.

"Would it be alright if I drink a beer?"

"Go ahead."

"You want one?"

"Yeah, why not, it's a holiday."

Lynette glanced back and forth between the road and Ben. She saw him wrap each can in a brown bag, before popping off the tops and dropping them in his coffee cup. He handed Lynette her can of beer wrapped in a bag. Taking a swig, she thought about Claude and how he must have felt when he woke up and found the letter on Christmas Eve. She thought about his Christmas presents already wrapped and in the trunk.

"Do you think I'm awful for dumping a guy right before Christmas?"

"You must a had your reasons." Ben stared out the windshield and took the first swig of his beer. "He just wasn't for you that's all."

Lynette took another drink. She thought about how she hadn't wanted to go on pretending to want a relationship that she really didn't, especially on Jesus' birthday.

"Thanks for the beer."

"You're welcome," said Ben. "Thanks for the ride."

Lynette set her beer between her legs and turned on the radio. The song *Rockin' around the Christmas Tree* was playing. She lowered the volume.

"Glad it's not raining so hard as it was," said Ben.

"Yah, that is good."

"So, what's in Santa Rosa?"

"My parents." Lynette took another swig from her beer. "Here's the Apalachicola River. We'll be passing Blountstown next."

And the small talk continued through Rollins Corner, onto South 231, straight through to Panama City's Salvation Army, where Ben picked up a voucher, that led to a motel stay down the road. While Ben checked in with the office to pick up his room key, Lynette waited in the car. Minutes later, Ben stood unlocking his motel room. Lynette was rummaging through the trunk of her car. Ben spoke from the open doorway.

"Would you stay awhile?"

"My parents are waiting on me," said Lynette. She closed the trunk with a thump. "I don't want them to worry, but thanks for offering."

"Yeah, they might be worrying now, since you're probably late." Ben stepped into the room. Lynette could see Ben taking off his raincoat, and underneath he wore a flannel shirt. She felt glad to see him getting comfortable. She never asked him how long he had been hitchhiking in the rain. The warm dry room must have felt good. In her hand she clutched a Christmas present, wrapped in paper of green with red poinsettias topped with a red shiny bow.

"Hey, I have something for you," said Lynette. Her arm outstretched close enough for Ben to reach. "Merry Christmas."

"Merry Christmas," said Ben. He accepted the small gift. Lynette smiled, waved, and rushed out of the room. Now inside the car, she gave Tashi a scratch on the head, and she thought to herself what a lucky girl she was to be going home for Christmas.

* * *

"This is one hundred one point five, All rock, all day. Current weather conditions are partly cloudy with thirty five percent chance of rain late this evening. One zero one point five Tallahassee." Lynette reached her arm out of the blankets and pressed the sleep button on the radio.

In her mouth a taste. Had something crawled in and died there? Under her cheek, marked a dry scrape of mascara hardening on the pillowcase. She wanted to puke, but her headache throbbed too much. Lynette mumbled to herself, now staggering to the toilet. A purge, a torcher, self-inflicted fun or hell. Which was the morning after? What the hell day is it anyway? Right, it's Sunday, she remembered, Lynette's shift at the bar was at three that afternoon, any earlier than that, she knew she would really be sorry. She reasoned that a planned misery was more justifiable. On Sunday morning, sleeping in was possible, and with no class to attend, she could spare a few dead brain cells. Now brushing the vomit from her teeth, Lynette crawled back into bed, gazing through her bedroom doorway at the air conditioning unit protruding from the brick wall in the other room. Well, at least the air conditioner is fixed, Lynette thought. Then she recollected how she got to feeling so rotten.

"Aw, man this is good shit," said Lynette. She drew another drag from the joint. It was Saturday night, and Lynnette was still trying to numb the guilt she felt for dumping Claude. "Where'd you get it?"

"My dad," Cameron was laughing now. He held the front cover of a wall unit air conditioner in his hand. On the floor of Lynette's apartment was a gauge meter, a can of R134 Refrigerant, and a small box marked piercing valve.

"You got a little cup of dish soap and some paper towels?" asked Cameron.

"Sure," said Lynette. She stood up from her green vinyl loveseat, and stepped over toward the metal kitchen unit, where she smudged out the joint on the edge of the sink. "What did you say you wanted?"

"Paper towels and dish soap." Cameron laughed beneath his horrid complexion. Lynette followed, now bursting into laughter, she walked over to hand him the towels.

"Thanks a lot for doing this." Lynette was squeezing dish soap in a bowl. "What are you gonna do with this?"

"I'm gonna see if there is any leak from this compression fitting? Come here, I'll show you." Lynette looked down at the unit, and Cameron pointed at the fitting he just put on.

"Oh, is that what came out of that little box over there?"

"Uh huh," said Cameron.

Lynette watched as he spread the dish soap on the valve, cradling it with a paper towel so that it didn't spill everywhere.

"Now, see that, no bubbles, means no leak. That's good." Cameron screwed down the meter and turned on the unit. He pointed at the gauge, the needle in the empty zone. "There's your malfunction." He looked over at the supplies on the floor. "Pass me that can."

Lynette handed off the refrigerant. "I'm getting the munchies," said Lynette.

Cameron smiled and hooked up the can, and they both watched until the gauge went into the full zone. "Well, another good sign. See that frost, mission accomplished."

"Aww, man, this is great. I can't thank you enough." Lynette turned and walked over to look in the refrigerator. She grabbed the bread. "I'm gonna make a grilled cheese sandwich. You want one?"

"No, thanks." I'm good with this." He lifted the can of Budweiser to his mouth. "We're just about done here." Lynette busied herself making and eating the sandwich, while Cameron finished up the job, including lifting the unit back into the big opening in the brick wall. Lynette watched him go outside to balance it properly. When he came back in, he grabbed his beer and his gauge off the desk. "That's it." He looked at his watch. "It's almost three o'clock in the morning. Hell, let's go for a morning ride."

"Hell ya. Let's go, then." Lynette grabbed her sweatshirt and her keys. "Oh, one more thing." She turned toward the counter, picked up the half a joint, then stuffed it into her pocket. From the top of the refrigerator, she grabbed a nip bottle of peppermint schnapps. Outside, it was still and dark.

"Should be a good sunrise," said Cameron. He stood holding open the door watching Lynette climb into his truck.

"You got that lighter?" asked Lynette. Cameron climbed in behind the steering wheel and grabbed a Bic from his dash and fired up the end of the joint Lynette now held in her mouth. Cameron turned the keys in the ignition, the radio already on, the tail end of Jimmy Buffet's *Margaritaville* burst into the cab.

"Oh, man, I love this song." Lynette was grinning, looking up at the dark sky out the windshield of the old truck. She was singing along, blowing smoke from her mouth. The bottle of Schnapps between her legs.

"Let me know if you need any, there's plenty more where this came from."

"Wait, did I hear you right earlier? Did you say you got this from your old man?"

Laughing Cameron said, "Yah, my dad. My dad got jammed up with the cops last month, but he's so damn old the judge gave him probation." Cameron swallowed the last drop from his Budweiser can, and was now crushing it in his hand. His complexion, though still unsightly was less so in the night's darkness. "Twenty years he's been working with some guy from Miami, moving shit up to Leon

County. Reaching his hand out the window, he tossed the can into the back of the truck. "No one messes with my old man."

"That's cool, Oh, I love this part. Can you turn up the radio?" Lynette was stoned and singing along to Don McLean's *American Pie*.

"Anyway, if you want any, let me know." Cameron was pointing his finger at something out the windshield. "Look, racoon." The head lights from the truck lit up their bandit faces, and ringed tails as they hurried along the line of trees on the side of the road.

"I love racoons. Looks like a mother and her babies," said Lynette. "Man, what time is it anyway?"

"It's fifteen minutes later than the last time you asked me what time it was," said Cameron. He laughed softly, then nodded his head. "Can you get me another beer? It's in the cooler behind your seat."

"I think I got it." Lynette was feeling around behind her seat.

"Yeah, the maroon one right behind the seat," said Cameron.

Lynette held up a plastic bag in the front seat. "Aw, man." Lynette saw the gallon bag of weed in her hand. "Oops, wrong cooler." Laughing, Lynette put it back. "What did you say you wanted? Oh, Right, a beer." Lynette then reached around to the maroon cooler grabbing a can of Budweiser and was popping off the top, when an animal ran across the road in front of the head lights. Cameron slowed the truck a bit and let him pass safely.

"Was that a coyote or a fox?" asked Lynette.

"A fox, he had a long fluffy tail. They walk like a cat."

"He sure ran fast. So, where are we going? Down the levy in your Chevy?" Lynette was laughing uncontrollably again.

"Yah, and I hope it's not dry." Cameron was laughing at Lynette's laughter.

"Old Plank Road. Wakulla County Jail is just up ahead."

"Oh, let's stay clear of that place." Lynette took the last drag from the joint before snuffing the roach out in his ash tray. "Can I open the window?"

"Absolutely!"

With the window cracked, Lynette lifted her head to feel the wind rush in on her face. "Hell, marijuana, should be legal. Can you imagine one day just going down the corner store and buying a pack of freshly rolled Acapulco Gold? Your dad could have his own store. He could call it Pop's Place" Lynette looking up, gestured with her hand imagining a big sign. Her wild side was out. The side that Lynette could easily trust with people like Cameron.

"I'm thirsty." Lynette had been unscrewing the cap of the peppermint schnapps and raised the bottle now in front of her. "Goodbye 1986. Cheers to 1987!"

"To 1987," said Cameron. He raised his beer can. Then he took a swig and Lynette swallowed the contents of the nip bottle, leaving it empty.

"Yah, that'd be something," said Cameron. "Legal weed."

"All I can say is thanks to your old man, that was good gangi."

"You think we'll ever see that happen?"

"See what?" asked Lynette.

"Legalized marijuana?"

"I don't know, man." Lynette listened to the sound of the old truck's tires roaring as they rolled and gripped the pavement.

"I'm so thirsty, Can I have a beer?"

"Yah go ahead," said Cameron. Lynette reached around the rear of her seat lifting the top off the maroon cooler.

"We're almost there. This is Lighthouse Road."

"Oh, man, I love lighthouses," said Lynette. The headlights revealed nothing but the dirt road, and the green shadowy bush on both sides. "Is there a lighthouse on Lighthouse Road?"

"Yes, there sure is. Been here since the eighteen-hundreds." Cameron stopped the truck, and all was quiet.

"Welcome to the St. Mark's River Lighthouse. That's the Gulf, well Apalachee Bay."

"I see the lighthouse. No sun yet." Lynette leaned into the windshield, then craned her neck to look upward at the waxing crescent of a moon steadying itself smack dab above the truck.

"Wait for it." He reached into the cupholder and pulled out a bag of beer nuts. "Want some?" He threw a couple in his mouth. "Breakfast of champions."

"What's the name of this river again?" asked Lynette, now holding a handful of peanuts.

"Hey here it comes." They both looked at the sky, it was a shade lighter than dark now.

"Yup, there it is."

The sun peeked out from the night sky. At first just a small yellow sliver, and then there was a crescent of light, until the whole sky was bright orange over a line of deep blue and purple, and the rays of light shot out in all directions. Three white birds took flight into the sky.

"Egrets," said Cameron.

"Oh wow, this is beautiful," said Lynette.

The Gulf of Mexico stretched out in front of them. The marsh pools shimmered behind them, the saber palms everywhere. Nearby an alligator was lying low in the river watching and waiting for a bird to land that he could catch for breakfast. The pied moss hung from the trees. The marsh grass looked like the African Savannah. Lynette stepped out from the truck and walked toward the water. The Great Blue Heron stood regally in the tall grass along the bank of the pool. A red dragon fly was hovering over a bright yellow flower. In a Cypress tree, a mother bird flew from her nest to find food, leaving two babies clinging to one another awaiting her return.

"So much life out here," said Lynette.

Cameron stepped out of the truck, "Yah, it's great isn't it. Peaceful terrain. Even those owls."

"Is that what that is. I thought it was a dog howling," said Lynette. With the sun out now, she was reminded it was Sunday. "Man, I gotta work tonight."

"Hold on, while I drop something off. If you want, you can wait in the truck." In his hand, he was holding a cooler.

"I'd rather go with you," said Lynette.

"Look, pelicans!" Lynette watched them flapping their big wings, pumping brown webbed feet. One diving, hitting the surface of the water, his body going streamline, head popping up with pouch expanded from the fish he caught.

"They gotta be the ugliest and clumsiest looking birds ever," said Cameron.

"They can't help it. Everything about 'em is useful. I used to love to feed them off my folk's dock. We'd throw dog food out to them and watch them catch it in midair. I think they look intelligent."

"If you say so. Come on, it's just down this trail."

The trail was narrow, and the ground was sandy. Both sides were full of yellow flowers, and butterflies in milkweed bushes. At the edge of the marsh Cranes and ducks were swimming, and fishing. And the water was thick with eel grass and hydrilla.

Lynette followed Cameron in the direction of some box on a pole.

"What the hell is that?" asked Lynette.

"It's a duck box. Like a bird house, where the birds can nest. Let's hope no one's moved in." Once they reached it, Cameron unhooked a latch on the bottom, and lifted the top that was connected by a hinge, then he looked inside and reached for a brown bag that was there. The cooler, he opened, took out the bag of weed, and dropped it in the duck box, closed the lid, and latched it down. The brown bag, he threw in the cooler. "All set."

Lynette noticed the Federal Express sticker on the top of the cooler.

"What, do you have your dope Fed Ex-ed to you or something?"

Cameron laughed. "Something like that," he said. "Let's go see if we can find a cup of coffee." Cameron turned looking beyond the duck box in the direction of someone standing at the edge of the water.

Lynette's eyes focused, her mind half buzzed still, she made out the shape of a person. "Oh, Shit, Who the hell is that?"

"Wait here, I might know 'em."

"No, I'm coming with you," said Lynette. "I'm not getting busted alone."

"Just stay back that's all," said Cameron. He walked in the direction toward the man. "And watch out for gators."

"Ooooh, Lord. What do I do if I see one?"

"You get away," said Cameron. "The trouble is not in seeing 'em, it's when you don't see 'em. Don't worry they're usually prowling at dusk, not dawn, it's not mating season."

"Good to know," said Lynette. She followed him down the bank of the marsh, hanging back near the bush line, so to be less visible, but close enough to recognize the two-tone khaki uniform, and olive-green safari hat of a park ranger. She watched Cameron jog down the beach about thirty yards. She could see the men's relaxed greeting.

Fist bumping, open palms sliding back and forth, until the final hand grip. So, they know each other, Lynette thought. She tried to listen to their conversation, but she wasn't close enough to hear the words, only the sound of their voices, blending in with the musical sounds of nature chirping, whistling, buzzing, screeching, rattling, flapping, quacking, and a plane flying over. After a full circle scan for gators, Lynette settled her eyes on the face of the man in uniform. The man was black, and he was shorter than Cameron. She could hear laughter between the men. Within minutes, Lynette heard the man, call out, *Chao.* Then Cameron turned and was headed in Lynette's direction, still carrying the cooler.

"Everything's cool," Cameron called out. "He's a friend."

"Was that a park ranger outfit?" Lynette could see the man was still standing where Cameron had left him. "Peaceful job, I guess when it's not gator mating season."

Cameron looked over his shoulder and waved bye to the man. Then he looked to Lynette. "Alright, let's go find that coffee."

Lynette followed him as they retraced their steps off the beach, and down the trail back toward the area where the truck was parked. When they got to the clearing, she spied a second vehicle now parked nearby, and assumed this belonged to the park ranger. Her eyes turned to the bumper of Cameron's truck, and the army green sticker with a star.

"You're vet."

"Yah."

"Vietnam?"

"Yah."

Lynette suddenly understood all the scars, the acne, the black-heads and the cysts. She looked down at the dirt and thought, *He lost his face to the tear gas, Agent Orange.* "Thanks for serving your country."

"We don't talk about that. And that's all I'll say about that."

* * *

Later in the afternoon in bed curled up in a fetal position with a hangover, Lynette pondered over her early morning with Cameron. The drug deal, the beauty of St. Marks River running through her mind. The ride back to town via Crawfordville Road, where Cameron said he lived. No wonder he always drank at the airport. It was the only watering hole for miles. Despite everything, she liked him. People like him accepted others at face value. No questions asked. They coasted along through life just giving themselves away. Perhaps because of their own peculiarities and trauma, human nature provided them with such a free spirit, likable no matter how irresponsible, rebellious, and cynical. They were realists, self-preserved survivors, simple and so damned likable. She remembered when Cameron had walked her to her door earlier that morning.

"Thanks again, for fixing my air conditioner, Cameron," said Lynette. Then she had hugged him and kissed him affectionately on the cheek. His hands had slid down to her waist and onto her ass. "Hey, watch it," she had said, breaking the embrace.

Then Cameron had looked up and shrugged his shoulders, "You can't blame a guy for trying."

Later that night at the Tallahassee Municipal Airport Lounge, when the crowd died down, and it was time to clean up and close, Lynette dropped a quarter in the juke box and played, Lee Greenwood's *Mornin' Ride*.

Chapter 6

Lynette looked up from her notebook to see Stewart entering the empty lounge like a sunrise. "Ah, Lynette, is it? Aren't you a sight for sore eyes?"

"Hey Stewart, how are you doing?" she asked. "Arriving or Departing?"

"Arriving actually." Stewart climbed onto a barstool at the middle of the bar and glanced at the television. Lynette set a napkin in front of him, secretly admiring his sideburns and the way they complimented his high cheek bones.

"Absolute and club soda?"

"Quite right. What are you watching on the tele?"

"In Search of the Trojan War." She held the soda gun in one hand and was reaching for a wedge of lime with the other. "I've got a research paper due for my Mythology course. I figured this would be a good source."

"I've always been fascinated with that sort of thing. Helen of Troy, she must have been some beautiful woman to have all those bloody Spartan blokes dash off to rescue her from the hands of Paris." He stirred his drink, his forehead puckering in reflection.

"This program is pretty good. This guy is an archeologist, who has spent his entire life trying to prove that the Trojan War was real, and not just a piece of Homer's imagination." Lynette returned to her former position at the end of the bar in front of her notebook, where she could jot down some notes.

"Lynette, at the risk of sounding too forward, I'd very much like you to join me for dinner."

"I'd like that," she said. She didn't recognize her own voice. Like when she heard herself say, *I'll give you a ride* to the hitchhiker.

"What time shall I call on you?"

"Seven thirty is good," said Lynette. On a napkin, she drew a map to her apartment. Then slid it in front of him. The lounge door swung open and three patrons shuffled in and sat at a table. Lynette finished their drink order, when a couple more people filed in, followed by two men, who entered through the restaurant doorway. They brought trays of food and mounted barstools. Muted fragments of conversation filled the air now.

"Things are picking up," said Stewart.

Lynette shot him a look of agreement, while setting a wine jug in the cooler. "Yah, so much for homework. Oh, well, money is money. Can't just learn, I got to earn."

Stewart smiled. "Alright then, I'm off, I'll see you at half passed seven, sharp." He rose from his stool and was now laying a twenty-dollar bill on the bar. "Keep the rest, Cheers."

"Thanks. See you later," said Lynette. She was loading up a cocktail tray, until she glanced up to see Stewart's stocky physique step out to the airport terminal.

After work, Lynette and the dog walked in the warm Spring air, under the light of the streetlamps. Tashi was busy nosing through grass and bushes. A couple of leg lifts, a squat, and the dog would be all set, then Lynette would feel comfortable leaving him for a while. "Tashi, I hate to leave you alone again, but I'll put on the T.V. for you." Lynette stepped into the apartment and bent to unfasten the leash. Tashi trotted to his water dish. "Maybe you'd be happier going back to Grandma's to live until I finish my Bachelor's degree." This thought simmered, while the excitement in anticipation of her date, grew.

After the break-up with Claude, she wanted to wait before starting another serious relationship. Why should her life be burdened with commitment, and evolve around the demands of someone else? Why not stay celibate for a while? What good was sex? She could always touch herself, if it came to that. She looked forward to dating other men. And she was looking forward to dinner with Stewart.

She decided on a fit and flare plum dress and matching shoes. With her curling iron, she transformed her head into a cascade of sandy waves and ringlets. To her face, she gave the works: foundation, blush, eye shadow, mascara, and lipstick. "Damn I'm good-looking!" she whispered aloud, while looking at her reflection. A muffled knock resounded through the apartment. Tashi barked. Lynette glanced at the clock, seven twenty-nine. She whirled from the bedroom to greet Stewart outside the front door, closing it behind her.

"Hello, you look absolutely lovely!" said Stewart.

"Thank you, you look handsome, yourself," said Lynette. She could hear music coming from the pristine sleek vehicle parked in front of her apartment. As for the make and model, she hadn't a clue, but before climbing inside, the glittering hubcaps caught her eye.

"Wow, some car," said Lynette. She was admiring the interior.

"It has a compact disk player," said Stewart. "What sort of music would you like to hear?"

"Ah, this is fine," said Lynette.

"One of my favorite jazz blues singers, Nancy Wilson." Stewart closed the door and made his way around the driver's side, then climbed in behind the wheel.

"So, I've never asked you where you are from?"

"London. And you?"

"I was born in a suburb outside of Boston. I did a lot of traveling out west with my folks while growing up. So, what is it you do for work, anyway?" asked Lynette.

"I'm an entrepreneur of sorts, in business for myself. I started when I was a boy. My Uncle gave me a loan for two thousand dollars, after me father kicked me out. Started out with nothing and now I can't spend money fast enough. I'm thirty-five years old and I should like to retire."

"What kind of business do you have?"

"I travel the world. Been to the Middle East, I've had popcorn in Pakistan, bought rice for peasants in Brazil, and seen drug crops in Middle America."

"So, you're in the travel business?"

"I'm quite ashamed to say, I'm in the drug business."

"Well, there's a lot of people in that business."

"I suppose so," said Stewart.

"So, where're we going for dinner?" asked Lynette.

"Tuto Bene's," said Stewart. "We'll eat there, and then afterwards, that is if you are up for it, we'll head upstairs to Maxin's for some jazz music."

Inside the restaurant, blue stained-glass windows shimmered. Candlelight twinkled over formal white-linen. Escargot sat on the table, where Lynette and Stewart sat. He poured out stories from his subconscious that were like an overflowing glass, spilling over the sides. Lynette drank them up. He had paused and was stirring the ice in his drink, when his expression suggested his mind was far off somewhere, possibly in the depths of decisions that made the course of his life so that there was no turning back.

"When I travel to Columbia, I pass money to complete strangers. I buy cartons of groceries at the markets and give them to anyone who looks needy. I do it with toys and children at the orphanage, near where I often stay in Brazil." Stewart gestured to the waiter.

"I'll have another vodka and tonic, and I think the lady is ready for another," said Stewart.

"Yes, I'll have another scotch on the rocks with a twist," said Lynette. "Thank you."

When the waiter had gone, Lynette picked up the menu. "What are you gonna have, Stewart?"

"Caneton a' l'orange, with carrots and potatoes."

"Have you had it before?"

"Yes."

"Is it good?"

"Quite good."

"I've never had it. I think I'll have Linguini Shrimp Fra Diavolo with sautéed spinach."

"Get whatever you like. Get two if you want. I have so much money, I can't possibly spend it all. I never expected to live this sort of life. In fact, I despise addiction and my contribution to it. It started as a way for me to get off the streets. I was taking out my rubbish, the day I met my cook. At first, I ran product to the country. I was somewhat chuffed in the beginning making easy cash, but now I can't get out, and well, these days I find myself quite gutted."

"What do you mean, chuffed?" Lynette hadn't heard that word before, but she had heard *cook and cash* often enough in conversations with drug dealing friends from her past.

"You know, chuffed, it's a bit slang. It means I was pleased with myself."

The waiter returned and set the fresh drinks, then removed the empties and took their dinner order. Stewart ordered a bottle of Chardonnay. The busboy picked up empty plates, refilled their glasses of water, then returned to deliver a bottle of wine tableside in a silver bucket on a stand. Not long after, the waiter delivered dinner. Lynette swallowed the last of her scotch and thought how all Stewart's adventures sounded like T.V. shows, not the real life that ever happened to her. After drinking up every drop that spilled from the overflowing glass of his history, she found a sameness between them. Not necessarily on the same scale, but a sameness just the same.

"Sometimes, I guess, the best way to get over the sting of hurting someone is to help someone." Pausing, she took a deep breath, and lifted her shoulder. Stewart had stopped eating now, and he was paying close attention. "Like you help those poor children in Brazil and how you give money to strangers and the homeless, and," She paused again and tilted her head. "Well, how you brought me here tonight." He moved a lock of her hair from her face and tucked it behind her ear. "Like I picked up an old hitchhiker on Christmas and gave him a ride, because me helping him, took away the sting I felt from hurting someone else. And I would think in your business it might cause hurt sometimes, but all the helping, somehow helps you go on." Lynette set her fork on the table, "Sort of a," looking down, she put her hands in her lap, and was searching for words, her brow knitting, she looked up at Stewart, "spiritual penance."

"Well," Stewart drew in a deep breath and sat relishing his thoughts. "Have a gander at you. I suppose there is truth in that." He picked up his fork and resumed his meal.

Lynette thought how reckless it seemed for Stewart to share the perils and secrets of his precarious life with a stranger, such as herself. But there was an honesty and a hardship in his eyes. Perhaps he saw the same things in her. Honesty is not an easy thing. But she had come to learn where there is honesty, there is trust, and where there is trust, there is safety.

"Lynette, you have taken away all my loneliness, tonight. Now tell me, to whom could you possibly cause harm?"

"Well, I dumped a guy, who loved me, because I wanted more."

"Oh, I see."

Lynette was glad that her answer was enough.

"Here, you must try this." Stewart spoon-fed her a bite of Caneton a' l'orange.

"What do you think?"

"I like it, it's sweet," said Lynette. She noticed a man approaching the table. As he got closer, she recognized his black rimmed eye-glasses.

"Hi Anthony, is that bloke, Josh in, your bar manager, is he working tonight?"

"Yes, as a matter of fact."

"He makes some good martinis, I'll say."

"Would you like a martini?"

"Oh, no thank you, perhaps later. I'll be seeing him upstairs in Maxin's. After dessert, we'll go up straight away."

"Hello Tony." Lynette spoke softly. Tony acknowledged her with a nod. Lynette figured he probably didn't remember her, or he hadn't expected to see her with Stewart. But with Stewart, what was to be expected?

"I used to work for him, well, not for too long, about two weeks before I took the job at the airport. He's a neat guy. He used to come downstairs and ask me how I was doing, and if I had any questions. Good rapport with the rest of the staff too, offered rides to a waiter who had car trouble one night. A real down to earth guy, not like your average too-good-for-the-staff boss."

"You're serious, aren't you? Tony and Josh, I've known since they were busing tables. Now Tony's a university grad and Josh attends university at FAMU," said Stewart. He stroked the neck of his wine glass. "I love this place and the food."

"I have to agree," said Lynette. "Thank you for dinner."

"It's not over yet." Stewart motioned for the waiter. "For dessert, what's good?"

"I have New York style cheesecake, crème brule, and Crepes fourre'es et flambés tonight."

"Anything chocolate?" Lynette asked.

"How 'bout chocolate tort?"

"Yes."

"And bring us a couple of glasses of champagne with dessert, alright."

The waiter repeated the order and dashed off to fill it.

"Now, let's talk about you." The inflection in his voice clearly indicated that he wanted to hear what she had to say, and the look in his eyes made it clearer than ever.

Lynette shared with him her aspirations to graduate from FSU and teach English. She talked about Tashi, her car, her jobs, her classes, her parents, how she'd bait the crab traps at her folk's place, and toss them out in the bay, and how tasty it was to steam the catch the next day. How she liked to feed the seagulls and the pelicans off the dock. And paddle out to the shrimp boats on a raft with her mom, to buy shrimp from the fisherman. And how on some days, if she were lucky, she would glimpse dolphins playing. She told him about selling flowers on the corner, shooting cans with a pistols and rifles in the Rockies of Colorado. But she did not tell him everything, not the things that she herself wanted to keep out of her present and future. What she did tell, Stewart listened to long after the tort and the champagne were gone.

"Now, gracious lady, would you do me the honor of allowing me to escort you upstairs for an after-dinner drink?" Stewart laid three hundred-dollar bills on the table.

Upstairs, the lounge was as it was when Lynette had interviewed for the job there a year before. This night, however, there were utterances of muted conversation and wisps of cigarette smoke from the Saturday night crowd that had gathered. The band played B.B. King's *The Thrill is Gone*. The lights were low. And after they found a booth, minutes later the bar manager came to the table.

"Well, Hello Josh, good to see you, mate." Stewart stood up.

"Hey, Stew," said Josh.

Marie saw that Josh was smiling affectionately. She watched the two of them fist bump, slide their hands together, open palm front and back, and hold a shake. Josh tipped his head, and opened his eyes wide, pointing at Stewart.

"Dry vodka martini?" asked Josh.

"Yes, yes that would be excellent."

"And for the lady?" Josh looked in her direction.

"I'll have a Bailey's on the rocks."

A candle burned at the center of the table. Lots of patrons were on the dance floor. But Stewart and Lynette were too intoxicated with passionate conversation and alcohol to dance, so they sat close in the booth absorbed in the freshness of each other's company until they were intruded by Josh, who was returning to the table with their drinks.

"Hey, ya'll have a good evenin' I'm heading out for the night," said Josh. "Good to see you, man."

"You too," said Stewart.

"Chao!" said Josh.

Lynette smiled and waved politely, observing Josh as he walked away. She was thinking that there was something familiar about him. She took a sip of her Bailey's and then it dawned on her. The park ranger at the river had said *Chao*, he was black too, and then there was that ritualistic handshake. What a weird coincidence. She shrugged it off. She thought it best to keep this to herself.

"Is your drink, right?"

"Yah, it's good, I love Bailey's." She returned her full attention to Stewart, who sat next to her in the booth. He was full bodied, probably from years of eating like this, she thought. She liked the scent of his cologne and his pleasant charm.

"How about your martini, is it as good as usual?"

"Quite right."

Trying not to act too shocked about all the truths with which Stewart entrusted her, and because she felt his need to lift from him some of the pressing burdens of his years filled with terrible secrets, she mustered up the nerve to counsel him.

"Your life seems to happen so fast that you barely have the time to realize what is happening to you before something new comes," said Lynette. "Kind of like a blip on a TV screen, you know something was there, but you don't know what it was."

Stewart smiled like a little boy, eased back glowing, and for what seemed like several moments, he reflected on Lynette's words and acknowledged that he was doing so. "I'm afraid you are spot on again," said Stewart. He wished he could take her in his arms, to feel the heat of this new and vibrantly honest person. Her blue eyes sparkled not with the practicality of sex, but with the promise of other things, another life, redemption.

"I can't speak freely often. Letting down my guard isn't good for business," he said. "But you have allowed me to do so, and I am most grateful."

"Sometimes, it's good to stop and smell the roses," she said.

Later they stood under the weak light of Lynette's doorstep. "Thank you so much for everything. The great food, drinks, and especially the great company," said Lynette. "I really enjoyed myself." She reached out to Stewart for a hug. He wrapped his arms around her and held her like he didn't want to let go.

"Did you really like dinner?" he asked. Lynette felt his breath on her ear.

"Yes, I did," she said. "I can't afford that sort of dinner, and I really appreciated being waited on for a change."

Gingerly, he pulled from the firm embrace. His arms outstretched now and his hands on her shoulders. He had a melancholy expression. "Well then, I am glad I could be of service."

"Me too."

"Promise me something."

Lynette nodded.

"Always, always stay as sweet as you are tonight." He kissed her forehead.

"Goodnight, Lynette."

"Goodnight, Stewart."

He turned and walked toward his vehicle, engine still running, parked at the curb. Lynette turned to her purse and found her keys. She was about to unlock the apartment door, when she heard him call out, "Oh Miss Autry." She looked over her shoulder.

"Yes." He was standing, his hand on the open driver's side door, ready to climb in.

"You will be a brilliant schoolteacher," he said.

"Thanks." Lynette smiled and waved, then watched him drive away until she could no longer see the posh taillights of his car.

* * *

Under the desk light, Lynette's hands tinkered inside the electric Corona typewriter. Why did the ribbon have to run out now? The final page with its three typed written lines, sat mocking her from the roller. Notes in cursive, books, index cards, and paper were strewn on the desktop. It was four in the morning and she just wanted to take a nap before her eight o'clock class.

The summer session was ending. Although it had only lasted six weeks, it felt much longer. And when she turned in this eighth research paper, she would be glad it was over. The Writing Workshop class professor made Lynette realize that she didn't really know as much about writing as she thought she did. She had considered herself a good writer, but this professor had made her feel like she knew nothing. *A well-written letter can change the world, it can start or stop a war, secure employment, save money, even save a life,* he had said in class. For six weeks, Lynette did nothing but work the airport lounge, go to class or the library and do homework. Never had she received the grade D on an assignment. Not in elementary school, middle school, high school, or college. Yet, there it was, a D. Until now, she had never got a D in her life.

She met with the professor in a writing conference. She worked herself harder, disciplined herself. She wrote every day. She realized it started with some sort of subconscious thing that happened with her mind, and her hands. Hour after hour, after hour, at the library, at the typewriter, at the paper with pen in hand, alone, trying to organize ideas, so that anyone could read them and understand exactly what she meant. Always notes in the margins, arrows pointing at this paragraph or that phrase. Tiny scribbles of sentences that needed to be inserted above or below another sentence. Maybe it was a piece of research or an explanation. First draft, outlines, final drafts, do it again. Rewrite. Add examples. Awkward. Question marks everywhere.

Then there were the deadlines. When everything else was going on around her, she had to avoid being distracted. She had to learn to shut everyone and everything out, becoming a hermit to create good writing. *Writing is reading, you're making something else for someone to read*, the professor would say.

Sometimes her brain was on fire and the ideas would roll out of her and other times, she couldn't sit one more second crunched up and cramped at the desk in her youthful body that wanted constant motion. Sleep became luxury, she learned to deny herself that, for the sake of the Bachelor's degree. Another cup of coffee, another cup of tea, more popcorn, another snack. Focus, Focus, stay with it. Even when other students were travelling to Europe for a semester, going to the football games, going to dances, rehearsing a play, swimming, playing squash ball, tennis, or golf, learning how to use leisure time, eating at Rax with a friend, studying together at the library, clubbing at night, studying their first choice of a major, Lynette worked for school or for the airport bar. Only three more hours until class. After work tonight, you can sleep, she told herself. There was just work, work, work, and survive. A paper for the Twentieth Century American Novel class, a paper for Mythology, a paper for Literature of American Minorities, another ribbon for the typewriter, out of correction tape again, a paper for a paper. Just writing one paper after another. That D paper for Writing Workshop.

May 5, <u>Alas! A Cure for Nail Biting writing conference (first draft).</u> Tap, tap, tap, ding, zzzzzzip. Ssssshhhhhp. D

May 9, <u>Glitter: A Taste of a Rich and Famous Lifestyle (final draft)</u>. Tap, tap, tap, ding, zzzzzzip. Ssssshhhhhp. *This is in no way an argumentative paper.* D

May 12, <u>A Motive for Mythology (first draft)</u> Tap, tap, tap, ding, zzzzzzip. Ssssshhhhhp *Too many sheer errors of mechanics, Too many intro. phrases and passive voice, Not parallel, Weak, Too often repeated, Spelling, You called the Exorcist TV, it's a movie.* D+

May 15, <u>A Motive for Mythology (final draft)</u> Tap, tap, tap, ding, zzzzzzip. Ssssshhhhhp. *Better, but too much correcting and not enough rewriting.* C+

May 22, <u>Undoubtedly a Festive Affair (final draft)</u> Tap, tap, tap, ding, zzzzzzip. Ssssshhhhhp. *Get the predicate and the subject up front, Wordy, Too many intro. Phrases, Too many wordy sentences, Much better writing, though.* C

May 29, <u>Freedom in Nazi Germany (final draft)</u> - Tap, tap, tap, ding, zzzzzzip. Ssssshhhhhp. *You need to be clearer, Not quite clear enough, Imprecise, Sp, Some pretty good writing, Who? What book? Document? Interesting comparison –meaty content, This is a good/bad paper: Good: some clean direct sentences good handling of difficult ideas, good comparisons. Bad: Weak Thesis, incomplete and badly worded, Still too many sloppy errors, Still too many passive and wordy sentences.* C

June 4 <u>The Classroom Cries Out for Change</u> - Tap, tap, tap, ding, zzzzzzip. Ssssshhhhhp. *Not parallel, Pretty good argument, but you must learn to comma correctly. The writing is better, but still needs work.* B-

Finally, a B minus. What a relief, *I'm not a failure after all,* Lynette thought. When the Writing Workshop class was over, she realized the power a letter held, the power the professor intended to convey to the class: the power to write something that could change things and change someone's life. Lynette had crossed an intellectual milestone. She learned the skill of playing God with ideas and words. To put them all together to tell a story or prove a point with enough evidence to persuade a reader. And when Lynette thought about how her great grandmother had signed her name with an X, she realized the value of her education.

* * *

Later, on the foot path, walking east from the Stone Building, Lynette felt the sun on her face, and heard power tools, and a jack hammer. Feeling like a flirt, she smiled and waved at the construction men whistling at her from high places. *Damn I'm good looking,* she thought. She felt fresh and new, even back in the car, driving to Alumni Village, pass the chain linked entrance and up Pennell circle to her little brick hovel, she felt like she had reached a new level. Until, the exhaustion returned, she felt free for just a little while. Then she sunk on the green vinyl love seat, switched on the television to *The Young and the Restless,* soap opera, just in time to see Victor Newman and Nikki in a lover's embrace. When the commercial break came on, she darted to the fridge and grabbed some cheese and bread. Placing a frying pan on the stove, Lynette added some butter, and grilled a cheese sandwich. She poured a glass of milk, sat down to eat. Then she glanced at her stereo, recalling the first night she saw it.

She had returned after Christmas, after picking up the hitch hiker, who *Jesus Christ*, she thought, *could have been a serial killer*. She recalled unlocking her apartment door only to stare at the tower of a stereo system with two large speakers. On top of it lay a key and an audio cassette tape. *To: Lynette, Merry Christmas* was written on the label. Lynette popped in the cassette and pressed play. The volume was turned way up, and Claude's recorded voice had filled the room. *I hope you like your Christmas present. A letter on the windshield, really. I'm returning your apartment key.* He ranted for half an hour on tape about being dumped. Aloud he read each line of Lynette's letter, and scrutinized it one sentence at a time. *You say you want to be honest with yourself, well, you've done nothing but lie to me and lead me on. You want to be in the fast lane, you'll never be a teacher.* Lynette still hadn't been able to listen to the whole tape. She had cried that night, but that was all. Even now, she knew she had done the right thing. *All I wanted for Christmas was freedom.* Without Claude, she had time to plow forward to her Bachelor's Degree. She prayed these days that she would meet some healthy people and friends that were spiritually and intellectually and physically healthy for her. Breaking-up was a dark place and Lynette had been here before. She had tried to return the stereo, but Claude wouldn't accept it.

When her plate and glass were empty, she decided to journal. *Things just don't seem to want to let up. If it's not school, it's work, if not work, then the messy apartment. The registrar's office, the declaration of domicile, long lines and bureaucratic bullshit. If not that, it's worry over bad eating habits, sex, exercise. No relaxation at all. There seemed to be no catching up with anything. The bills nagging all hours of the day and Claude, had been more in the way, just another added pressure to everything else. Picking him up from work at three thirty in the morning, loaning him money for a rent-a-car when going grocery shopping was the plan. Although there had been love, whatever that was, no wonder I broke up with him. Mom's words run around in my mind, you could do better, you deserve money, youth. What does he have to offer? You have so much going for you. Running on adrenaline, noodles, and coffee, and nerves. Late for class again, walking across campus, rushing always rushing from one place to another. Four jobs in one month, moving, two flat tires. Math class, trigonometry, bad moods, loneliness on top of it all. The doctor says, you're burning the candle at both ends. Worry, worry, worry. So exhausted some days it feels like my eyes are pasted shut, and my back pack feels like it weighs five tons, and as if I've been carrying it for one hundred years, like I'll never make it through the next day. Claude was always borrowing things, leaving clothes and dirty towels around. Jesus Christ, why do I feel deserted, when I was the one who broke up with him. That damn stereo. Going out with Stewart and Cameron was fun, but right now I'm just exhausted.* She lifted her pen and closed the notebook. Then she moved from the kitchen table to shut off the T.V. In silence she dropped onto the love seat, her head back, she stared at the ceiling. Her thoughts whipped around like ingredients under the beater blades of a mixer. She reflected on the previous semester and she thought about a grade in World History, that *B* she got on her French Revolution paper.

She had stayed up all night to finish it. No more correction tape meant bottled white out. Still wearing the jeans and t-shirt from the day before, white-out smeared on her hands and face, she had staggered, exhausted into class. She took a seat in the second row, looked at the professor when she handed in her paper, and remembered thinking that he looked like an ancient dusty trinket. She had no idea at that time, that the paper she had turned in wasn't *B* quality. That the history teacher only cared about the facts and not her writing. She hadn't known the difference, until now.

She recalled listening to the murmur of voices in class that day. She had folded and laid her wet umbrella on the floor underneath the desk. Then sunk into her seat. Had she fallen asleep in class? She couldn't remember, but she must have closed her eyes, because she had opened them to the startling sound of her own textbook hitting the floor. She remembered feeling embarrassed and exhausted. Always exhausted. And always alone, alone on campus, alone when she mounted the stairs of the library, alone when she returned her books, alone under the great southern live oak, and alone under her umbrella. The rain had been friendly that day. There was something charming about a rainy day on campus. So many umbrellas, moving about like a flow of water itself that fell from the sky. All different colors, sizes, and patterns.

Was being a student nothing but a game? Or one of Shakespeare's seven ages of man? Lynette knew how to meet the deadlines. How to take notes about the facts, to listen to the lecture. It had been so comfortable just sinking into her seat listening until she was in a notetaking coma, copying down bourgeois, peasants, nobles. No challenge at all. Memorizing the notes, coughing it up for the test. At community college, she had done theatre, from when learning by rote was a skill on which she could easily rely. She knew how to act like a student, while resting her body from a long shift on her feet at the bar.

Had she been a privileged FSU student, who didn't need to work to support herself, Theatre would have been her extracurricular activity of choice. She recalled auditioning for a musical, being cast as a dancer, and declining the offer. How could the rehearsals fit into her work schedule? There was consolation. In Theatre Improv class, a requirement had been to attend the play and write a review. She got an *A* on that paper. She recalled sitting in the audience. Seeing her name listed in the play bill. Why had the director left her in the program? Had he not proofread his own playbill? On the loveseat now, Lynette reached for a pillow. Her mind flashed to seeing the movie, *Going Back to the Future*, with Claude. She hadn't needed to write a paper about that.

She knew when she didn't know. Metacognition, the word she learned in Psychology class. That's why she had gotten a tutor to help with trigonometry last year. She remembered thinking. How are these people getting the answers so fast? The tutor told her to buy a calculator. Who knew she was the only one using the back of the textbook to look up decimal numbers for cotangents, and tangents?

But when it came to writing, why hadn't she known that she didn't know? The whipping of her thoughts had stopped now, and she settled on the thought that she knew now, and she was grateful for the Writing Workshop challenges. No longer staring at the ceiling, Lynette's eyelids drooped, and then she dozed with limbs bent and drawn up to her torso.

A couple of weeks later, she heard a metal scraping sound outside the door. The mailman, she thought. Her first summer session report card had come. All *A*'s and one *C* plus. In that *C* plus for Writing Workshop, had she learned more than in the courses, where she saw the grade *A*? She looked heavenward. *Thanks God, for helping me conquer another semester.*

* * *

Close to midnight, the full moon glowed upon the towering perimeter pines casting divinity over the night. The air was especially warm, the night Marie jogged obsessively around Pennell Circle, the main street that was the perimeter around Alumni Village. With her Walkman headset volume turned up full blast, sweat pouring down her neck, her ponytail like a pendulum swinging back and forth wildly, she didn't see the driver in a white Continental stalking her. Side one of her cassette tape concluded, silencing the music in her ears. She heard a horn, and instinctively looked over her shoulder to see a car pulling near her.

The passenger window was open. The driver, a black man, called out, "Hey, Babe, do you know where we can find West Gaines Street?"

"Sure, turn around and take Levy out of here, then turn right on Lake Bradford. Lake Bradford runs right into it." Careful not to lean into the vehicle, the woman jogger stayed on the grass still jogging in place.

"Thanks," said the stranger.

Marie lifted her headset to her ears, but intentionally kept the sound off. She just ran. Beside her, the Continental drove, matching speed with her running. "Hey Baby, you sho looks fine runnin' in this moonlight! Why don't you ride wit' me and my boys to find Gaines Street?" Two more men in the car snickered.

Attempting to appear reserved, a faint fear simmering in her belly, the jogger spoke through rapid breathing, "You know what? I would love to, but I'm on my way to my boyfriend's house. Sorry!"

Now her palms were sweating. She looked ahead and saw the last line of brick apartments. She veered toward the end unit. Crossing the black top, running up a patch of grass to the sidewalk, she was at the door. She lifted her sweaty fist and banged hard. She understood the sounds within the apartment, the clinking, the clicking, the barking. Under duress, she recalled the bite of a Doberman that once put a gash in her leg. Curtains lit up behind the windows. Then relief resulted from learning that someone was home. A woman's voice inside the apartment yelled, "Just a minute." The outside light exposed Marie to the person looking at her through the peephole. She looked over her shoulder and for now the white Continental was out of sight.

"Who is it?" the voice behind the door yelled.

"It's Marie. Is Beverly home?" Marie asked, yelling through the closed door. The door handle rattled. Marie felt more relief.

Fumbling to throw on a purple furry robe, Lynette opened the door as wide as the chain lock would allow, and she peeked out.

"No Beverly lives here." Lynette scanned Marie from her sneakers, to her shorts, up to her black tank top, and sweat band.

"I'm looking for a girl named Beverly," said Marie. "I go running with her sometimes and she said she lived in this apartment."

"At this time of night." Lynette shook her head. "Man, you better be careful jogging around this neighborhood in the dark." Lynette swung the front door wide open. Tashi jumped and barked behind the closed bedroom door. "Jogging around this neighborhood at this time a night is a bad idea. I had a peeping tom last year and it turned out the guy did a lot of peeping. You better come in," said Lynette. Marie stepped inside. Her eyes were on the bedroom door. Lynette closed and locked the door, the dead bolt, and the chain. "That peeper came over to my apartment out of nowhere and asked to borrow my basketball. So, I'm thinking, now, how did he know I had a basketball? He must have been totally looking in my windows."

"Do you have a dog?" asked Marie.

Paranoid that the apartment manager was in cohorts with this midnight stranger, Lynette answered a question with a question. "You friends with the manager?"

"No, Why?"

"Ok then, I got a dog. You gonna report me or something?"

"For what?"

"Having a dog. The apartments' no pet policy, and all. Are you going to call maintenance or management to evict me?"

"No," said Marie.

"Ok, good." Lynette moved to open the bedroom door.

"Does he bite? I got bit once." Marie retreated when Tashi approached her feet.

"No, he doesn't bite. Sorry! Tash, come." Lynette called out as she lifted the rusty Lhasa Apso from the floor and held him under her arm. "Really, like I was saying being a woman out alone at night around here is a bad idea. We're sitting ducks for a mugger."

Marie replied, "Oh my God. You'll never believe it, but I believe you. Some black guy was just scaring the shit out of me. He drove by me twice. So, I knocked on the first door I could find."

"Whose? Beverly's?"

"No, I made her up. I had to do something. I heard the dog, I thought, Oh, great, I have to knock on a door with some wolf in it." Marie laughed at herself, and the situation, while she looked over at the cute little beast.

"By the way, I'm Lynette."

"Glad to meet you, you just saved my life. I'm Marie. I live in the front apartments, on Crenshaw."

Lynette stationed the dog on a blanket on the green vinyl love seat, pulled out a dog treat from her pocket and handed it to Tashi, who contently chomped it into smaller pieces and sniffed for any fallen crumbs. Then he circled and laid down.

"Let me give you my phone number in case you need me to call the police about a peeping tom or something." Lynette laughed and moved to the kitchen table. Marie, staying clear of the dog, followed. They exchanged numbers writing them on a sheet of paper Lynette now ripped in half.

"You look like you could use a drink of water," said Lynette.

"Yes, I can, thank you."

Lynette filled a glass from the tap. "I'll give you a ride to your apartment."

"No that's alright," said Marie. She reached out for the glass. "I'll be ok."

"No, I think it's better you have a ride." Lynette watched Marie gulping down the water. "Besides, I have to let Tashi out for last call, anyway."

"Ok, then." Marie cast her eyes about the room. "Nice stereo."

"Yeah, my ex-boyfriend gave it to me for Christmas. It's a touchy subject right now."

"Oh, I know about those touchy subjects: love and passion, thinking you can't live without him, until one night lying in bed at night, listening to him breath sends you into a rage." Marie gestured toward her crotch with her index finger, then pulled her fist to her chest. "My hole my soul." She paused with closed eye lids. Then when she opened them, they sparked with intensity. "In that order. So, what happened to you and your ex?"

Lynette fell about laughing. "That is priceless, 'my hole my soul in that order'. I'm gonna remember that. Anyhow, in a nutshell, I dumped him and broke his heart." Lynette grabbed her keys, then slid her bare feet into her slippers. "Come on, Tashi, you wanna go for a ride?"

Tashi lifted his head from the love seat and wagged his tail. Then he sprung to the floor and trailed behind, stopping in the grass to take care of business on the way to the car.

"You know, I've been praying for a friend," said Lynette. "I've been in this City a year already, and well, so far the only memories I have are of work, college, professors and textbooks. I'm so glad you knocked on my door."

"You know what, I'm glad too," said Marie.

Lynette unlocked the driver's side door and reached around to the back to unlock the back door. "Up, Tashi." Tashi hopped in. Lynette climbed in the driver's seat and reached across the passenger side to unlock the door for Marie.

"I am so grateful you're driving me home. What kind of car is this?"

"A Toyota Corona. Good on gas mileage," said Lynette. "What do you drive?"

"I have a Chevy Impala. It's bad on gas."

"I had a beautiful metallic blue Mazda sports car with a sunroof before this Toyota, and I totaled it," said Lynette. "Oh, well, no car payments with this one."

"So, what are you studying?" asked Marie.

"English Education."

"How about you?"

"Pre-med. Turn here on Crenshaw Drive." Marie pointed to her building. "It's that one."

"Well, here's your stop," said Lynette. "I'll call you."

"Be careful when you get back to your place," said Marie.

"I will, I have my killer dog with me."

"Thank you so much." Marie climbed out of the car.

"Nice to meet you," said Lynette. The door shut with a thump. They both smiled and waved. On the way home, Lynette couldn't stop thinking, how she had just found herself a friend.

Chapter 7

"So, what's this I hear number ninety-nine made an emergency landing here last week?" The short man with a receding hairline, Roman nose, dark features spoke. "What the hell happened?"

"Not sure, I'll look into it. All I know is that the shipment was received."

"What about this weekend. All set at the Frat house?"

"Yep, all set."

"Flight nine-one-two-eight is boarding for Miami," the intercom interrupted.

"Excuse me, Miss."

Lynette turned around from the table she had been wiping, to see a man with his hand in the air.

"Can we have the check please. We gotta plane to catch."

"Sure. I'll be right back." Lynette returned to the bar, where Becky totaled out the tab. "Hurry, cause…"

Becky cut in, "Don't tell me, they have a plane to catch." She smiled accentuating her pudgy cheeks. Both girls laughed sarcastically. Lynette filled a bowl with pretzels, while watching the Fed Ex jet outside.

"Oh, I'm so glad Lori's here," said Becky.

"Who's Lori?" asked Lynette.

Becky pointed out the window toward the tarmac at someone in uniform throwing packages on the belt loader. Then she turned to the cash drawer. "She'll probably stop in later, she usually does."

Lynette reached out to accept the customer's change Becky had laid on the bar, then returned to the table with the suits followed by a stop at another table with a woman and a child.

"Becky, I need a Shirley Temple and a glass of Chablis." Lynette glanced up to see Cameron slide in through the restaurant entrance. He sat at the end of the bar, where his back was against the corner. From there, he could survey every inch of the lounge and the entrances.

"Hey Cameron."

"Hey," The corners of his mouth turned up under his scars and boils. "Love that uniform."

"Yeah," Lynette looked down at her white jumpsuit with the zippers everywhere, pinched her collar to make sure it was popped. "It kinda looks like a flight suit, don't you think?"

"Sure does," said Cameron. "Just stay outta those space shuttles."

"How's it going?"

"Good, how's that air conditioner running?"

"A, ok," said Lynette.

"Hey Becky," said Cameron.

"Hey, nice haircut. You want a Bud?"

"How'd you know?" Cameron was ready for banter.

"Just a good guesser." Becky set the Chablis on the cocktail tray and now shot Sprite into a glass with the soda gun. "I'm gonna count the till and then I'm leaving," said Becky. "After that, the bar's yours."

"Alright," Lynette picked a cherry from the fruit tray, waiting for a grenadine pour. A woman wearing navy blue uniform shorts, and a collared shirt with a red, white, and blue Federal Express patch appeared. In her hand, she held a Styrofoam cooler. Lynette watched her set the package on the floor next to Cameron.

"Hey everybody!" said the woman in uniform.

"Hey Lori," said Becky. "Good to see you, girl!"

"Hey," said Cameron.

"Hey, Lynette, meet Lori."

Lynette said a quick hello before turning away to deliver drinks.

"I'll have a coke with a lemon," said Lori. "I'm gonna grab lunch next door and I'll be back."

"Alright," said Cameron.

Becky was at the register, when Lynette returned with an empty tray and a wet bar towel. "I'll get Lori's drink."

"Thanks," said Becky.

The lounge door swung open, revealing a man wearing a dungaree jacket. Lynette poised herself with napkin in hand to greet Dillan. He took a seat next to the cocktail waitress station.

"Hi Dillan, what can I get ya?" Lynette noticed his mildly foreign features, a small eagle like nose, and almond shaped eyes.

"Hey everybody," said Dillan. He smiled from thick lips and glanced at Becky, then Cameron. "Well, it's my day off, so I think I'll have a beer." His eyes landed on Lynette. "I'll take a Budweiser."

"Wooooo!" said Cameron, now raising his beer glass. "How'd you get a day off?"

"And what are you doing here on it?" asked Becky, now at the cash register.

"Well, it's pay day," said Dillan. "I came in to pick up my check."

"Pay Day," said Cameron. "Why don't you celebrate by buying me another round."

"You want another beer? I'll buy you a beer."

"Naw, man, I was just kidding."

"What? Cameron's refusing free beer," said Lynette, looking toward Cameron. "Are you dying?" Then she slid a beer across the bar in Dillan's direction. Dillan gripped the glass in his cigar sized fingers and thumb. Then he smiled, revealing a dimple on the left side of his mouth. His expression was sweet.

"Cameron, let me get you a beer."

"No thanks, man. I'm heading out." Cameron stood, and reached around to his back pocket, pulling out his wallet. "Maybe next time."

"Put it on my tab." Dillan looked to Lynette, who was setting Lori's Coke next to Cameron, now tossing money on the bar.

"Next time, man. Later, you guys." Cameron turned to leave through the restaurant doorway. Under his arm, he cradled the cooler that Lori had delivered.

"What's that?" asked Dillan. "Omaha steaks?"

"Yeah," said Cameron glancing over his shoulder with a grin, "Somethin' like that." Then he disappeared into the restaurant.

"Well, they're good steaks," said Dillan. "I order those for my mom."

Lynette was picking up the money, and the empty glass, when Lori burst into the room carrying a plate of burger and fries.

"I'll be right back with the new drawer," said Becky. She held the register tray under her arm and disappeared into the restaurant.

Lynette moved to the table from where the woman and the little girl had been seated. She loaded glasses onto her tray and picked up the newspaper someone had left behind. Then stepped back to the bar.

"Is that the Democrat?" asked Lori with her mouth full.

"Yah," said Lynette. "You want to look at it?" She handed it off.

"Yah, I wanna read my horoscope." Lori popped a fry in her mouth and began flipping through the pages. "So, how do you like working here?"

"It's been great so far," said Lynette.

"Ok, here it is, 'People would be wise to get out of your way today. You might find yourself feeling like a steam engine, stoked to the brim with fiery hot coals. You are likely to be adamant about the course you are on, and no one is likely to pull you off track.'" Lori paused, "Well, guess I'll stay on track." Becky returned with the new cash drawer. Lori looked up from the paper. "Beck, What's your sign?"

"I'm a Leo." Becky had just slid the cash drawer into the register, and stood listening now.

"Ok, here we go, 'Leo. Arguments that may have been slowly brewing are now rearing their head today. Most likely, this is a result of your own doing. Cycles of anger are reaching a critical climax, and your stubborn character is coming head-to-head with an equally strong force.'"

"Uh oh, did I hear stubborn character," said Dillan. "Becky, are you stubborn?"

"Ummm, sometimes." She bit her lower lip and tossed her long blonde hair. "Alright, you guys, I gotta get out of here."

"Bye," everyone murmured.

"Ok, what does it say for Taurus?" asked Dillan.

"Let me see," said Lori. "Ready, here it goes. 'Taurus. Luck is surely smiling down on you. Doors are opening that you hadn't even known were there. But your response is strange. Why is it that you hesitate to accept what is being offered? Spend some quiet time today and see if you can figure out what the problem is.'"

Lynette was smiling and she noticed Dillan's dimple again.

"What's your sign Lynette?"

"I'm a Taurus too."

"Uh Huh. Two stubborn bulls, having a lucky day," said Lori. "Now what do you suppose that means?"

The lounge door swung open and in walked a stout smiling black man wearing a dark blue apron.

"Hey," he flashed a big smile showing off his front tooth with its gold filling that formed the shape of a star." "Let me know when you mix up a mistake?"

"A mistake of the vodka tonic kind?"

"Oh, that'd be good."

"Ok, Tyler," said Lynette. "I'll save 'em for you."

"I am ready for all those customers to roll on in." Tyler held his hands in front of his body rubbing his palms together like he was about to shoot some dice. "It's busy season. I gots a lot work to do today, so I won't be ready for a mistake until much later this evenin'."

"Tyler, what's your horoscope?" asked Lori.

"Ahhh, I don't know."

"When's your birthday?"

"August," said Tyler.

"August what?"

"Thirty."

"You're a Virgo," said Lori. Tyler's eyes widened. "Ok, here we go, 'You may find yourself wanting to go in many directions today, yet something is holding you back from going anywhere. This annoying conflict makes it difficult for you to make the most of your day, but you can handle it. Consider all your choices before making your decision.'"

"Uh, huh. What holds me back from going anywhere, is money. My kids in Miami spend it as fast as I can make it. My kids." He shook his head. "You know what I call 'em? Mr. and Mrs. Need More. Because they always needing more." He moved behind Lori. Scratching the back of his neck, he looked over her shoulder at the newspaper. "What's that like a fortune teller?"

"It's your future," said Lynette, "from the stars in the sky."

"Oh," he looked upward and held out his hands palm side up, then shrugged his shoulders. "Well, if the stars do smile on me, I'm gonna make some money this afternoon, when all them fancy shoes be walkin' through here." Tyler paused. "Good to see ev'rybody. I'm gonna get me some coffee."

"I'm heading out too," said Lori. She dug in her pocket and left money on the bar.

"Good to meet you," said Lynette.

"Bye Lori," said Dillan.

"Bye," said Lori.

After Lori and Tyler had disappeared, Dillan had scooped up the remains of the paper and sat flipping through it.

"Anything good?" Lynette picked up Lori's empty glass and turned toward the sinks.

"A lot of bad news, 'Federal judge dismisses lawsuits sought by Oliver North.'"

Dillan turned a few more pages and read another headline aloud, "American televangelist Jim Baker resigns." Dillan looked over the paper at Lynette. "What a mess that guy is."

"Do you think he really raped his secretary?" asked Lynette.

"I don't know," said Dillan. "She says he did."

Lynette postponed cutting fruit. Instead, she took a few minutes to scan the want ads. And when she finished, she was satisfied that nothing listed was better than the job she had. She heard voices coming from the restaurant. A tall woman and a skinny blonde guy, who was holding cases of beer, burst into the lounge.

"Hey, Lynette. Where do you want these?"

"Hey, Sam," said Lynette. She gestured toward the floor mat next to the beer cooler. "Here's fine."

"Good morning Kim," said Dillan and Lynette.

"Hey you guys, Where's Beck?" Kim spoke in a soft voice with surprise. Her blue eyes widened. "I thought she was scheduled for today?"

"Yah, she worked for a couple hours, but I'm finishing the shift for her. She had a doctor appointment."

Kim hung her jacket on the coat rack in the corner. "Do you want to do tables or the bar?" asked Kim.

"We can take turns," said Lynette. "Good money today. Another Legislative session, Thank God."

"Hey Dillan," said Sam. He threw his shoulders back and flashed a big teeth grin. "How are you?"

Dillan folded his arms across his chest. "I'm fine. How are you?"

"You're looking mighty good today." Sam smoothed his blonde hair with his hand. "That denim suits you."

Dillan shook his head, then bowed it into the newspaper to shield himself with reading.

"Girl," said Sam, now looking to Kim. "Who forgot to empty this trash last night?"

"You," said Kim.

"Damn, it was busy yesterday." Sam removed the lid from the can and was sliding out the bag of trash. "You forgive me, don't you, girlfriend?"

Lynette looked up. She had been pouring orange juice into a white plastic bottle. "Can I get you another beer, Dillan?"

"No, I'm gonna be heading out in a minute." Dillan looked through his billfold. "I gotta go to the bank."

"Oh," said Sam. His lips pursed. He dropped the trash bag he had been tying, and now stood with his hands on his hips. "You're leaving so soon?"

"Bye, Sam." Dillan used his voice like a fly swatter.

Sam huffed, then picked up his trash bag. "I could get you something from the kitchen."

"Bye, Sam," said Dillan.

"I love the way you say my name." Sam clicked his tongue, turned on his heel, then passed through the restaurant doorway, and yelled back, "You don't know what you're missing."

Kim and Lynette looked at each other, giggling. Dillan rolled his eyes.

"Let me settle up, a dollar seventy-five, right?"

"Yes, Sir," said Lynette. "That's right."

"So, how's school going?" asked Dillan.

"It's going." Lynette screwed the spout neck onto the plastic container now filled with juice. "I got one year down, and one to go."

Dillan set three dollars on the bar. "The rest is for you." His eyes averted to the television screen. "Liberace died today. Oh, man. He was a great piano player."

"Yah, he was. My grandmother liked him a lot," said Lynette. "She saw him in concert, once."

"My grandma saw him in Vegas," said Kim. She looked up from the cabinet, she had been reaching in. A pile of napkins was in her hand.

Lynette picked up Dillan's cash from the bar, "Thanks, Dillan."

"See you later," he said.

Lynette watched as he walked to the Lounge door, which swung open revealing three men carrying briefcases. They settled on a table close to the door.

"Well, Kim, it's noon time. Time to make some money."

"Alright, I got the floor first," said Kim. "Let's switch off around four."

"Sounds, good," said Lynette. She opened the cooler to take out the fruit she had postponed cutting earlier. Kim moved out to greet the three men at their table.

* * *

Dillan woke from a sound sleep with a hard on. He stretched, then sat up slowly. He noticed a ray of sunlight casting itself on the keyboard in his room. He was reminded of the strict practice schedule during his childhood. Fifteen years he had been making music on the keys. With that synthesizer he had rocked the Marine Corp. barracks in Arizona. He stood up and walked around the bed, to the connecting bathroom, relieved himself, and then showered. He couldn't get Lynette off his mind. He wondered what it would be like to date her. She was beautiful, had brains, was going to college, was a hard worker, and that white jumpsuit with the zippers. *Woo hoo.* He had to ask her out. But how could he do it? How could he not sound like every other perv who asks out the hot bartender? He grabbed a towel, and stood now, looking in the mirror. He flexed his bicep, which called his attention to the bird tattoo, a colorful macaw, covering his upper arm. He saw his strength and muscles left behind from years of military drills. His chest was smooth and hairless. He was still in top shape and strong. He wanted her. She was the one. Wearing the towel around his waist he returned to his bedroom, then dressed into his old favorite jeans. Shirtless, he stepped into the kitchen to brew a pot of coffee.

"Hey, Paul, you want coffee?" asked Dillan.

A groan came from the hallway. "Yeah, I'll take some."

Dillan sat down with his coffee at the piano in the living room and began turning pages of sheet music. Then softly, the adagio sostenuto of Beethoven's *Moonlight Sonata* welled up in the room. In the kitchen, ghost-like and looking half asleep, Paul absorbed the melody while pouring his cup of coffee. He turned to face the living room through the opening in the wall, looking at Dillan's back swaying to the rise and fall of the notes. Dillan's thick fingers on his adept hands were tenderly meeting the piano keys. The triplet rhythm breathing, drifted calm out the open windows. The song had a life of its own, a beginning, a middle, and an end. And when the last note declared itself, Dillan reached for his coffee.

"Outstanding, man." Paul said, now stepping to the couch.

"Not bad for a grease monkey." Dillan lifted his coffee to his lips, then spun around on the piano bench. "The C sharp minor I get, but the second and third parts I don't."

"It's Greek to me," said Paul. "Can I watch the news or are you still playing?"

"Ah, I'm getting more coffee and then I'm cooking eggs." Dillan walked toward the kitchen. "Go ahead, put on the news."

"Check this out," Paul was taking something out of his pocket.

"It fell out of a suitcase yesterday. You want some?"

"You took weed out of someone's luggage?"

"No, I confiscated illegal contraband from the aircraft." Paul tossed the weed on the coffee table. "It's not like I touched the shaving lotion and the nice shirts. Just the weed."

Dillan looked down at the contents of the bag. "Nah, I'm good. You better make sure it's not laced with something." He picked up the baggie, opened it, sniffed it, closed it back up and fondled the buds through the plastic. "What are you doing after work today?"

"Nothing."

"It's my day off. Come hang out with me at the shop and help me work on my truck?"

"What's wrong with it?"

"Needs an alternator," said Dillan. He stood at the refrigerator reaching for the carton of eggs. "I'll buy the beer and you can meet me at the ground maintenance carports."

"Alright," said Paul. He pressed the power button on the television remote.

"Good morning," broadcasted the reporter. "It's Tuesday February 3, 1987. Coming up next, Donald Joel Aronow, American designer, builder and racer of the famous Magnum Marine, Cary, Cigarette, Donzi, and Formula speedboats, was found dead in his car in Miami Beach."

The dirt road leading out to the ground maintenance corrals was lined on both sides by tall white pine trees. Dillan pulled his truck under the car port. He climbed out of the driver's seat and stood for a minute looking out at the airport runways in the distance. He checked the sky for any signs of bad weather, then walked around to the bed of the truck to retrieve a toolbox and a cardboard box, which he opened. He laid out wrenches and screwdrivers on a work bench. Then turned his attention to the red Ford Ranger. Just as he popped open the hood, Paul pulled up in the driveway.

"Where's the beer?"

"In the cooler in the back. Help yourself."

"Hang on, I gotta take a leak." Paul stepped into the thicket, outside of the dirt parking area, and noticed a shiny object on the ground. He bent to retrieve it. It was a coin. After brushing it off, he could see that it was gold in color with something on it that looked like a praying mantis or a boat with oars. He flipped it over and saw the number one. He slipped it into his pocket.

"Hey man, where's the beer?" asked Paul.

"I told you, it's in the back of the truck. Are you stoned or something?"

"Yes, I am," said Paul. He bent over the cooler. "Hey, why'd you get Budweiser again? I wanted Miller."

"You didn't tell me you wanted Miller. Do you want a beer or not?"

"Alright, hey I just found this," Paul took the coin out of his pocket and showed it to Dillan.

"Looks foreign for sure." Dillan took out a rag and poured some beer on it to clean it. "It's from Israel, huh."

"How do you know it's from Israel?"

"Because it says it right next to that picture of the little candle thing." Dillan handed it back to his roommate. "Here. Now drink your beer and then you can take this bag over to the trash can for me."

Just then Cameron's truck pulled into the clearing blaring *Love Stinks* from the radio. He parked next to Paul's car and got out. "Hey, you guys, what's new?

"This case a beer," said Paul, now pulling a can out of the cooler in the back of the truck. "Hey, Man. What's up?"

"Just stopped for a beer at the airport," said Cameron.

Dillan was all ears. "Who's working the bar today?"

"The college girl, Lynette."

"I'd let her eat crackers in my bed," said Paul.

"Can I have one of your beers?" asked Cameron.

"Sure. Paul, grab Cameron a beer."

"That chick is hot," said Paul.

"Are you asking her out?" asked Dillan.

"She'd never go out with me anyway," said Paul.

"We got drunk together once," said Cameron. He popped the top off his can. "And watched the sunrise at the river."

"No way," said Dillan. He was trying to hide his jealousy. "Did you get any?"

Cameron chuckled, "No, just being neighborly and friendly and all. I had to check her air conditioning unit." Cameron took a swig from his beer.

"I heard she had some boyfriend." Dillan wanted more information.

"Nope, she told me she broke it off with him. He moved back to Pensacola or Destin or something."

"Hmm." Dillan was disconnecting the battery cable.

"What's wrong with the truck?" asked Cameron.

"Replacing the alternator. Trying to fix this up. I'm going back home to get my boat."

"Where's home?"

"Kansas." Dillan pulled out a duct assembly and handed it to Cameron. "Lay that over on that towel."

"Never been there." Cameron walked toward the work bench and found a rag to wipe his hands.

"A lot of Indians. Hey, Paul, pass me a socket wrench, ten millimeter." Dillan pointed to a set of wrenches on the ground. He released the tensioner to remove the alternator belt. "And we have an alternator." Dillan dusted it off with his hand. He laid it down next to the new one, cross referencing them side by side and inspecting the new one for any defects.

"I wrote her a poem on the napkin," said Paul.

"What the fuck?" Beer spewed from Cameron's mouth when he began to laugh, "You mean to tell me you write poetry?"

"Yes, I do."

"Shut the fuck up," said Cameron. He spoke with a tone of disbelief.

Dillan's hands were now on the belt checking to be sure it stayed in the grooves all the way around. He slid the duct back in. "Cameron, can you find that 10 millimeter bolt, before Paul writes a poem about it."

"Don't pinch that vacuum hose under the platform," said Cameron.

"Hey, I think I got it." Dillan was wide eyed and his expression testy. "I've fixed a thing or two before. I'm an aircraft mechanic, remember, I have an A&P license."

"Well, aren't you in a mood." Cameron bent over the work bench looking at the bolts. "Man, it's a nice day. I love this time of year. Not too hot."

"Feels like a perfect sixty-nine degrees," said Paul.

"Yeah, is that what temperature it was in your poem?" said Dillan.

"Are you replacin' the filter in the air box?" asked Paul.

"Yes, I'm gonna replace the filter in the air box."

"Man, I'm just trying to help," said Paul.

"Well, go in the back of my truck and grab the new air filter then, since you're so worried about it. "

"So, what did your girlfriend say when you wrote the poem on the napkin?"

"She's not my girlfriend, yet." Paul now held the box with the filter.

"Who's not your girlfriend?" asked Cameron.

"Lynette, the new bartender." Paul's attempt to pass off the air filter to Dillan, failed, when it fell onto the ground, rolling into the dirt.

Dillan sighed. Cameron, who had been leaning under the hood of the truck ready to hand off the air box housing, straightened up to see where the filter landed.

"Next time, I ask you to help me with something," said Dillan. "No beer for you until the job's over."

Paul successfully handed off the air filter on his second attempt. Dillan stood wiping it down with a towel. His full lips blew off the residual dust. "So, you wrote the poem to Lynette?" Dillan was trying to wrap his mind around this idea.

Cameron snickered, "Man, what did she say?"

"I don't know. I was shitfaced when I wrote it."

Dillan's dexterous hands were busy tightening the exhaust hose clamps. "Well, did she read it?"

"I don't know. I left it sitting on the bar next to my empty glass."

Dillan's head was shaking back and forth, and his lips now pressed together in a tight smile. "Oh, brother." He was now plugging in the IET sensor.

"Paul, grab me that voltage meter, and try not to drop it."

"What? Do you think I should ask her if she got the poem?"

"Aw, man, I think she'd tell you herself if she was interested," said Cameron. "Her being a college girl and all."

"Cameron, will you hop in the truck, and get ready to crank it up? I just have to hook up the battery cable."

"Dillan, what do you think?" asked Paul. Cameron was behind the steering wheel.

"Alright, start it up," The sound of the engine running was followed by Dillan throwing his arms in the air in victory, "Ooh-rah!"

"Well, what do you think?" Paul persisted.

"I think fourteen-point-five volts is a good number, that means my battery is charging." Dillan set the voltage meter on the towel. "And I think, it's time for a beer."

* * *

The leg in the immobilizer brace lay stretched and elevated over the length of the green vinyl loveseat. Momma, who had come to visit Lynette, sat with her back propped against the armrest that was cushioned with pillows. She held an ice pack in her hand.

"Mom," said Lynette, now looking up from a book on the desk. "Are you sure you don't want me to drive you home tonight?"

"Yes, I'm sure. You have a final exam tomorrow. Like the orthopedic doctor said, it'll be better to go home for surgery and be local. I don't want a two-hour commute for doctor appointments. I'm iced and splinted. Tomorrow I'll call for an appointment with a doctor at home."

"Alright, then," said Lynette. Her nose back in her book, until a knock at the door interrupted. The dog barked, she flipped on the porch light, and when she looked through the peephole, there stood Marie with some guy. "Mom, I'll be right outside the door." Lynette opened the door, then stepped outside, closing the door behind her.

"Wanna party?" asked Marie.

"Nah, I can't. My mom's here and we just got back from the hospital. She broke her leg."

"No, way. What happened?" asked Marie.

"She slipped over there in the radio station parking lot, while we were walking the dog. Split her kneecap in half."

"Dios Mío, I'm sorry to knock so late. This is my friend Vahid."

"Hi," said Lynette.

Vahid hesitated, "You're the witch."

Lynette looked at him like he was nuts. She noticed his bubbly eyes.

"I met you at the airport," said Vahid.

Lynette cocked her head, lifted her eyebrow, and rolled her eyes up, trying to remember. Had she ever met this guy? She shook her head. Then settled on not bothering to make any sense of it since Marie and this guy were obviously drinking. "Listen I gotta go, I got a final tomorrow and then I have to drive my mom home to Santa Rosa Beach. I hope you guys have a good time."

"Ok, Bye," said Marie.

"Bye," said Lynette.

Lynette shut the door, locked the deadbolt and the chain. She heard her guests' voices trailing off outside as they staggered from her front door and onto Pennell Circle.

"You know, you should never hang around with a witch," said Vahid.

"She's not a witch." Marie told him, "She goes to FSU just like you and me."

"She says she is," said Vahid. "Her mom's leg is broken, that alone is fair warning."

"She's magical to me for sure," said Marie.

"I am talking about black magic, I am Muslim, and we protect ourselves from witches and black magic. They can ruin you."

"Really? Like voodoo in Miami."

"I'm serious, Marie. In Jammu in India, where I'm from, Hadith tells where a witch cast a spell on a Prophet Muhammad and made him sick."

"What's a Hadith?"

"It's a report," said Vahid. "Listen to me, the witch then tried to possess Muhamad."

Marie looked at Vahid and thought maybe it was time to take him home.

"Performing black magic is therefore one of the worst sins." Vahid's tone sounded urgent.

* * *

Inside the apartment, Lynette returned her attention to Momma.

"What was that all about? asked Momma.

"Oh, just this girl, Marie, from school. She wanted to go out."

"Kinda late, doesn't she have an exam tomorrow?"

"Guess not." Lynette turned the desk chair to face Momma. Then she sat.

"Well, being out this late at night, she better be careful, or she'll end up on a slow boat to China. Nothing good ever happens after midnight."

"Ok, Mom, I'm gonna sleep on the love seat, so I don't hurt your leg."

"I'm sorry, honey."

"It's not your fault. I'm just sorry that I can't drive you home right now. I can't thank you enough for staying here for the night until my exam is over in the morning. I should be home by ten. The exam is at eight."

"It's alright. If I were home, I wouldn't be at the hospital anyway, until tomorrow, and even then, I probably won't have surgery until the next day, because I'll have to wait for the surgeon."

"Ok, then it's settled. Are you hungry?"

"Ohhh, you're taking care of your momma." She pulled the blanket up to her chin. Well, I could use a little something, you got a yogurt? And a piece of toast?"

"Sure, how about a cup of tea with it?"

"I'd rather have a diet coke."

"I could run out and get you some down the Quickie Mart."

"No, forget it, just give me the tea."

"Besides the tea's better for you."

"Ok, Boss," said Momma.

Lynette moved to the kitchen counter and opened a box of tea bags. "I'll pick a good one." Tea bag in hand now, her eyes went to the tag. "It says, *Love is the ultimate law of life.*"

"I like that," said Momma. "I love you."

"I love you too."

Lynette tucked her mom into her bed with the snacks, tea, and prescription ibuprofen, and then settled onto the loveseat with a blanket and pillow and her notebook. Before studying, she sat in the quiet for a minute. A collection of Shakespeare's Works lay on the coffee table. *Damn this college degree.* Pursuing it weighed doggedly on her and now on her mom. Was an exam taking precedence over her mother's broken knee? *Jesus Christ,* thought

Lynette. While pondering her mother's logic about waiting until tomorrow to go home, Lynette let out a heavy sigh. Glad for her time working as a nurse's assistant in a nursing home, Lynette pulled from her experience. She planned how best to manage the two-hour drive back home. Mom would ride in the back seat with her legs stretched out, elevated on pillows, with an ice pack. Lynette anticipated that every bump of the ride would feel like an earthquake to that knee. She glanced across the room through the doorway, where her mother now lay sleeping. *There are many moms in the world, but she surpasses them all, what strength she has*, thought Lynette.

Lynette rubbed her eyes and felt the pressure of tomorrow morning's exam hanging over her. Then she focused her attention on Shakespeare. She opened her notes and studied the themes for his tragedies. *Memento Mori,* her professor had said was one theme that ran in all thirty-three Shakespeare plays. She opened her book, turning page after page, reading the penciled notes she had written in the margin's during class, during her silent readings. She landed on the notes for Macbeth and the three witches. Looking up from the page at the front door, her mind drifted to Marie's visit with that guy calling her a witch.

She realized that she must have waited on him at the bar. He had probably asked her where she was from, like a lot of customers usually did, and she must have responded with Salem, Massachusetts. Yup, she remembered toying with someone about being a witch, but she never would have imagined that the guy would show up at her door, with Marie of all people. *Well, after all, I was a witch*, thought Lynette.

She recalled her sophomore year at Salem High School, where the football team was known as the Witches, and she had even played trumpet with the Witches' Marching Band. A black image of a witch flying on a broomstick was darned into the uniform.

Curiously, this guy seemed to believe in witchcraft. She remembered how he had asked her, "You're a real witch? Really?" And how with conviction, she had said she was. Never would she have thought he was serious, but tonight at her door, his tone was clear, he and his culture took it seriously. *Huh, the world is full of all kinds of people*, Lynette thought. *Imagine being scared, of witches*. She felt guilty for making him afraid. That had not been her intention, but this was the result. Being the cause of someone's fear would never be an objective of Lynette's. No, this playful toying with Vahid, which was meant to be entertaining and possibly inspire a big tip, had created a big misunderstanding instead. Guilt was her consequence, and she decided she would tread more lightly with people in the future. Lynette turned her attention to *Macbeth. More witchcraft, Oh my.*

* * *

Lynette wore a red and white candy-cane-striped bikini. Marie, a solid white one. On towels, the sun kissing their skin, they sported sunglasses, and sat massaging themselves with oil. They felt concealed on the lawn between the building and the hedges, and with the back door open, they listened to music coming through the screen door. George Michael's song, *Father Figure,* played on the stereo, *I will be your father figure, put your tiny hands in mine, I will be your preacher teacher, anything you have in mind...*

"I think it's time to change the channel," said Marie. She pursed her lips, eyes aglare.

"Oh, my God. Tell me you're not smitten with that priest?"

"And if I was?"

"It would be a total sin for him and you. And he could get kicked out of the priesthood. And I'm telling you, you're asking for," And before Lynette could finish chastising her friend, her attention was averted to a man passing through the open area between the end of the hedges and the end of the building.

"Hey, nice day, do you know how to get to Bullwinkle's?" asked the stranger. He now stood about six feet away facing the girls. He was a clean cut handsome young black man. Lynette noted that he was wearing a sharp looking black and white striped collared polo shirt, white shorts, and matching sneakers.

"Sure, it's about ten minutes from here," said Lynette. She felt Marie poke her in the arm and turned to look at her with perplexity. "What? That's right, you've been there." Lynette returned her attention to the visitor. "Go out this road turn right on Levy, then," Another elbow jab from Marie. Then a hand clutching her forearm. Lynette turned toward Marie and jerked her arm away. "Then left on

Lake Bradford Road. What's that street that connects to Macomb?" She turned her furrowed brow to Marie and saw that Marie had lifted her glasses above her eyes and was glaring wide eyed nervously back at her.

Lynette's glance turned again to the stranger, when she saw it, the reason Marie was acting so annoying. The man's penis was staring out of the barn door of the white shorts like a cyclops from a cave in Homer's Odyssey. *Stay calm. Pretend not to notice,* Lynette thought. She decided getting to the phone was the best course of action. "Let me go call Warren, he's got a map." She stood up and opened the sliding screen door, and as soon as she passed the threshold, she bolted for the phone and dialed nine-one-one.

"Lynette Autry here three-two-seven Pennell Circle apartment one, some guy just flashed my friend and me. I don't know if he's still there because I'm inside now." Lynette looked up and could see Marie had stepped into the apartment and was locking the glass door. She exploded into the room.

"Girlfriend, what the fuck did you leave me out there with him for?"

"Is he still there?"

"He took off when he saw me getting up off my towel."

"No ma'am, he's gone now," said Lynette. She looked up at Marie. "Did you see which way he went?"

"I think he went out toward the trails around the farming co-op," said Marie.

"Yes, ma'am he's gone." Lynette repeated what Marie had said to the woman on the phone.

"Ok, thank you." Lynette stared at Marie and hung up the phone. "Did you lock the back door."

"Yes, I did."

Lynette's eyes focused on the front door, confirming it was locked also. Then she sunk into the chair at the kitchen table. She put her head in her hands. "My fucking head." She laughed, nervously.

"What the fuck is so funny?"

"I can't fucken believe this is happening again."

"That's not funny."

"Sorry, I always laugh when I get upset," said Lynette.

"What?"

"Yah, I know it pisses a lot of people off. Well, no wonder we got flashed, everyone wants to bone us."

"No, everyone wants to bone you." Marie was laughing now.

"No, everyone wants to bone both of us," said Lynette. "I was really enjoying laying in the sun too."

"Me too," said Marie.

"Shit the cops will be here soon," said Lynette. "I'm putting on a shirt."

"Why don't you just leave it off, then the cop will want to bone you."

"Not that again," said Lynette.

"Well, I'm going to clean up my stuff," said Marie.

"No, don't go out there until the cops get here," said Lynette. "At least the guy was an exhibitionist and not a rapist. They just get off on being looked at."

"How do you know?" asked Marie.

"One night, my mom heard cat noises out her bedroom window, so she opens the curtains and looks out. Some guy's laying on the grass masturbating," said Lynette. "When the police came that's what he told her. That the guy was most likely harmless and just wanted to get a reaction."

"Hey, there's the police now," said Marie. She ran to slide open the door in time to see the officer climb out from the car. Waving her hand, she stepped outside. Lynette trailing right behind, now back in the sun, it felt like a nice day again. The officer stood near the hedges.

"Hi, are you the girls who reported the flasher?"

"Yeah, he went that way." Marie pointed in the direction of the trails.

"What was he wearing?"

"A black and white polo shirt with a collar and white shorts and matching sneakers," said Lynette.

"Did he say anything to you?"

"Yah, He was asking if we knew where Bullwinkle's was. I just started giving him directions, because I didn't notice at first that, well, his thing was hanging out. It seemed to blend with his outfit."

"Ok, there's a couple of officers looking for him now, just sit tight for a bit, go back inside and wait. I'll be back here with an update." The officer climbed into his car and sped out toward the dirt road behind the building. Marie slung her towel over her arm and held a bottle of suntan oil in her hand.

"I kept trying to elbow you. And tell you," said Marie.

Lynette was bent over picking up her book, a bag of popcorn and towel. "I was looking at his face, not his crotch," said Lynette. "I have a clean mind, unlike you." Marie turned to step into the apartment, and Lynette was right behind. After tossing her stuff on the bed, she locked both doors, the screen, and the glass, then closed the curtains.

"Man, I'm hungry," said Lynette. She sunk onto the bed, and grabbed the bag of popcorn, popping a few pieces into her mouth.

"How can you eat in this situation?"

"Oh, I can always eat," said Lynette. "Man, I'm gonna go ahead and take my shower and get ready for work. Alright?"

"After the cop comes back, I'll head back to my apartment."

The ring from the phone drove Lynette off the bed. Marie stood by with anticipation as Lynette lifted the receiver.

"Hello," Lynette peered out through a slit in the closed curtain. "Yes, I see him." She paused. "Thanks, Bye."

"Was that the cops?"

"Yah, they're coming to the front door."

They both startled when they heard the knock. Lynette went to the peephole and peered out to be sure it was the police.

"Just open the door," said Marie. "You know it's them."

"Yah, yah, yah." Lynette swung it open. Marie standing by her side, they both stared into the face of the uniformed officer, who had spoken to them just minutes earlier outside the back door. They saw two police cars parked behind him at the curb about fifteen yards away. There was an officer standing outside the passenger side of the car.

"Ladies, we have apprehended a suspect. Do you see the police car and the officer right behind me?"

The girl's peered out and nodded.

"The suspect is in the back-seat. The officer outside the car is going to open the door, and I need you to take a good look at the man sitting inside, then tell me if he is the man who flashed you. Do you understand?"

They nodded again.

The officer at the door turned and signaled to the officer standing outside the car.

Lynette and Marie watched the car door opening to reveal the man inside. They heard the officer yell, "Stay in the car and keep your head down." There was no mistaking the black and white striped shirt, white shorts, and matching sneakers.

"Yes, that's him," said Marie.

"It's definitely him," said Lynette.

"Ok," said the officer. "We'll take it from here. I want you to go back inside the apartment, close the door, and don't come out until the cop cars are gone. Got it?" Lynette and Marie nodded.

"Ok," said Lynette.

"Got it," said Marie.

"Thanks officer," said Lynette.

"You're welcome, you ladies stay safe."

Marie stepped back, and watched Lynette close the door, lock the handle, the dead bolt and the chain.

"Oh my God. I wonder if it's the same guy who asked to borrow my basketball." Lynette was shaking her head. "If it is, he fucken needs to get some help."

Marie spurted out her catch-all saying, "My hole, my soul, in that order."

Chapter 8

Dillan was prepared and ready to make his move. He had borrowed his parents' boat, then hauled it from Topeka, Kansas to Tallahassee. Today he would ask Lynette out on a date. Would she go out for a ride? Would she go for a grease monkey? At the airport maintenance shop, he had finished scrubbing the day's work from his hands with lava soap, and stood now, combing his hair. Minutes later, he walked through the airport terminal to the lounge.

Lynette held a knife in her hand and was cutting limes. She looked up and smiled at the familiar face approaching. A solid guy she thought, and tan. Looking at his jean jacket and clean jeans, she wondered if he changed at the shop or wore those clothes under his work coveralls. She had often seen him through the window on the tarmac, but she hadn't seen him in the bar for a few weeks. "Hi Dillan, what can I get you?"

"I'll have a vodka tonic," Dillan said. "Quiet tonight, huh?" Dillan sat in his usual spot at the end of the bar where the cocktail waitresses picked up drinks for table service. There were no waitresses now.

"Typical Sunday. The last flight just went out," said Lynette. She poured his drink and added one of the freshly cut limes to the glass. "Haven't seen you in a while, what've you been up to?" Lynette grabbed a napkin and placed it in front of Dillan, then set his drink on it. She walked to the other end of the bar, then stopped at the cooler to continue cutting limes.

"I just got back from Kansas, from visiting my parents," said Dillan. "They let me borrow their boat."

"Oh yah," she paused, and looked up, then over her shoulder at Dillan. "When I was growing up, my folks had a boat. We used to go camping a lot. Grand Canyon, Big Bear, Flagstaff. Lot of fun. I probably told you that already."

Dillan took a sip from his drink, and asked, "Are you working tomorrow?"

"No, I'm off, good thing too, I have to work on a paper," said Lynette. She stepped to the pouring station, now near Dillan, and plonked some limes into the fruit trough. "I was supposed to be off today, but Little Miss Muffet called in sick, again."

"I'll take you out on the boat. That is, if what I hear is true, you dumped that boyfriend of yours." Dillan awaited confirmation.

"I really need to work on that paper." She reached for a bottle of sanitizer at the sink.

"And I have a dog."

"Well, I guess I can ask Little Miss Muffet." Dillan's eyebrows raised, and he was tapping his fingers on the bar.

The thought of Becky going out on that boat and enjoying herself pushed Lynette to consider the opportunity for herself. "Can I bring my dog?" Lynette slid her hands into yellow gloves. "And can we be back by four, so I can work on my paper?"

"I think we can manage that. Anyways, what is your paper about?"

"It's for my Marriage and Family class. I'm writing about a book called *Living, Loving, and Learning* by Leo Buscaglia."

"Well, is it any good?" Dillan lifted his glass to his lips.

"Yah, it is. One of my favorite quotes from the book, goes something like this," She paused from plunging glasses onto the brushes in a sink full of soapy water, "Love is the definition of me leading you gently back to yourself."

"Hey, that's pretty good."

Dillan was smiling. Lynette pictured the boat ride. "I can pack us a lunch for tomorrow."

"Like a picnic." Dillan drank his glass down to the ice. "Very nice."

"Last call, do you want one more?"

"No thanks, I'm driving," said Dillan. He reached for his billfold, while Lynette peeled off yellow gloves.

Dillan persisted. "Hey, you never answered my question. Did you break up with your boyfriend?" Lynette was walking toward him now.

"Yes, I did." Her eyes were on the cash, laying on the bar.

"Alright then, I'll pick you up tomorrow at eight." Dillan stood up. "Where do you live?"

"Alumni Village apartments," said Lynette. Pen in hand, she reached for a clean napkin, and on it jotted down her contact information. "Here's my address." Lynette handed him the napkin. "I'm in the last row of buildings at the very back of the complex, it's an end unit. Pennell Circle is off Levy, which is off Lake Bradford Road. And my phone number is there, in case you can't find it."

"Oh, I'll find it, you just get that picnic squared away." Dillan reached out to accept the napkin. There was a brightness in his eyes. He opened his jean jacket and placed the napkin in the inside pocket. "See you tomorrow."

"Yes," said Lynette. "See you tomorrow."

After locking the lounge door behind him, Lynette grabbed a clean towel and began wiping down the length of the bar. She was feeling competitive. What was that shit about I can ask Miss Muffet? What did she know about going boating or picnicking anyway? Lynette created a grocery list in her mind. She pondered caviar, champagne, cheese, crackers, grapes, and sandwiches. She could already see the water, the lily pads, and the open sky, already hear sounds of all the flying, crawling, and swimming creatures and the putter of the boat motor. She smiled to herself about how good it was to be making such a day.

* * *

It was seven-thirty in the morning, when the Ford Ranger pulled the boat over the speed bumps at Alumni Village. Dillan checked his rearview mirror and side mirrors to make sure the boat wasn't jostling around too much. Now on Pennell Circle, he searched the rows of brick tenements for Lynette's building number. The napkin with the address lay on the seat next to him. The last building was in sight. He fixed his eyes on the three-two-seven. Then made a wide right turn and circled the parking lot, pulling up at the curb in front of her apartment, now in perfect position for driving out of the complex.

He looked at his Casio wristwatch, climbed out of the truck, and circled the trailer, inspecting the hitch hook up, tires, and lights, until he was satisfied that everything was secure. He looked across the lawn toward the apartment door, and then over to the line of cars, abutting the sidewalk. Lynette's Toyota was parked in the end space. He opted to back track, so he could take the sidewalk. Walking by her car, he smiled at the collection of figurines on her dashboard. The California Raisin Band. There was a puffy cheeked sax player, a finger snapping raisin with pink eyelids wearing orange sunglasses, and a singer with a blue bow tie holding an orange microphone. They were all wearing black shoes with white spats. He shook his head when he saw the empty Hardee's coffee cup, biscuit wrapper, and bag on the floor. He looked at her tires, then noticed some bird-shit on the hood. He pulled a napkin from his jacket pocket to wipe it off. After folding it and returning it to his pocket, he glanced at his watch once more, then stepped up the curb and made his way on the sidewalk, passing apartments three and two, until he stood in front of number one.

He knocked on the door and could hear the dog barking and the chain lock sliding. Then there stood Lynette, dressed in jeans and a pastel turquoise sweatshirt. She had a cooler in one hand and a canvas bag in the other. The dog trotted out and sniffed Dillan's leg. Dillan squatted to pet the dog, "Ooh, good boy."

The door of apartment two swung open. "Going somewhere?" asked Warren. He had on a playful smile.

"Good morning, Warren," said Lynette. "Warren, meet Dillan, Dillan this is Warren."

Dillan looked up and waved his hand.

"You kids have a good time!"

"Thanks," said Lynette. "Bye now!" She was smiling but her tone said, *All's well, you can mind your own business.*

"Bye," said Warren. He disappeared into his apartment.

"That's Warren, a good neighbor. Ever since I had a peeping tom, he's always watching."

Dillan reached for her cooler and canvas bag. "Are you all set?" he asked.

"Just about," said Lynette. "Tashi, come."

"I'm gonna load this stuff up," said Dillan. "And you go finish getting ready."

Lynette ducked into her apartment. She shut off lights and the coffee pot. Then she loaded Alpo Snaps into a plastic baggy, threw a towel over her shoulder, stuffed keys into her pocket, and stood scanning the living room, when Dillan strolled through the open doorway.

"Ta-a-ashi-i-i, I brought something for yoooou!" He held a cannister in one hand and was prying off the lid with the other hand.

Lynette flashed a smile.

"Ta-a-ashi-i-i," said Dillan.

Tashi answered with bright eyes and a wagging tail. Dillan squatted and poured a tennis ball into his hand, then offered it to the dog. Tashi gladly accepted the ball into his mouth, then strutted back and forth on guard. Dillan looked around the room, then at Lynette. "Are you ready?"

"I just need to find Tashi's leash."

Dillan, still squatting, and now petting the dog, answered by pointing at the floor underneath the love seat. Lynette got down on her hands and knees and reached for the leash.

"Ok, now I'm ready."

Dillan lifted the dog and stepped outside, waiting for Lynette to lock the door.

"So where are we going?" Lynette walked across the lawn toward the truck. Dillan followed.

"The Ochlockonee River or Dead Lake? Take your pick."

"Let's go to the River. The dead lake does not sound very," Lynette clicked her tongue. "alive."

Do you know what Ochlockonee means?"

"I definitely do not."

"It's Native American. It means black."

"Hmm, you learn something new every day. Never been there, I've been out to St. Mark's River once."

"With Cameron, right?"

"Yah, How'd you know?"

"He mentioned it."

"Wow, nice boat."

"Well, it's my parent's boat; they're just letting me use it."

"Hey, set Tashi in the grass, I'm going to leash him up and just walk him for a minute in case he has to potty before we leave."

Dillan stood watching Lynette lead Tashi to the hedges alongside her apartment. After Tashi lifted his leg, Lynette turned and could see Dillan was holding the truck door open. "Good boy," said Dillan.

Lynette pulled at the towel on her shoulder. "I brought this for the dog to sit on, so he doesn't get dirty paw prints all over your seat."

"I appreciate that." Dillan gestured toward the floor. "Your bag's right there, if you need it."

Lynette already feeling comfortable, spread the towel across the seat. Dillan bent down to pick up Tashi. "Ok, climb in and I'll pass him to you." He waited until Lynette settled.

"Ready?" He was scratching the dog's head. "Good Boy."

"Ok, give me Tashi Two Shoes."

"Here you go," He set the dog in Lynette's lap. "Elbow in," said Dillan. He closed the door and walked around the front of the truck to the driver's side and climbed behind the steering wheel. He picked up a map from the dashboard and showed Lynette the route to the river. Then he pulled onto Pennell Circle.

"Thanks for taking us on your boat," said Lynette.

"Yah, well, we haven't got on the boat yet. Did you want to stop and get a coffee?"

"No, I already had some."

"Ok, let's go then," Dillan turned the key in the ignition, and maneuvered the truck and trailer onto the road leading them out of the complex.

"So, how's school? what are you taking?"

"I'm majoring in English Education. When I graduate, I'll be a teacher."

"Oh, a teacher, huh, Wow."

"I like the idea of having June, July and August off."

"I was in the Marine Corp."

"Oh?"

"I did bootcamp in San Diego and was stationed in Yuma, Arizona."

"What did you do, or are you allowed to talk about it?"

"Aircraft maintenance. I flew jump seat."

"How long have you been in T-town?"

"Almost a year. I was working up in Walla Walla, Washington before I moved here. The airline I worked for, *Cascade,* went out of business."

"That sucks."

"It's getting to be a pattern with me. The airline I worked with before that, *Pacific Express,* went out of business too in Chico, California. I love Chico, I used to go fishing for salmon up there. Once, I caught one with my bare hands."

"How'd you do that?"

"I just stood over the stream like a bear does, and when the salmon are running there is a swarm of them, it's really beautiful, and well, I reached in and snatched him right out of the water."

"I never caught a fish with my hands before. When I was little, I caught fish with a drop line. Other than that, I always caught them with a pole. One fish I hate is catfish. They creep me out."

"Yah, they got those barbs on their head, they can hurt you if you're not careful when you're taking 'em off the line."

"Yah, I know."

"So, no more Claude, huh?"

"No, no more Claude. When we broke up, he moved back to Destin."

Lynette noticed they were on Crawfordville Highway south. "So how long do you think it will take to get there?"

"Oh, maybe an hour. I like to go the speed limit."

"Oh, that's good. I got a couple of speeding tickets this year already around Blountstown on my way to and from my mom's house."

"That's a bummer, the fine's go up every time you get one, don't they?"

"Yup, they do."

"So how do you like working at the airport?"

"The tips are great, and the schedule is good. How about you?"

"Well, I'm an aircraft mechanic, and if I'm at the airport with my planes, I'm happy. Tallahassee airport is small, so everyone knows everyone. Do you know the new girl that works at Avis? Her mom is the other bartender that you work with."

"I didn't know that."

"Her dad's a pilot for Federal Express. My boss, Bob, he works for Aero Associates, and I used to work with him out west. Now I work for *Oceanair*.

"Wait, *Oceanair*? I saw you on the tarmac, working on an Eastern plane."

"Right, *Oceanair* is a contract maintenance company. Tallahassee Airport is a regional airport. It's small, and there's not enough flights for each airline to have a full-time mechanic. So, they contract *Oceanair,* and what I do is on call emergency aircraft and ground support maintenance for Fed Ex, Delta and Eastern. When their planes need regular maintenance, their own mechanics do it at their hubs."

"No way, so you work on all the planes that come in."

"I can, but there are some other guys, who work general aviation, that do what I do."

"You must know everybody."

"Not too much, because, I always have my head in an airplane."

"Well, all the airport employees are friendly at the bar," said Lynette. "How about that shoeshine guy, Tyler,"

"He's funny," said Dillan. "That bar can get busy."

"It's Legislative session time, so right now money is good, no worries about paying tuition."

"Let's turn on the radio." Dillan turned the knob. The radio announcer's voice filled the truck's cab. "President Reagan has just addressed the nation on the Iran Contra. He promises to tell the nation the truth about the scandal, and he has introduced new personnel and policy and wants to ensure the integrity of National Security Decisions in the future. 'I want the American people to know that this wrenching ordeal of recent months has not been in vain,' quoted President Reagan. For more on the President's address, tune in to ABC News at five' o'clock." Dillan lowered the volume.

"I voted for President Reagan," said Dillan.

"I've never voted."

"You should."

"Maybe." Lynette looked out at the trees.

"I love this song, is it ok if I turn it up?"

"Sure, I like this song too, nice key-board. I have the sheet music. It's called, *Give me a Higher Love* by Steve Winwood.

"What instrument do you play?" asked Lynette.

"Piano."

"I played trumpet in high school," said Lynette.

"I played tuba," said Dillan, "Marching band was a lot of fun."

* * *

When the Ford Ranger parked in position to back up the trailer on the ramp at the Ochlockonee River, Lynette hopped out from the truck to walk the dog around the beach area. Then she stood watching Dillan skillfully perform a one-man boat launch with perfect precision. First, he walked to the rear of the truck, leaving the trailer wench hooked up, he removed the boat straps. At the bow, he jacked up the motor. Then he climbed back into the cab of the truck and backed up. Lynette could hear the transmission shift to neutral, and the boat headed the truck to the water's edge. When the boat began to lift off, Dillan stopped the truck, jumped out of the cab and climbed into the bed of the truck and onto the boat trailer. There he balanced like a gymnast, while unhooking the wench. Then he jumped onto the boat, climbed into the captain's seat, and started the engine to back up the boat, where he drove it to a nearby Lichgate oak tree and tied it up. Lynette yelled, "Do you want me to park the truck?"

"I got it," Dillan yelled back.

Lynette looked at the sky. The sun was bright and warm, surrounded by the blue only the sky knows. She could see the white underside and wide brown wingspan of a river hawk soaring overhead. It was a beautiful day. The clearing was fringed with dense long leafed pine forest, decorated with the red berries of coral ardisia, and saw palmetto. She realized they were the only ones there.

After parking the truck, Dillan waded in the water. He called the dog, then lifted him, onto the boat. When Lynette bent over about to remove her shoes, Dillan gestured to her over his shoulder. "Hop on," he said. "I'll give you a piggy ride."

"Ok," said Lynette.

Now wading in the water with Lynette on his back, Dillan turned and stepped backward, making it easy for Lynette to sit on the stern, where she was now, legs dangling and dry.

"This looks like the world of the dinosaurs," said Lynette. She looked toward the other side of the river. The moss hung on the trees. The forest looked untouched by humans. There were two turtles bathing on a fallen tree trunk. A white squirrel perched on a branch. A white doe with brown spots pranced by over low-growing fan-leaved palmettos. Dillan and Lynette looked on in awe. Tashi stood on the deck at the bow, wagging his tail, now barking, he stole all the attention.

They road for a long while down the river through the banks of thick forest. Twisted vines ran around tree trunks and their branches. Dillan at the helm, slowed the boat.

"Are you ready for lunch?" he said. "This looks like a good spot. What do you think?"

Lynette saw the small beach area, "You're the Captain."

Dillan cut the engine. The water was gently lapping the hull. He stepped swiftly to the bow, where he removed the anchor from the seat compartment, and tossed it ashore. He climbed into the water and now stood knee deep in the river, pulling the boat onto the sand. He secured the anchor into the ground. The excess rope, he wrapped around the cleat. "Look, there's a wood-pecker," He pointed upward at the trunk of a tall pine. "See his red head?"

Lynette listened to his beak jackhammering the bark, "Yah, I see 'em." With the boat safely beached, Dillan called Tashi, and then lifted him to the sand. Lynette jumped ashore and headed straight for a great big fallen tree.

"Smile," said Dillan, now back in the boat holding a camera. Lynette mounted the trunk, and struck a pose, Click went the shutter.

"What kind of camera is that?"

"A Nikon," said Dillan. Lynette thought it looked professional and expensive. She kept an eye on Tashi, who was now nosing through pine needles and sand.

Dillan was reaching into the seat compartments. "I brought my tripod, so I can get a picture with both of us."

"Ok. Do you want to eat on the shore or on the boat?" asked Lynette.

"Probably be easier to eat on the boat?"

"Alright, I'm gonna have beer," said Dillan. "Would you like one?"

"No, thanks, I have to work on my paper later." Lynette called Tashi. Then she lifted him back into the boat, after which she climbed aboard herself. Dillan climbed ashore, taking with him the tripod and a can of beer.

Lynette laid a towel on the deck at the bow. Then she opened the cooler and lay out an assortment of boxes and containers. She pried off the wire on the champagne bottle and covered the neck with a dish towel to pop the plastic top off. Careful not to spill it, she placed it back in the cooler to stay cold. Then she pulled champagne glasses from her canvas bag and held the glasses up for Dillan to see. "Ready for some celebration?"

Dillan, still on the beach, looked up from the camera he had secured to the tripod. The camera now aiming at the boat.

"What'd you bring?"

"We have fruit, olives, crackers, cheese, and caviar with sour cream, and chicken salad sandwiches."

"Geez, Caviar, this feels like that show." Dillan stepped toward the boat. "What's it called?" He looked down at the spread.

"Lifestyles of the Rich and Famous." He climbed aboard. Tashi sat nearby sniffing the picnic. "Can he have a piece of the cheese?"

"Sure," said Lynette. She watched Dillan telling Tashi to sit. After Dillan handed off the cheese, he sat next to Lynette.

"Would you like a grape, your royal highness?"

"I'll take one," said Dillan.

"Open wide," Lynette said, playfully popping one into his mouth. Dillan bit down on the berry.

"Mmmm, ripe and juicy," he said.

"Ok, my turn." Dillan held out his hand to receive the cluster of grapes. Then he repeated after Lynette. "Would you like a grape, your royal highness?"

"Why yes, thank you." Lynette parted her lips to receive the fruit. She bit into the flesh of the grape and the juice burst into her mouth, "Oh, these are sweet and juicy, and satisfying."

"Hey, let's get a picture." Dillan hopped outside of the boat, then trotted to the tripod. He set the timer, hauled back again, positioning himself, one arm around Lynette's shoulder and the other holding up the cluster of grapes. "Smile, wait for it." Click went the shutter.

"I hope it comes out good," said Lynette.

"Geez, this is a nice picnic," said Dillan. "So how do you eat caviar anyways? I've never had it."

"Well, I mixed it with the sour cream, see." Lynette scooped some on a cracker and showed him.

He took it in his hand, scrutinizing it, tilting it this way and that, before taking the whole thing in his mouth, "Mmmm, not bad."

"Here." She handed him a glass, then poured in champagne. "You gotta have a little champers with it."

"Where's yours? Shouldn't we toast?"

"Ok," Lynette poured herself a glass, and held it up waiting. "Cheers," said Lynette.

Clink

"Cheers," said Dillan. "Thank you for this picnic."

"We're not done yet," Lynette handed him a plastic baggie with a sandwich inside. It's chicken salad with chopped celery, onions, and a little garlic powder, and onion salt."

"Sounds good." Dillan bit into his sandwich. "Uh Huh, it is good." Tashi sat in front of him staring up at the sandwich. "Can he have a bit of this?"

"Sure," said Lynette.

"Ta-a-a-shi-i-i, sit." Dillan handed him a bite of his sandwich. "Good boy."

When the food was eaten, Lynette began packing up.

"I'll go get the tripod and the camera," said Dillan. He hopped ashore, then turned facing starboard, now patting his hand on the boat. "Come, Tashi, let's go recon on the beach." Lynette watched Dillan lift the dog to the sand. She loaded up her canvas bag with the glasses and the empty containers. The champagne, she corked and left in the cooler.

She noticed Dillan bent over. Both hands reaching into the water, making swishing sounds. Tashi near his ankles. Then the swash and trickle of the water fell from his hands, now cupped together, lifting something from the riverbank. "Hey look what I found," He walked toward the boat, Tashi trailing behind. "See." He squatted and offered his treasure to the dog, who had a sniff. Lynette squinted to see. As Dillan drew nearer, he opened his palms and showed off a small green shell. Lynette stepped portside for a closer look.

"Aw," she said. "It's a baby turtle." Dillan handed off the creature to Lynette's open palm. She held him close to her face and peeked inside his shell to see his tiny reptile eyes staring back at her. "You look like my little Charlie and Henry I had when I was a kid." Lynette was talking softly to the baby turtle. "They lived in a bowl with a plastic palm tree." She turned him round to study his little tucked in tail, and webbed feet.

Dillan stood, towel in hand, wiping sand from the tripod. The camera now dangling from the strap around his neck. He approached starboard-side and laid the tripod on the seat at the bow. "Did he come out of his shell yet?"

"No, he's scared."

"Alright, time for you to go home." Dillan looked at the turtle and cupped his hands. He waited for Lynette to return the little green visitor. After she had passed him back, Dillan looked at the tripod still on the seat. "Will you lay that in the cabinet under the seat?"

She responded with a nod, while she lifted a seat cover. She watched as Dillan, gently returned the shelled creature to the same place, where he had been found.

"Well, how about we head a little further down the river, before we turn around?"

"You're the Captain."

Dillan pulled up the anchor from the beach, shoved off the boat, and hopped aboard. He used an oar to push the boat out further, then darted to the helm and started the engine. They tooled along for close to a quarter of an hour. The river growing narrow. Vines twisting and snaking themselves everywhere. The forest growing thicker around them. Dillan cut the engine.

"Lots of downed trees from the hurricane," said Dillan.

"Yah, I noticed that."

"I'm gonna take a swim," said Dillan. He undressed, except for his cut off shorts. "Tell me if you see any alligators." He walked to the stern of the boat and bent down to pick up the anchor, hurling it into the river. Then he jumped into the cold water with a splash.

"Do you want to come in? It's nice." Dillan swam away from the boat.

"No, but I'll take your picture." Lynette grabbed the camera from under the helm, and snapped a quick shot, then put it back where she had found it. She became aware of his lean biceps and strong back, and legs kicking in the water. His jet-black hair shining in the sun.

The water dripping off his face. Then a story she read in the paper last summer barged into her thoughts.

"Did you hear about that art student at FSU?" She stood up, turned around as her eyes began scanning her surroundings.

"What art student?"

"He went snorkeling at Wakulla Springs and ended up inside a ten-foot gator." She sat down and leaned over the edge of the boat to put her hand in the water.

"Yeah, I think I do remember that. Some tourists riding on a glass bottom boat saw the guy laying inside the gator's mouth. Dillan began doggie paddling toward the boat. "So, I guess that means you're not coming in for a swim?"

Lynette pulled her hand out of the water. She was surprised how cold it was. "I don't like swimming until it's at least eighty degrees outside," she said.

Dillan splashed around for a few more minutes and dove under water. For a second it was quiet. Lynette could hear a seagull cry and she looked up to see it soaring passed the line of trees.

Dillan's face popped out of the black water.

"There's a body under there," he said.

"You're kidding."

"No, I'm not. Can you see it, it's right at the base of that tree, about three feet down toward the riverbank."

Lynette ran to the starboard side of the boat, but with the sun glare on the water she still couldn't see anything. She was starting to feel uncomfortable.

"It looks like he's in military fatigues," said Dillan. "I think if I pull this tree trunk off of him, he might come up to the surface and I can get him on the beach."

Dillan swam back over to the stern and climbed aboard. "Man, there's somebody under there."

"What are you gonna do?" Lynette handed Dillan a towel.

"I don't know, we can't just leave him there."

"Why don't we mark the place and then we can go to a pay phone and call the police. He can't be alive down there, anyway." Lynette tipped her head and lifted her eyebrows. "Where's he gonna go?"

"I wish I had a mask, so I could see better down there." Dillan, still dripping wet, opened the compartment under the seat and took out some yellow nylon rope and a knife. He cut a piece of the rope and then jumped back into the river to tie the rope around the end of the tree trunk, sticking out of the water. The other end of the tree pinned the body under the river. Lynette mumbled to herself, "God help us."

When Dillan was done, he climbed aboard, and pulled in the anchor. After drying off, he started the boat motor, and pushed on the throttle. He drove about three more minutes down the river to where it widened enough to turn around, so they could head back.

"Look, Dillan, over there." Lynette pointed at a grubby yellow raincoat hanging from a tree, next to a makeshift camp. It was marked by a tarp tied at three points at what looked like an attempt to create shelter.

"I picked up a hitchhiker last year wearing rain gear like that," said Lynette.

"Let's get out of here and call the police." They rode pass the trunk tied with the yellow nylon rope. Dillan pointed out landmarks on the way back that he would later tell police to help them locate the man at the bottom of the river.

* * *

A dirty wet towel in one hand and a spray bottle of cleaner in the other, Lynette moved about the airport lounge wiping down tables and chairs. While she worked, she thought about Dillan and the boat, and the body of the man. She remembered the make-shift camp, and the yellow raincoat and wondered if they might have belonged to her hitch hiker, Ben. She had given the police his name out of speculation. What else could she do? With only a first name, there was not much to go on, but she would have to keep the faith that somehow, someone, if not divine intervention perhaps, might connect the dots. She sighed heavily, and she conceded to the fact that she may never really know.

When all the chairs were pushed in, she had resumed her position behind the bar, and stood now, looking at the newspaper article that

Dillan had read aloud earlier that day, *Sopchoppy, FL. – The Leon County Sheriff says two boaters reported a body they found in the Ochlockonee River Monday afternoon. The body was a male, wearing military camouflage, probably fifty to sixty years old. It is likely that he was a military veteran. The body was found in a forested area about a mile from Highway three-nineteen. Sopchoppy residents reported that there had been a homeless man camping near the river during the past few months. Post-Traumatic Stress Syndrome may have contributed to his unstable mindset. The man's identity is unknown.*

After her second re-read of the article, she redirected her concentration to inventory. She marked down bottles of cordials, premiums, calls, and wells. She moved about swiftly opening and closing coolers, making a count of beer and wine. Then while she was making a list of liquor to be re-ordered, Tyler ducked in through the restaurant entrance holding a plate of food.

"Hey, how's it going?" he said.

"It's quiet, how about you?"

"It's dead. I'm fixin' to finish these wings, and then I'm cleaning up and getting ready to go," said Tyler, "Can I get a ride?"

"Sure, where you going?"

"Home, Frenchtown."

"I'm almost ready to go. Give me about thirty minutes," said Lynette. "I just need to finish up this inventory and cash out my drawer." She held a clipboard in her hand, and was reviewing her list, when she heard brittle cracking sounds. She looked over at Tyler, now gnawing at his saucy wings. "Are you eating the bones?"

"Well, no sense wasting." Tyler stood and threw his Styrofoam plate into the trash. "Ok, thanks for giving me a ride, I gotsta clean up my stand, I'll see you later."

"Yup." Lynette watched Tyler return to the terminal.

It was almost closing time. Lynette was kneeling behind the bar counting cleaning supplies when she heard the lounge door swing open and a man's voice call out.

"Are you open?"

Lynette burst up from beneath the bar, then stood looking into the face of a surprised chubby middle-aged man approaching. Instantly his expression turned smirk, then he puckered his lips and wolf whistled.

"How'd you do that?" he said. He swung his head to one side causing the curls in his dark hair to bounce. Lynette ignored the question, then answered the first one.

"We're open for about twenty more minutes," said Lynette. She could see the man's eyes were half-mast. "What can I get you?"

"I'll take a gin and tonic with a lime, please." The man claimed a bar stool.

Lynette walked to the pouring station, then mixed him a drink that was light on the gin. She set the glass in front of him.

"So, what's there to do in this town?" asked the man. He slurred his words.

"Depends on you I guess, there's theatre, the civic center, night clubs, church." Lynette was being a smart ass with the last suggestion. She could see he clearly had enough to drink. His elbows on the bar, he looked over his shoulder around the room. Then lifting himself off the stool, he leaned over. He spoke with a dubious demeanor. "Do you know where I can get some tail?"

Lynette looked up from the sink she had just drained, and attempted to answer with lucidity. "Perhaps, you can pick someone up in a night club."

"Aw, come o-o-on, don't you know where I could get some tail?" His eyelids drooped and opened again.

Lynette remained unflappable. "How about the Slipper or Bullwinkle's?"

"Naw, I just want a little tail." He held up his hand with his index finger and thumb close, but not touching. Then he lifted his glass to his mouth and swilled down the rest of his drink. "Can I get another one of these?"

"I'm sorry sir, that drink was last call. We closed at ten."

"Isn't there anywhere else we can get a drink tonight. I'll buy you a drink."

"No, the little bar is closed too. How about I call you a taxi?"

"I already called one." He flashed some cash. "Come on, go with me to have a drink."

"No thanks, I'm going home to study."

Tyler, the shoeshine man popped in from the restaurant. This seemed to prompt Mr. Middle age to admit defeat. He stood, threw money on the bar, turned, and staggered to the door and out into the terminal. Lynette could see him stopping at the Avis counter. *He's probably hitting on the Avis agent*, she thought.

Larry stepped into the lounge, "Are you done with the inventory?"

"Yes, here's the sheets."

"Thanks, Great work today. The place was pretty busy."

"Hey, you guys see that guy out there," Lynette gestured toward the Avis counter. He's a real creep. Go see if Terri is alright."

"Sure," Larry walked out into the terminal. Tyler trailed behind. Lynette watched as both men stood lingering by the Avis counter. Less than a moment later, the creep wandered toward the sliding glass doors that preceded outside. Larry disappeared into the restaurant. Tyler returned to the lounge.

"How'd it go?" asked Lynette.

"He's drunk fo sho. All we did was look at him, and he got on his way."

"What a pig," Lynette picked up her cash drawer and was about to carry it to the office, when she heard a plane on the tarmac. "Hmm, must be a private plane."

"Uh Huh, All the schedule flights have come and gone. You want me to lock the door?"

"Sure, thanks," Lynette handed Tyler the keys.

"I'm ready to get outta here. I'll meet you at Larry's office."

Minutes later, Lynette was driving Tyler home.

"Where are you headed, again?" asked Lynette.

"French Town. I'm gonna pick up some smoke, you want some?"

"No thanks, I'm good."

"Turn here on Copeland Street, then take that turn there by the next streetlamp. I can get you some, no problem."

"No, really, I'm set."

"This is it, pull into the driveway. Keep the car running and doors locked until I gits back. Then if it be ok, I need to get a ride just a few more blocks from here, ok? I'm going to see my girl."

"I'll be here." Lynette locked the door, and let her head lay back on the seat. She closed her eyes. Knocking sounds woke her up. The streetlamp lit up Tyler's apron, where he stood outside the passenger side door. Lynette leaned over to unlock it.

"Hey that was fast, I didn't have time to finish my nap."

"Good, I didn't want you waitin'."

"Well, where to now?"

"Just up the road apiece."

"Take this left. That's North Woodward Ave."

"So why do they call this French Town?"

"Well, see after that war between the north and the south, lotta black freed folks moved here. The land wasn't so good, lotta flooding, but it was here for the takin'." Tyler pointed at the intersection out the car window. "Ok, turn here on Preston.

You know, Ray Charles lived around here. In the sixties, things changed, lotta crime and stuff. Here, turn here, that's Birmingham Street. The house gonna be on the right. Slow down. See that big magnolia."

"I love magnolia trees."

"Here it is."

Lynette pulled over to the curb.

"Can you find your way outta here? We're Northwest of downtown Tallahassee, and that be where this shoe shine man lives." He flashed a smile showing off his gold filling that formed a star on his front tooth.

"Yah, I'll just go back the way we came."

"Well, thank ya kindly for the ride."

"You're welcome," said Lynette. "Good night."

Tyler climbed out, then turned and leaned in, "Lock up," he said. Then he closed the car door.

Minutes later at Alumni Village, Lynette lumbered up the walk toward her apartment. Her eyes fixed on the front door. There was something sticking to it. Her consternation was rising. At a closer look, it was recognizably an envelope. She grabbed it, tucking it under her arm, to free her hands to manage the keys and the door handle. She flipped on the exterior light, revealing Tashi, who was doing his greeting dance. After tossing her purse and the envelope on the love seat, she squatted down to return Tashi's hello. "Aww, my sweet boy, I missed you too." She scratched him all over, nuzzling his neck with her head. "Come on, let's go potty." Lynette walked beside him on the front lawn under the streetlamp, then down the walk passed Warren's lit up apartment. After all the potty business was done, they returned home, locked up, and sank onto the loveseat. With Tashi in her lap, Lynette opened the envelope.

Please be advised you are in violation of the no pet policy at Alumni Village. This is a violation of your signed lease, which has subjected you to a fine equal to twenty-five percent of your monthly rent. You must remove the pet from the premises within seven days. If you do not comply with this timeline, Alumni Village will serve you with an Eviction Notice.

Tashi stretched upward, lapping at her face with his long pink tongue. "Well, my friend," said Lynette. "It looks like you're moving back to Grandma's."

Chapter 9

Wearing curlers in her hair and staring into the open birth control pill cartridge, Marie was troubled that she had missed a day. She pressed out a tiny tablet, popped it in her mouth, then drank water from the spicket. It had been a while since she had been to a bar. Feeling lonely, reckless and presumptuous, tonight she would attempt it alone. She had decided on panty hose with her black mini dress. Now removing her rollers, she thought about where she would be going. She had heard a lot about the Silver Slipper at the hospital. One of the nurses had told her it was a few miles north of the Capitol, on Silver Slipper Lane. "They have secluded dining rooms with curtains that you can close off," her co-worker had said.

Later inside the Slipper, Marie took in the ambiance. There was a crystal chandelier in the lobby, the lights were dim, the walls, paneled in pink. She wandered the premises and saw well-dressed patrons filing into a large dining room with tables covered in white and red linen, surrounded by chairs of blue. Just off there, was the hall of private rooms, some with booths, some with chairs, all with mirrors, and a lamp mounted to the wall. The damask patterned curtains were closed on three of the rooms. What might she do, should she find herself in one of them? She admired the hall of autographed photos of former Presidents John F. Kennedy, Lyndon B. Johnson, Jimmy Carter, and President Ronald Reagan, among other photos of football players, coaches, and politicians. At the end of the hall, she peeked into the Ball Room. Then she settled in the lounge at a bar stool. Shortly after ordering her first drink, a tall blonde innocuous gentleman rushed in and leaned on the bar, eyes on Marie.

"Hey, do you know where there is a pay phone?"

She tossed her bouncy brown hair and smiled. "That depends on who you call."

He reached his hand up to loosen his necktie. "Well, not that it's any of your business, but I'm calling my office." He smiled. "And how about, after I make this call, I buy you a drink."

"Don't keep me waiting too long, my glass is almost empty." Marie lifted her drink to her lips.

"I'll tell you what." He signaled to the bartender, who came running. "Ron, can I get this beautiful woman, a drink, and I'll take a Jack and Coke, and let's run a tab."

Marie looked at the bartender. "I'll take another martini, please." She watched the tall blonde leaving the lounge then focused on the bartender flipping bottles, bottoms up. "So, Ron, how do you know this guy who just bought me a drink?"

"He's a good tipper," said the bartender.

"Does he come in here a lot?"

"Why don't you ask him." The bartender set drinks near her. After downing the first martini, Marie pushed it aside. Then pinching the neck of the fresh drink, she slid it in front of her. The blonde returning, caught Marie's eye, stirring her up.

"Hi, the name's Bill," he offered his hand for a shake. Marie liked his deep-set eyes and lustrous brows.

"Hi, the name's Marie."

"How come, I've never seen you in here before?"

"I just moved here from South Florida."

"Me," He glanced at his gold Rolex. "I've lived here all my life."

Marie's gold-digging antennae went up. "Oh, I think I'm getting just a little hungry."

"Hey Ron," said Bill. He gestured to the bartender. "When you get a minute, we'd like to order some food."

"I think I'll have a shrimp cocktail," said Marie.

"Suit yourself, but this place is renowned for its steak. I'm having their bacon wrapped fillet mignon. It's two-inches-thick." Bill licked his top lip. "They char it just enough to make a crust and it melts in your mouth."

"So, you come here often?" Marie pinched the sword with the olive in her finger and thumb, then slid it into her mouth.

"I like it here." Bill lifted his drink and swiveled his bar stool around to gaze around the room. "It wasn't always at this location."

"Really?" said Marie.

"It caught fire in the seventies." Bill sipped at his drink and swallowed. "Back then it was on South Monroe Street, about a mile from the Capitol."

"I like how they named the street after the restaurant," said Marie.

"Cute, huh," said Bill. He spun his seat, and now faced Marie. "My dad comes here a lot. I remember when I was a kid, we had a party in the ballroom for their anniversary."

"How about those curtained rooms." Marie crossed her legs and swiveled slightly in Bill's direction.

"Good place for business meetings and state politics," said Bill. "During legislative session, this place is packed with legislators, waiting for lobbyists to pick up the tab for anything a lawmaker can eat and drink in a single sitting."

"How boring," said Marie. "I can think of better things to do behind a closed curtain."

Ron intruded, "Would you like a menu?" Bill set his glass on the bar.

"No, not necessary, I'll have my usual, filet mignon, medium rare, with a baked potato, and Italian dressing on my salad. The lady will have a shrimp cocktail to start."

"Got it," said Ron.

"So, what do you do, Marie?"

"I'm a medical student. And you?"

"I'm somewhat of an entrepreneur. I studied Business at Duke University. "

"Where is that?"

"In Durham, North Carolina." He lifted his drink to his thin lips. "Have you been there?"

"No, never."

"So, what's it like studying medicine, and all? What sort of medicine do you want to practice?"

"Probably pediatrics, or obstetrics," said Marie. "I love delivering those babies."

"Babies, huh." Bill smiled revealing his straight teeth. "Sounds like you've done it before."

"I have, in fact, I delivered one a few weeks ago at the hospital. I'm working per diem as an RN." She stood up. "Would you excuse me for a minute?"

"You're not leaving, are you?"

"Before the shrimp cocktail? No, I'll be back."

Marie felt Bill watching her. In the tight dress, her ass wagged with each step out of the lounge. She returned after a trip to the ladies' room just in time to see the waiter deliver the shrimp cocktail and a salad.

"I was lonely while you were away." Bill took a bite of his salad.

"I had hoped you would be. You didn't steal any of my shrimp, now, did you?"

"No, ma'am. Did you see any movie stars out there?"

"Not yet, but the night is young." Marie sat, then toyed with her first shrimp. "I can't believe my glass is empty, already."

"Would you like another one?"

Marie nodded. "I would love one."

"Ron, Another martini for the lady."

"Say, after dinner, I'm heading to a party, a buddy of mine, a frat boy invited me. Do you want to go with me?"

"I thought you'd never ask."

"Great, now I don't have to go stag," he said. "How's your shrimp?"

"Oh, it's delicious, thank you for asking," said Marie. She saw a waiter stepping into the lounge. He was carrying a plate and silverware. "Here comes your steak."

"Ahhh! Looks great." Bill's deep-set eyes shot up at the waiter. "Thanks."

Bill put a knife to his meat. "Pink and juicy, just the way I like it."

"Oh, I know what you mean."

"Do you?"

"Doesn't everyone like it pink and juicy?" asked Marie. She squeezed a lemon on her shrimp. Her social filters were off. She nibbled at the tiny tails, while nursing her third martini. She chattered away, while Bill finished his dinner.

* * *

An hour later, Bill drove Marie down Live Oak Plantation Road. Music and loud voices could be heard out the open car windows. Bill climbed out of the drivers' side and walked around the rear of the vehicle to open the door for Marie. She purposefully pointed her leg out of the car, while Bill took her hand. The three martinis had created more than a fair buzz. Marie could feel her inhibitions dissipating and her desire to have sex congealing. They walked past clumps of trees. A crescent moon hung above. Mars and Saturn shined, perfectly visible, should anyone know the difference between them and the stars. The neighborhood seemed isolated from the rest of Tallahassee.

They stepped down a long horseshoe driveway leading to a large two-story stately brick house nestled among pine trees, groomed with dogwoods, crepe myrtle and symmetrical shrubbery. Four white pillars lined the front, giving it the face of a mansion. Cheering, yelling, and laughter got louder. Marie's shoes were getting wet from walking on the grass. A man was approaching.

"Hey Bill," said the man. He spoke in a deep voice.

"Hey Tom." They met with a handshake.

"Glad you could make it," said Tom, now handing Marie and Bill a beer. A girl stepped over from behind Tom. She offered a tray of coke. Marie watched Bill partake first, then she snorted a line.

"The party is just getting started," said Tom with a lustful smirk.

Once they reached the rear yard of the house, there was a huddle of people and bright lights beaming down. "What the hell is going on over there?" asked Bill. He was speaking loudly, so to be heard over the crowd.

"Go on over an' take a look, you'll love it."

Marie took her shoes off to walk more easily in the grass. She looked over at the pool deck and wanted to sit down, but Bill grabbed her arm and guided her to the huddle of cheers. He was tall enough to see what all the excitement was about.

"Awwww… Bill now felt the superhero cocaine high.

"What? I can't see," said Marie, now feeling her own sense of invincibility from snorting the cocaine.

"Here I'll give you a lift." He kneeled, reaching for Marie's hands. "Climb up on my shoulders."

Marie threw her spiked shoes in the grass, hiked up her skirt, and then one leg at a time, climbed onto Bill's shoulders. When he stood up, Marie could see above the crowd. She could see all the people yelling and chanting, cheering, whooping, waving their hands in the air. There were lights on tripods, cameras on tripods, a man squatting on one knee. On his shoulder was a video camera that he pointed at the spectacle in the center of the huddled crowd. A young brunette female lay naked, on her back, eyes closed, knees bent, legs spread. A medium-built brunette male, wearing nothing but jeans, was burying his face in her groin while he held his hands on her hips. All the while, the shouting and the applauding from the crowd continued with a life of its own. The male giving the oral pleasure lifted his face. Marie could see the camera man motioning to him. He stood, unzipped his jeans and dropped them to the grass. He was ready to penetrate. The female rolled over and rose-up on her hands and knees. Her back was covered in leaves and grass. When he entered her from the rear, the huddle ascended to a roar. The female wailed with carnality. The man mouthed, "I am fucking you." The woman mouthed "Fuck me, fuck me." The copulation continued slowly. People in the huddle shouted, "Fuck her," "Oh yah." Groans, moans, cries, cat calls, yelps. Marie could hear her own yowling. The male began to pump faster, enjoying the pleasure. He fucked feverishly as if there was no one watching. The female was no different. She looked possessed. They were sweating and breathing heavy like animals, coming close to climax. The camera men motioned to each other. The female's face contorted wildly, she screamed in orgasm, but kept her back arched to meet her partner's pleasure. The crowd intensely reverberated in a frenzy. The man pulled out and exploded on her ass and lower back. The squatting camera men yelled, "Cut. You two, get dressed."

Everyone applauded and the huddle broke up. Bill's shoulders were aching. He squatted to allow Marie to climb down from his back.

"Some party," she said.

"Nothing like sex as a spectator sport." He spoke with his lips touching her ear. The crowd circle was breaking up. "Come on, let's check out the house."

Marie trotted to the house, trying to keep up with Bill's long strides. She held her beer in one hand and her shoes in the other. The brick stairs on the front porch snagged at her panty hose. The front door was framed with stained glass panels, and once inside the foyer, the marble floor was smooth, but slippery under her feet. The plantation shutters were closed over the large windows. The dangling chandelier fixed in the high ceiling, twinkled light over the partiers. There were people everywhere. They were talking in front of the fireplace, drinking under the white pillars, smoking at the bottom of the giant curved stairwell. She thought she recognized someone in the sitting room off to the right. Bill led Marie toward the stairs, where they passed a couple seated near the bottom, peering through the railing at the crowd, smoking a joint. Now on the second floor, they stood at the railing looking down. A Bon Jovi song played underneath the many voices of all the people.

"What do you think?" asked Bill. He reached for her forearm.

"This place is beautiful," said Marie. The heat of Bill's strong hand spread arousal to every inch of her. Marie swallowed the remains of her beer that hadn't already spilled earlier. She set the empty can on a bookshelf. A door opened behind them. A couple with tossed hair, burst into the hall.

"Come on." Bill led her by the arm into the room, closed and locked the door behind them. The walls were painted red. Marie threw her shoes on the floor and sashayed to the four-post bed. She sat down, and smoothed the covlet in a circular motion, looking at Bill, who had sunk into a chair, "Look, Bill, it's a playground. Wanna play with me?"

"Fuck, yeah." He smiled, then lunged at her.

Writhing and knotting themselves on the bed. Clothes tearing. Hands, fingers, lips, and tongues everywhere. Bill paused, speaking through his heavy breaths, are you sure you want me to fuck you?"

"Fuck, yeah," said Marie.

* * *

It was Sunday morning when Marie surprised Lynette at the airport lounge.

"Hey, Marie, what are you doing out here? You flying home for Spring Break?"

"No, but I think I did some flying last night." She climbed onto a stool. "Can I get a Bloody Mary?"

"Sure." Lynette iced down a tall glass and poured in a jigger of vodka. "So, tell me, what the hell happened last night?"

"You won't believe it."

"Try me." Lynette was now peeling the top from a can of tomato juice.

"I went out to the Silver Slipper and met a guy."

"Never been there. They say it's pretty nice. What'd did you get to eat?"

"Shrimp cocktail, I drank most of my dinner."

"It's a steakhouse, isn't it?"

"Yeah, I guess so, Bill, that's the guy I met, he got a steak. He said it was pink and juicy, and that's not all that was pink and juicy about last night."

"Oh, I can't wait to hear more."

Marie glanced over her shoulder. "Why is it so quiet today?"

"It's early yet. Most people are drinking coffee right now." Lynette pinched a lime from the fruit trough and dropped it into the Bloody Mary, before setting down the glass in front of Marie.

"We went to a party after the Slipper."

"Where?" Lynette stood at the end of the bar filling a bowl with pretzels.

"Up in that rich neighborhood behind the Publix on Monroe Street. It was wild."

"Here." Lynette set the bowl of pretzels next to Marie's drink. "I figure this will help with the hang over."

Marie reached for it, then tossed the salty snack in her mouth. Her eyes darting back and forth. She spoke softly. "There were people having sex. And we all watched. It was fucken loco."

Lynette looked up from the sink she was filling with water, her expression was shock, straight up. "Oh, My, God." She cut the faucet, her eyes darting now, Lynette stepped directly in front of Marie.

"There were cameras and lights, and it was..." Marie shook her head, mulling over her memory of the night before.

"Oh, my God. Sounds like you watched people making a porno film," said Lynette. "You better hope you're not in it. Or there goes your reputation as a medical student, and you can forget being a doctor." Lynette watched Marie's eyes looking off to the side. "Oh, man. Do you think you're in it?"

"I don't know. I was on Bill's shoulders. Hell, I had my hands and my beer in the air cheering 'em on like the rest of the people. I was pretty wasted." Marie put her elbow on the bar, lowered her head, and covered her brow with her hand. "Dios Mío, a porno movie, I never thought a that."

"Man, are you gullible."

"Gullible?" Marie's pronunciation was weak, "What does that mean?" She tapped her red painted fingernails on the bar.

"Easily fooled," answered Lynette.

"He said his friend, a fraternity guy invited him to the party."

"Fraternities, I fucken hate fraternities." Lynette went back to her sinks, filling up the sink for the rinse cycle. "Making porno, sounds right up their alley. Bunch of rich spoiled brats, they think they can do whatever they want." Seconds later, Dillan stepped in from the restaurant.

"Good morning." Dillan smiled, flashing his dimple in Lynette's direction. He held a cup of coffee in his hand and laid the newspaper on the bar.

"Good morning," said Lynette. She flashed her smile Dillan's way. "This is my friend Marie, she's studying medicine."

"Medicine, really, wow, nice to meet you." Dillan unfolded the paper. Lynette noticed his strong hand and she remembered how he had handled the boat.

"Dillan took me on the fun boat trip."

"How's Tashi?" asked Dillan.

"Oh, well, he's back living with my folks. The no pet policy at my apartment, caught up with us."

"Oh, no way," said Marie. "You got away with it for a long time, didn't you?"

"Yah, almost a year. Well, he's better off, he's got my mom's dog he can play with. And I don't have to feel guilty anymore about leaving him alone. It wasn't good for him."

"How's your mom's leg?" asked Marie. She sat swirling the straw in her drink.

"Better, she got her cast off, and is finally walking without crutches."

"I didn't know your mom broke her leg," said Dillan.

"Yah, she's much better now." Lynette looked out the window. "Looks like a private plane. Do you know who it is?"

"I'm not at liberty to discuss it at this time," said Dillan. "Let's just say, it's a very important person." He was looking up from the paper through the window at the tarmac, when he heard someone coming in from behind and turned to see.

"Hey, Bob," said Dillan, "Lynette this is my boss, Bob."

"Hello, Bob, nice to meet you," said Lynette. "Can I get you something to drink?"

"I'll have a Coors on tap, thank you." Bob was clean cut with smooth skin. Lynette figured him to be in his mid-forties. "Southern Air Transport has a charter flight coming through tomorrow, from the Turks and Cacaos," said Bob.

"What time?" asked Dillan.

"Probably late, just stand by," said Bob. He smiled at Lynette when she delivered his beer.

"How you doing, Marie?" asked Lynette. "Can I get you anything? More pretzels?"

"No, thanks." She lifted her drink and looked at it, still half full. "This will be it for today. I think I've done enough damage this Spring Break, and I still have seven days to go. How about you, are you going home this week?"

"No," said Lynette. "I have so much homework, and I'm picking up extra hours here."

"Dillan, are you still good with the coffee or do you want something from the bar?"

"I'm good, thanks, my boss tells me I'm on stand-by." Dillan flipped a page in the newspaper. "Looks like they still haven't caught anyone in that Don Aronow murder from last month."

"Who's Don Aronow?" asked Marie.

"Says here he invented the Cigarette Boat in Miami. In a place called Thunder Alley." Dillan read the paper aloud. "They don't call 'em cigarette boats for nothing, they leave everyone behind them in a cloud of smoke." Dillan looked up from the paper. "Someone left him in a cloud of smoke alright, he was shot several times in his car. When he was found, the engine and the air conditioning were still running."

"Yah, his boats are something," said Bob. "Expensive too, they run from the thousands to the millions depending on the size. I saw on the news, he built boats for the Drug Enforcement Agency and Customs."

Dillan read some more out loud. "If the sea were outer space, these damn things like a rocket, would shoot you to the moon." He looked over the top of the paper. "Guess they're pretty fast."

Lynette held a jar of cherries, and stood now, glancing out the window. "Is it President Reagan?"

"I told you I am not at liberty to discuss it."

"It's the Governor, what's his name?" asked Marie.

"Martinez," said Bob.

"You guys," said Dillan.

Marie and Lynette giggled. "I know, you're not at liberty to say," said Lynette. She unscrewed the lid on the cherries and was reaching in to refill the trough, and she saw Bob smiling.

"Hey, Ada," said Bob.

"Well, Hey, everybody, how's it going?"

"How's Gene?" Bob asked.

"He's good. He's flying to Miami. We're looking at some property around Lake Talquin."

"Very nice," said Dillan.

Ada walked behind the bar and stowed away her purse in a cabinet. "Good spot for you to put your boat in, Dillan." said Ada.

"Yah, it would be."

"So, girl, we ready to make some money this afternoon?" Ada gave Lynette a hug.

"Yes, ma'am."

"Hey ya'll, Gene and I were wantin' to have you guys over sometime."

"I'll bring the caviar," said Lynette.

Dillan set down his newspaper. "I'll bring something too."

"Ada and Bob, this is my friend Marie, from FSU."

Bob raised his beer glass. "Hey."

"Well, good to meet you." said Marie, now smiling. "Lynette, I'm going home, I have to recover from this hang over." Marie stood, opening her purse. "How much for the drink?"

"Don't worry about it, it's on me," said Lynette. "Here, wait, I need to unlock the lounge doors. We officially open in about ten minutes." Marie trailed behind Lynette, sashaying across the lounge.

"Thanks for the drink," said Marie.

"You're welcome. I'll see you around. Meanwhile, try to stay out of trouble. Like my grandma used to say, 'If you can't be good, be careful.'" Lynette jiggled the key in the lock and opened the door.

"I gotta remember that one, say it again."

"If you can't be good, be careful," said Lynette.

Marie stepped out into the terminal repeating it. "If you can't be good, be careful."

"Bye," said Lynette, still holding the door open. Marie waved before walking away. Lynette approached the bar. Dillan was standing. "I'll be heading out too," he said. "The crowd'll be coming in soon. Let's have dinner this week."

"Crab legs?" requested Lynette.

"Ok, crab legs. I've never had them, but I'll try them," said Dillan. "I'll call you tomorrow."

"Hey, ladies, good to see you." Bob stood, looking through his wallet, and left money on the bar. He and Dillan walked out together.

"Hey Ada, I'll be right back," said Lynette. "I'm going to the bathroom before the rush starts."

* * *

Lynette mounted the stairs to the second floor of the building marked two seventeen on Crenshaw Drive. She knocked on the door, then stood waiting for someone to answer. She glanced at the parking lot and could see Marie's Chevy parked in the line of cars out front. She could hear music coming from inside the apartment. She should be home, Lynette thought. She knocked a second and third time. The face that appeared when the door finally opened, was not the face she had expected.

"Hello," said Lynette.

"Hello," said the man wearing the Cassock shirt. Marie appeared behind him, as the door opened wider.

"Hey Lynette. Come on in." Marie sat on a green vinyl chair, tucking a leg under her. Lynette sat on the edge of the sofa, folding her hands in front of her. She could see the table had been set for two, a candle burned in the middle, and there were dirty dishes in the sink. The aroma of some tasty meal filled the air.

"Lynette, this is Father Juan from St. Thomas Moore's Co-Cathedral. We were just having a Bible Study."

Lynette gritted her teeth, and looked down at her hands, to prevent herself from rolling her eyes, or speaking on the matter. "Nice to meet you," Lynette trying to appear sincere, now offered her hand for a shake.

"Likewise," said Father Juan. He sat down on the other end of the sofa.

"Would you like an expresso?" asked Marie.

"No, thanks," said Lynette. I can't stay. I'm going grocery shopping."

"Well, I'll leave you two to visit," said Father Juan. He gathered his Bible from the coffee table.

"Ok," Marie watched him with hungry eyes. "I'll see you at church."

"You don't need to leave on account of me," said Lynette.

"Oh, I was on my way out anyway." The priest stood, the door in arms reach, he opened it, stepped out on the balcony, turned, and looked inside for one last goodbye, before shutting the door.

Lynette turned around in her seat, gripped the curtain, cracking it open just enough so she could see the priest heading down the stairs. Jerking the curtains closed again, she snapped. "What the fuck are you doing? He's a man of the cloth. You can't date a priest. It's a sin, the guy has a celibacy vow."

Marie just looked back at her with wide guilty eyes. She swallowed and twirled her hair. Lynette went on. "What the hell is wrong with that guy. Is the whole world corrupt? I can't be anymore disillusioned." Lynette was standing now looking over toward the kitchen. She saw the bowl with the salad.

"He didn't do anything he didn't want to do. He was a man before he decided to be a priest," said Marie.

"Yeah, well, you better get your shit together, because this is not good for your reputation and he is gonna get thrown out of the church." Lynette stood over the salad bowl now, looking down at the spinach leaves, black olives, avocado, and chunks of chicken. "This looks really good."

"You want some?"

"Hell, yeah."

Marie had moved to the kitchen. She stood now filling a plate with salad. Lynette was about to sit at the table when she saw on the floor, a pair of eye-glasses.

"What happened to these?" Lynette lifted them onto the table, where Marie was setting the salad plate and a fork.

"Dios Mío," said Marie now reaching for the glasses.

"Nice salad, what kind of dressing is this?" Lynette sat down at the table.

"Vinaigrette," Marie was taking a closer look at the glasses. "I can't believe this. One of the lenses is cracked, and the frame's bent. And I cannot afford to fix these, right now."

"Well, I can front you a few bucks, just let me know what you need."

"Oh, my hole my soul, in that order." Marie folded the glasses and placed them in a case. "Ok, I'll take 'em in and then let you know what the bill is."

"You wanna go to Publix with me?" Lynette's mouth was full.

"Ok," Marie moved about the kitchen opening and closing cabinets. I'm all out of Café Bustelo, eggs, and granola."

"Do you eat that stuff dry? I never buy that stuff."

"It's crunchy, like a bag of tortilla chips."

"You're weird," said Lynette, now stabbing up the last forkful of spinach. "I gotta get quite a few things, I made a list." She set down her fork, then pulled a paper from her pocket. After unfolding it, she read aloud from it. "Bread, milk eggs, cheese, peanut butter, popcorn, butter, coffee, and chips ahoy, and I almost forgot." She grabbed a pen lying on the table and scribbled. "deodorant."

* * *

Later, from inside the beige Toyota Corona, the Publix was in sight.

"Hey, turn here," said Marie.

"What, Why?"

"I think that's the street where that frat porno party was?"

"Oh, man." Lynette was curious. She made the right turn.

"I know it was some Plantation Road off of Meridian Street."

"I hope no one is there," said Lynette. "My virgin eyes, ya know."

"Just drive."

"What do you mean just drive, I'm driving, and you're driving me crazy."

"Drive slow, so I can read the signs," said Marie. She was leaning toward the dashboard.

"There it is." Marie pointed at the street sign. "Live Oak Plantation Road, that's it."

Lynette flipped on the blinker and turned the steering wheel.

"Go slow."

"I'm going slow."

"Do you see it?"

"There, there it is," said Marie, now pointing at the house outside the windshield.

Lynette pulled the car to the curb and looked out at the big brick house with the four white pillars. "Oh, brother, look at the pillars of hypocrisy. I can't hack it."

"Go, go, go, get out of here, before someone comes out," said Marie.

"Can we go grocery shopping now?"

"Yes, please," said Marie.

Then Lynette turned the car around.

* * *

The night Lynette went with Dillan to his boss' place for a party, she wore an embroidered bell sleeved blouse, her hair teased, and tight jeans. At the front door, they were greeted by a broad shouldered, clean shaven, giant of a smiling man. He held a Coors beer in his hand.

"Hey Dillan, glad you could make it. How you doin', man?"

"Good," said Dillan. "Gene, this is Lynette."

"Hey, Lynette," said Gene. "I've been hearing a lot about you, lately."

"All good, I hope."

"All good. Glad to finally meet you." Gene ushered them through the door into the foyer of the ranch style home. He was still wearing his Federal Express pilot uniform.

"I didn't even know you were back," said Dillan.

"Yeah man, I already clocked too many hours this week. Just flew the Miami run." Gene looked toward the six pack in Dillan's hand. "Can I put that in the fridge for you?"

"Absolutely," said Dillan, now handing it off. "Thanks, man."

Lynette spotted Ada in the living room. "Well, Hey, Lynette," said Ada. She set her beer down on the coffee table and faced Lynette to greet her with a hug. She smelled of perfume. Her hair was freshly styled. Her make up just glamorous enough to suit her gentle features.

"Hey Ada," Lynette was recalling how Ada had called in sick to work, making Lynette work a double shift, last week on the day before an exam. She spoke, trying not to show her agitation. "Glad to see you are feeling better."

"I'm not as young as I used to be." Ada sat down, then picked up a burning cigarette from an ash tray near her beer. "What a big ole bug I caught." She took a puff. "I didn't sleep all night for two days." Smoke was coming out of her mouth and swirling above her head. "Gene, honey, pull another one of these chairs out for Lynette."

"Yes Ma'am," said Gene.

Dillan stood greeting his boss, who was sitting on the sofa. Gene approached carrying a chair. His friendly blue eyes could now be seen in the light of the living room lamp.

"Here you go, madam," said Gene now setting the chair near Ada. He made a grand gesture with his hand, motioning Lynette to sit.

"Thank you, kindly," said Lynette. She took her seat between Ada and the sofa.

"Lynette, you remember Bob," said Dillan. He spoke loudly over the country music playing on the stereo.

"Hi, good to see you again," said Lynette. She noticed his eyes were half-mast. "You have a beautiful home." Bob looked down at the beer in his hand.

"It'll do," said Bob. He spoke softly.

"Thanks for covering for me at work last week," Ada said.

"You're welcome," said Lynette. Dillan bent to speak softly in Lynette's ear.

"They have Bartles and James. Would you like one?"

"That's perfect, thanks."

She watched him walk toward the kitchen, stopping to talk to a petit Korean woman sitting in a kitchen chair next to a round middle-aged man in a recliner.

"It's so nice to see Dillan so happy. You look real fine on him," said Gene.

"We've gone out a few times," said Lynette. "And I really like him."

"He's a good catch, if you ask me," said Ada. "He pays his rent, on time, and he keeps the place so nice and fixed up."

"You're his landlord?"

"I'm his landlord."

Dillan returned leaning down to hand Lynette her wine cooler.

"I didn't know Ada was your landlord," said Lynette. She kissed Dillan's cheek. "I guess I still have a lot to learn." Lynette crossed her legs and shook her sandaled foot. "So, Gene tells me, he's your sweetheart."

"Yes, ma'am, I am. I met him in Homestead, where he was stationed. He's a pilot, you know," said Ada. "Served in Vietnam, flying helicopters."

Lynette chugged some wine cooler. She wanted to shake off some social anxiety. "Wow, He works for Fed Ex, right?"

"Yes, for Fed Ex." Ada lifted her can a beer in the air, she spoke loudly. "Baby, what's a woman got to do to get a fresh beer around here?" Lynette looked over at Gene, who was getting up from the dining room table and smiling. His childlike face come in close to Ada, "You have to give me a kiss to get a fresh beer, baby."

"Oh, boy." Ada stretched up to meet his intention.

"Awww, that's so sweet," said Lynette. Then she glanced over to see Dillan elbow Gene and gesture with a tip of his head and glance of his eyes toward Bob and Paul, who had just entered from the hallway. Paul was smoking a joint and had passed it to Bob.

"Geez, you guys, I don't believe my eyes. Bob is smoking weed." Dillan walked closer to them.

"Go easy on him, Dillan." Gene looked sincere. "His wife just left him."

Dillan's eyebrows lifted over his almond eyes. "Wha-a-at?" said Dillan. "Geez, I'm sorry."

Everyone's attention was on Bob now. Lynette could see in Bob's eyes that the pot was taking effect.

"Shhhhhhh…" said Bob. "Sorry, Lynette, I'm not usually like this."

Lynette wrapped both hands around the wine cooler. "I see no evil and hear no evil."

"Hey, Lynette," said Paul. He offered the half smoked joint. "You want a hit?"

"Nah, I'm good, thanks, Paul," said Lynette. She could see Dillan was affected by the news about Bill's wife. The Korean woman now stood near and introduced herself.

"Hello, Lynette, I'm Mee-Yon, Charles' wife. Dillan has told us much about you. He like you lots."

"I like him too," said Lynette, now feeling the alcohol relaxing her. "It's a pleasure to meet you. Now, how do you and Dillan know each other?"

"Charles' owner of Aero Associates, his boss' boss. He's helicopter pilot in war. Maybe you and Dillan will come to my restaurant."

"Yes, that would be great. Does Dillan know where it is?" asked Lynette.

"The food is super," said Ada.

"Yes, Dillan come before," said Mee-Yon. The sound of the doorbell drove her from the conversation. "Excuse me."

"I'll get it," said Bob, now pointing his index finger toward the ceiling. He stood, then tripped on the coffee table. "So sorry." Bob patted the table and staggered toward the door. "Coming," he yelled. Everyone got quiet and swiveled their heads toward the hall leading to the front door.

"Hey, Becky. Hey, Kim. Come on in," said Bob. Lynette watched as he hugged Becky and led her to the living room. Becky was carrying a bottle of Jack Daniels.

"Now we can get the party started," said Paul.

"Hey, girls, was it busy tonight?" asked Ada.

"Busy enough, we split almost two hundred dollars," said Kim, now ripping open a bag of Doritos.

"Hey, Becky," said Lynette. "Hey, Kim." Lynette reached in and grabbed a handful. "You read my mind."

"Hey, ladies, let's head in the kitchen," said Ada. "Ya'll need to try some of my artichoke dip."

"To the kitchen, I go," said Lynette. "I'm ready for another wine cooler." She walked over to Dillan and sat on the arm of the couch. "Do you need a refill?"

Dillan looked down at his beer. "Yah, I'm about ready. Thanks." He handed off his empty bottle.

"Sorry to hear about Bob's wife," said Lynette, speaking softly. "I can tell you were surprised."

"I can't believe it. I just saw her at Bob's office just a few days ago."

"Yah, well, you never know." When Lynette reached the kitchen, Mee-Yon was pouring crackers onto a plate. Ada stood at the counter pulling foil wrap from a casserole dish.

"I love Miami Beach," said Mee-Yon. "Charles flies there a lot. And to Honduras. Next time he goes to Miami, I go too."

Lynette opened the refrigerator and pulled out bottles, one for herself and one for Dillan. She left the kitchen and headed back to the den. She could hear the murmur of the men's voices down the hall.

"Here's to humanitarian aid," said Bob. Beer bottles clinked in salute.

"What do you think about Senator Kerry's investigation?" asked Dillan.

"Here's to gun running, narcotic's trafficking, and the well-being of the contras," said Gene.

Lynette stepped into the room and handed Dillan his beer. "Thanks, Lynette," said Dillan.

She sat down on his knee.

"I'm not up to speed on this whole Iran thing, what exactly is a contra, anyway?" She lifted her wine cooler to her mouth. Everyone's eyes were on Lynette. Dillan tipped his bottle and took some gulps off his beer.

"My dear, contras," he took a deep breath, "let me see, contras," said Charles. Lynette could see he was drunk. "They're a militant group in Nicaragua."

"They're fighting against socialism," said Gene.

"And thanks to them, the money I paid for this pot, will go to help their cause," said Bob. "That's what Kerry's investigative committee is trying to say."

"Here's to democracy!" said Paul. He took a drag from a joint. Smoke trailed from his nostrils.

"This contra war against Nicaragua," said Gene. "Makes me want to drink Jack Daniels."

Ada popped her head into the room. "Ya'll come on to the kitchen now and try my artichoke dip."

In the kitchen, Gene slapped Ada on the ass. "Baby, didn't someone bring Jack Daniels?" Ada pointed to the bottle on the dining room table. "Ah there you are," said Gene. Ada handed him a glass. He poured himself, a shot and drank it down.

"Baby," said Gene. I'm flying cargo for a couple of days on Friday and Saturday."

"Where are you going?" asked Ada.

"Down to Homestead," said Gene. "Then possibly Costa Rica or Panama."

Bob stood looking through the refrigerator. "Did you drink the last Coors beer?"

"Like Oliver North," said Charles. "I'm pleading the fifth amendment."

"What are you eating?" asked Bob. "I want to try some." He watched Gene eating out of Ada's hand.

"Here, you'll love it." Ada scooped dip onto a cracker and popped it into Bob's mouth.

"Mmmm, that's nice." Bob grabbed a cracker and made himself another one.

"Ok, Dillan and I are ready for this dip," said Lynette. She held a cracker in her hand.

"Man, Ada, this is good," said Dillan. He gestured to Lynette with another cracker full of dip and fed it to her. Dillan turned to Gene.

"Hey, you still got that come-along?" asked Dillan.

"Yeah, why?"

"Can I borrow it?"

"Sure, I got it in the truck," said Gene.

"Is it unlocked?" asked Dillan.

"Yah, I think so, just help yourself."

"Thanks, I'll get it on the way out," said Dillan. He stepped close to Lynette. "Hey, are you close to ready to go?"

"Yah, pretty soon. I just need to use the restroom."

After discovering the main bathroom occupied, Lynette headed to the second bathroom off the master bedroom, where she saw all the decorative touches, the lace shower curtain, ceramic seashells hanging on the wall, a large bottle of hand lotion on the counter. She thought of Bob's wife and wondered why she left. Finished with nature's call, Lynette washed her hands, and checked her reflection in the mirror. She stepped out of the bathroom and into the bedroom, where she saw a desk, scattered with letter head marked Aero Associates and Ocean Air, and a packet marked United States Government contract. She heard voices outside the door in the hall.

"I'll see you for lunch then," said Charles. "Before we pick up the Southern Air Transport flight."

"Alright," said Gene. "Be careful."

"Don't worry, I'm not gonna be another "Barry Seal.""

"Semper Fi."

"Yah, Semper Fi."

Lynette stepped out from the room and went to meet Dillan standing near the front door. He held her jacket and raised it to help her slip it on. "Thanks, Dillan." Lynette hugged him.

"Alright everybody, we're heading out," said Dillan. "See you tomorrow."

"Dillan," said Bob. "The logbooks look great."

"Well, I always keep my note pad in my pocket while I'm working," said Dillan. "That way I can make maintenance notes as I go."

"Thanks for everything," said Lynette.

"Good night," said Bob.

Dillan opened the door and he saw a gray sedan pulling up to the curb. "Looks like Bryan. Come on, I'll introduce you to the airport Manager. Have you met him?"

"No," said Lynette.

"Come on, I'll introduce you." He led her toward the driver's side of the sedan.

"Hi Dillan, How's the party?" asked Bryan. "Did I miss anything?"

"No, everyone's still here, we're heading out now, though. This is Lynette, she works in the lounge and goes to school at FSU."

"Hi Lynette, it's great to meet you." He stepped out of the car and met Lynette for a handshake. His mouth smiled under a full beard

"You too," said Lynette. Bryan turned to Dillan.

"Hey, I heard you got a boat," said Bryan.

"Want to go out to the river some time?"

"Really," said Bryan. "Yes, I would."

"Alright, we'll set something up."

"Bye," Lynette waved and climbed into Dillan's Ford truck. She watched through the windshield as Dillan pulled the come-along from Gene's truck. Minutes later, the Ford backed out of the driveway.

"Dillan," said Lynette, "I need to finish a paper tomorrow for my Teaching Reading Class. I'm working with this little girl. She's in the sixth grade and can barely read. I'm gonna start reading books about airplanes with her. And I'd like to bring her to the airport for a field trip."

"I can get her on a plane if you want."

"Really, can you?"

"Yah, let me know when you want to bring her out, and I'll take her aboard. It will probably be a DC – 6."

"That'd be perfect. I'll have to get permission. Thanks so much. You're the best."

"Well, anything for the kids," said Dillan. The corners of his full lips turned up showing off his dimple. Lynette scooted close, then planted a thank you kiss on his face.

* * *

Lynette studied how learning to read is a complex process: emotional, affected by self-concept, attitudes, and culture. And in all that mix, a vital ingredient needed to learn to read is prior knowledge, also called schema. On Thursday mornings, while fulfilling a requirement for her *Teaching Reading* course, Lynette saw firsthand the power of schema. At the Belle Vue Middle School Library in Tallahassee, Lynette tutored Tina Smith, a sixth grader struggling to read. Tina was reserved, shy, a real wallflower.

"You see all these books around here, Tina." Tina studied the many shelves at the library. Her two thick braids moving when she turned her head. "Inside those books your mind can travel places," said Lynette. "If you could go anywhere you wanted, where would you go?"

After a long silence, she said, "I don't know, but I'd go in a plane."

"Ok, I'm going to find you some books about airplanes," said Lynette. "Have you ever been inside an airplane?"

Tina shook her head to say no.

And after reading with Tina for the following three Thursdays, Lynette asked her supervising teacher about taking Tina on a field trip to the airport.

"You will need field trip forms, you'll need permission from her parents, the principal and me," said the supervising teacher.

"Ok, Do I have your permission?" asked Lynette.

"Yes," said the teacher.

"Ok, then," said Lynette. "I'll write up a slip and a note for Tina's folks asking for theirs."

The following week Lynette was glad to hear the airport trip had been approved. Dillan gave Tina a big welcome with a tour of the aviation maintenance hangar and a Piedmont jet. He dubbed her with a plastic pilot wings pin. All the while, Tina only spoke when spoken to. And her eyes smiled a lot, but her mouth did not.

Later, in the car on the way back to school, Lynette realized Tina had missed lunch period.

"Are you hungry, Tina?"

Tina nodded.

"Would you like to get a burger at Hardees?"

She nodded again.

Minutes later, Lynette turned the car into the parking lot, climbed out and went round to open Tina's door. She did not come out of the car. Instead, she sat silently, facing front staring out the windshield.

"Are you ready?" asked Lynette.

"I don't go in."

"You don't go in?" asked Lynette. "You mean you don't like to eat inside the restaurant?"

"I eat in the car, we don't go in."

Lynette saw the worry of an old woman on Tina's face. "Well, I go in and you can go in with me. It's nice and cool in there, like your cafeteria at school, and there's tables and chairs to eat at." Lynette couldn't understand the wariness, the apprehension. Tina turned to look up at Lynette standing outside the car. Her knitted brow and wide eyes pondered thoughts that Lynette would never know. And after about ten seconds, Tina climbed out of the car. Her eyes surveyed the parking lot and the street nearby as they walked into the restaurant. Tina looked as if she was overcoming some obstacle.

Minutes later they sat at a booth inside Hardees. "Would you like some catsup?" Lynette asked, now pinching packets between her thumb and fore finger.

Tina nodded, and reached her hand across the table to accept the catsup. Her skin dark against Lynette's. At eleven years old it was the first time Tina ate a burger inside the Hardee's restaurant.

Chapter 10

In Lynette's Marriage and Family class, the girl swayed back and forth supporting herself on forearm crutches. While she moved across the floor, her long brown hair moved to the rhythm of her gait. Her face was determined under black rimmed glasses. Lynette watched her swivel and take a seat two rows away. The crutches were set neatly on the floor against the legs of the desk. The isle remained open. A red book bag dropped to the floor, followed by the sound of a zipper. Had anyone else in the class felt a sense of awe in the presence of such courage? Lynette turned away, to stop herself from gawking.

When the professor counted the students off to organize groups, Lynette dragged a desk to the forming circle of all who had been dubbed a number two. It was after the introduce-yourself part and during the write-down-one-positive-thing-about-each-person part of the activity, when she met Jesse.

The first folded paper Lynette opened was from Jesse. And on the paper was the word, *sophisticated.* "Me, sophisticated, really?" said Lynette. She watched Jesse's glance shoot downward and back up.

"Why not?" asked Jesse.

"No one's ever called me that."

"Well, now they have."

* * *

Weeks later someone had taken Lynette's parking space, forcing her to park at the opposite end of the building. Cutting the engine, swearing, then gathering her bag, Lynette spied Jesse swaying with only one crutch carrying a brown bag. Lynette swung open her car door, stood and called out over the roof.

"Jesse, it's Lynette."

Jesse peered out of her glasses in the direction of the voice.

"Hello," said Jesse.

Now waving her arms, Lynette darted across the small patch of grass and down the sidewalk to meet her. "Can I carry the bag for you?"

"No, I got it, but you can take my keys and open my door." Jesse gestured toward the building marked three-twenty-eight.

"I didn't know you lived here, I live here too, I'm the first apartment down the other end." Lynette unlocked the door and held it open. Jesse stepped inside.

"Thanks. Would you like to come in?"

"Sure," said Lynette. "Well, your place looks exactly like mine, and I see you enjoy the same airplane-galley-sized kitchen that I have."

"I'm just about to graduate," said Jesse. "Getting my degree in Social Work." She set her bag on the kitchen table. "This is my last semester. I'm doing my internship at the Welfare Department."

"Oh, man, I wish I was finishing up."

"You will." Jesse sunk into a kitchen chair.

"I still have a year to go before my internship." Lynette noticed the open curtains. "Hey, be careful leaving your curtains open. I had a peeping tom and a flasher outside my apartment." Lynette turned her car keys over in her hand. "I still don't know if they were the same guy or not."

"No way," said Jesse. "No trouble like that for me."

"Well, my unit is more isolated than yours," said Lynette. "Last unit, last building. Anyway, they caught the guy or guys. Geez, I'm psyched that you live so close by."

"I'm glad too."

"Hey, you wanna come over sometime later in the week. I'll cook something, and I can introduce you to my new beau."

"Ok, that'd be fun."

"If you got some paper handy," said Lynette. "I'll write down my phone number."

"On the desk." Jesse pointed across the room.

After stuffing Jesse's phone number in her pocket, Lynette stepped toward the door.

"Well, I gotta go get ready for work."

"Oh right, you work at the airport lounge."

"You remember from class." Lynette smiled.

"Call me if you need to borrow a cup of sugar or anything," said Jesse.

"You too." Lynette stepped out of the apartment and shut the door behind her. She walked and thought about how amazing Jesse really was. Finishing school, doing an internship, living on her own in a strange town, with all that trouble walking. Given that disadvantage, would Lynette be that brave? She'd like to think that she would. But how different her life would be. Her mind wandered to Dillan, and she smiled to herself. He was so incredibly kind and mindful. She couldn't wait to take a ride on his motorcycle. The sound of a door opening startled her. She swung her head around.

"Hey Lynette," said Warren. He was wearing short jean cut offs and an apron covered in paint. Standing next to him was a sandy haired guy in white shorts.

"Hey," said Lynette.

"You wanna come in for a minute and tell me what you think of my new paintings?"

"Ok," Lynette stepped into the apartment. There were five of them, all splatter designs on canvas. "You're moving from paper now, huh?"

"Lynette this is my friend Randy. Randy's a Biology major. Randy this is Lynette. She's an English education major." Lynette reached out and shook hands with Randy. "And you two will probably get a real job before I do. Do you know why I'm getting my PHD? Because I don't want a real job." He threw his head back and laughed loudly.

"Don't you just love this one?" asked Randy. He held a canvas for Lynette to have a closer look.

"This is my favorite," said Lynette pointing to a smaller one with only three colors, that had a symmetrical shape.

"Here, you must take it," said Warren. He picked it up and handed it to her.

"Are you sure?"

"I insist, I want you to have it."

"Thanks."

"So how was your boat ride? Are you and that boater an item yet?"

"Well, yah, I suppose we are."

"Ahhh, I knew it. A man doesn't take a girl on his boat unless he's serious."

"Hey, that reminds me, I have a roll of film in my camera from some pictures I took while we were on the boat. Let me take a few pictures of you and Randy with your paintings."

"Oh, yes, that would be really nice," said Warren. "And you'll give me copies of the pictures?"

"Of course," Lynette set her purse, books, and painting on the table. She stood taking out her camera next to an open bottle of wine and two empty glasses. "You two look like you've been partying it up."

"Oh that, sorry," said Warren. His hands were on his hips and his eyes darted left. "We drank it all, or I'd offer you some."

"I'm working tonight anyway."

Warren touched Randy's shoulder, "Lynette's a bartender at the airport."

"Alright, come on." Lynette directed with her hand raised. "Now you two up on the love seat behind the paintings."

"Oh wait." Warren leaped at Lynette. "Can I borrow this?" He reached for the umbrella that dangled from Lynette's wrist. He popped it open and twirled it like a Burlesque dancer in front of himself. Lynette held up the camera. Click went the shutter. Then he climbed up on the love seat, and Randy met him in the middle. They struck a pose and click went the shutter.

"One more left," said Lynette.

"Let Randy take a picture of you and me," said Warren. He swiped his hand in front of him in a grand gesture. "We'll call it, Neighbors."

"I love it," said Lynette. She wrapped her arm around his shoulder. He returned the affection with the same.

"Smile," said Randy. Click went the shutter.

Lynette gathered her purse, books, camera, and new painting, "Gotta go," said Lynette.

"Hey, maybe we'll come out and see you at the airport tonight."

"Ok, sure." Warren held the door open.

"Bye," said Lynette. The door closed with a thud. Lynette stepped toward her own apartment door.

* * *

A couple of hours later, voices filled the airport lounge with the Happy Birthday song. It was a hot July day. A water mirage appeared on the tarmac outside the window. Dillan pushed a black man in the wheelchair, to give him better view. Kim blew out her candles and the airport family cheered and clapped. Kim raised a knife to cut into her cake. Her hand pushed down on the knife and nothing happened. Her brow crossed and she pressed a bit harder. Kim searched the quiet faces surrounding her for a hint that someone knew what was happening.

"What did you guys do?" asked Kim. Her expression, suspicious.

"Geez, why is that cake so hard?" asked Dillan.

"Who baked this cake?" asked Jan.

"It's a trick," said Jackson now leaning forward in his wheelchair, laughing out loud.

"It's a brick," said Becky.

"Gotcha," said Lynette. She held up a camera. "Smile." Click. Jan disappeared into the restaurant. "Happy Birthday." Lynette gave Kim a hug.

"Good job on the cake," said Ellie.

"Thanks, I never frosted a brick before," said Lynette. She raised her eye-brows. Then looked to Kim. "You still good to go out on the boat with us Saturday? I think Dillan said we're going to St. Mark's River. Bryan, the airport manager's coming. Should be a good time."

"I wouldn't miss it for anything," said Kim. Jan reappeared with a real cake. Sam lifted the flap on a small carton of birthday candles.

"Should we sing again?" he asked.

"No," said Ellie, "let's eat."

"Happy Birthday!" said Ada, now giving Kim a hug. "I'm working the little bar today, so I'm going to take my cake and run." She placed her cake onto the cart filled with beer, a bucket of ice, cash box, a bottle of vodka, and her purse. Sam trailed behind her.

"Lemme hold the doors for you," he said.

"Thank you, everybody," said Kim.

"Jackson, would you like a beer?" asked Becky.

His eyes grew big. "Are you serious?"

"I wouldn't lie about that?" said Becky.

"Jackson lifted his good hand near his mouth, touching his lips with his finger. His crippled hand lay lifeless on the arm of his wheelchair. He spoke in a garbled voice." Shhhhh, I won't tell."

Lynette moved close to Becky, who stood at the beer tap. "Only one," said Lynette. She spoke softly. "His nurse got upset when she picked him up drunk last week. He couldn't empty his catheter bag by himself, and I had to help him."

"Alright," said Becky. "I'll just put his beer in a highball glass."

"Yah, good idea," said Lynette.

Tyler joined Jackson at a table, where they sat eating cake and making conversation. Kim stood reading her card with handwritten birthday wishes from all the bartenders and the kitchen staff. Lynette saw Dillan coming toward her with two plates of cake.

"I'm taking my cake back to the shop," said Dillan. He set the other plate on the bar. "I'll pick you up after work for that motorcycle ride."

"Can't wait." Lynette met his lips for a peck. "Bye."

Dillan raised his hand to wave. "Bye, Everybody, Happy Birthday Kim!"

* * *

Lynette basked in the rush of Dillan's skin. "Welcome to my world," she said, her fingers, now tracing the lines of the macaw tattoo on his bicep. She felt all his joy and wonder, when he sprung from the bed and scooped her in his arms, cradling her against his chest.

"Come on," he said. Now at the front door, he swung it open. His hazel almond eyes were smiling.

"What are you doing? We're naked, it's three in the morning." Lynette was giggling now, "Oh, my God."

"Howling at the moon." He stepped out into the moonlight, under cover of the cypress and fringe trees, the hedges, and the side of the building. She felt his lips on her forehead. Then he lifted his face and let out one big howl, before running back into the apartment, slamming the door shut, and tossing her back onto the bed.

* * *

The next few months were a blur, with work, school, and Dillan. Where had the loneliness gone? How could she be so blessed with friendship, financial security, and hope for the future? Lynette's tip money provided not only enough for living expenses, meals, tuition, and books, but also plenty extra to pick up restaurant and bar tabs for everyone.

With Dillan, there were dinners out, squirting crab legs, cheesy fondue, spicy Thai food, backyard barbeques. There were sleepovers. Big breakfasts in the mornings. Motorcycle rides, boat rides, looking through the telescope at the stars, sing-a-longs at the piano with new sheet music, roses, and love notes on napkins. He fixed her bike and car, cleaned the apartment, and stocked the fridge. He met Lynette's mother. He filled her life with encouragement, support, and love.

One day, Lynette went out to her car after work, and had to dig her way into the driver's seat through a hundred balloons. He had blown them up himself. Balloons of red, green, blue, yellow flying from the windows of the car as she drove down Capital Circle all the way to Pensacola Street, where she parked to race across campus to take an exam. Had Lynette ever been so truly minded, tended, and loved before now? Could Dillan be the healthy relationship she had prayed for? Without effort his love dwelled in her. Their affinity felt like home. Every day now had Dillan in it. And where Dillan left off, neighbors, work buddies, bartending, schoolwork, or Marie picked up.

Marie came over one day and didn't leave for two weeks. She rearranged Lynette's apartment. After Lynette surprised Marie on her birthday with a dinner party at Applebee's restaurant, complete with guests, and a birthday cake topped with a statue of a doctor holding a medical bag, Marie surprised Lynette one night while sitting on the floor at the Japanese restaurant by telling the waitress it was Lynette's birthday, when it really wasn't. There was the night they slept on the beach at St. George Island in the itchy plants, then woke up later with a rash and couldn't stop scratching. There was scotch, lots of scotch. Drinking one day with Kim from the bar, the three girls had their picture taken with the Easter Bunny. There were ironed clothes, waxed floors, scrubbed bathroom fixtures, fresh expresso, and homecooked meals, where there hadn't been before. Lynette had swallowed a large portion of Marie's history, and in her found an ally, who like her had come from a past removed somewhat from mainstream. Their friendship felt like gypsies dancing.

There were times the three of them, Lynette, Dillan, and Marie did things together. Once they camped overnight at Alligator Point. Marie slept in the front seat of Dillan's truck, Dillan and Lynette in the truck bed. There were days in the sun, sand dollar hunts, hermit crab, and sea urchin finds. There was white sand that looked like snow for miles. A photo shoot in matching tank tops in front of the fountain and castle-like towers at FSU's Westcott Building. Lynette brought them to her parent's home for a visit. If it wasn't Dillan at the apartment, when Lynette came home from work, it was Marie at her apartment, when she came home from school. The three of them became a pack.

The Spring semester now over, and Summer semester not yet started, alone and grateful to be so for one night, Lynette lay dozing on the love seat. She was disturbed by a knock on the door. Her eyes fluttered open. The apartment was dark, except for the flickering light from the television. Lynette turned toward the screen and saw the news reporter speaking. "And more on the Washington Melodrama of the Iran Contra and the unfolding of crimes in high places, and mercy killing in the Netherlands." The knock continued at the door. Lynette stood, "Who is it?"

"It's Marie. Party-time!" Lynette heard the muffled voice through the closed door. She flipped on the light. Then when she opened it, Marie stood looking in, with a bottle of Chivas Regal in one hand and a lemon in the other. She wore a peach romper and flip flops.

"Oh, Man, come on in. Is that the bottle I left at your place?"

"Yah, Sorry I forgot the key you gave me."

"So, what's going on?" asked Lynette.

"How are you and the grease monkey?" asked Marie.

"Well, that wasn't very nice."

Marie pulled a pack of cigarettes and matches from her shorts' pocket and tossed them on the table.

"You smoking now?"

"Yup, you should try one, they're clove." Marie was helping herself to glasses in the cupboard.

Lynette turned the pack over in her hand reading the package. "Looks like a healthy cigarette." Tapping the pack on her hand, a couple cigarettes popped out, and she pinched one between her thumb and forefinger. Marie was loosening ice from a tray.

"So, how's it going? I can't believe you're still seeing that priest."

"What?" asked Marie. Lynette shook her head.

"You two looked a little too comfortable the other night when Dillan and I stopped by." Lynette was sucking on a cigarette now. A plume of smoke rising around her face." She held the cigarette up for a closer look. "Hey, these aren't too bad."

"Let's drink to that," said Marie.

"Cheers." Lynette lifted her glass with one hand and her cigarette with the other. Her tone shifted from celebration to monotonous lecture. "You have to quit seeing that priest. It's a big fucken sin that will put you straight in hell, you know. A priest, man. A man of the cloth. Do you know what you are doing? A mortal God damned sin." Lynette reached for a can from the trash to use for an ashtray. "He's probably got tons of girls that he is seducing besides you. You think you are the only one? He's gonna get thrown out of the church for this crap. You better cut it out. I got a good mind to call the church myself and nark on him." Lynette took a big drag from her cigarette, then threw back another swig of scotch. She continued ranting. "You know priests are supposed to be celibate, it's a vow they take." Marie's eyes were wide. She had that childlike expression that Lynette took for naivety, guilt, or a conviction of this is none of your business. Lynette couldn't tell, but at the very least Lynette hoped to see some shame. "Hell, priests are not even allowed to touch themselves."

"That's not healthy," said Marie. "Sex is like brushing your teeth." Her pitch was egotistical. "You should do it every day."

"Yah well, tell that to the Pope." Lynette raised a brow, now blowing smoke over her shoulder. Her expression of reprimand suddenly soured to scrutiny. "Staying celibate for your whole life does seem like it would kill you, like a fasting that turns into starving to death." She paused. "But, until there is a term limit on celibacy,"

Lynette aimed the end of her cigarette over the can, now flicking in ash, "priests are stuck with the vow the way it is, not the way we want it to be. And it's supposed to mean something."

"Like what?" Marie was toying.

"Like staying pure and whole and committed to God and the church. That's his marriage."

"Well, that's not healthy."

"Maybe not, but it's his choice."

Marie's eyes glossed over. She drank the last of her scotch. It seemed like she realized, if only for just that moment, maybe there might be some truth in what Lynette had to say. The alcohol, however, made her forget about the epiphany, the minute she had it. Lynette sat at the kitchen table squashing out her cigarette butt on an empty soda can. Marie turned on the stereo. "Oh, man, I love this song, Sweet Child of Mi-i-i-i-ne." She sang along to Guns and Roses.

"I'm hungry," Lynette swallowed the last of her shot of scotch. "Let's go to Hardee's and get a burger." Lynette poured scotch into an empty bottle of apple juice and shoved it into her purse. Then she slid into her flip flops.

"You comin'?"

"Hell yah, I'm comin'," said Marie.

Lynette set the full apple juice bottle in the cup holder of the car. When they returned from Hardees, the bottle was empty. Wearing sunglasses now, they sat parked with the windows rolled down all the while singing along to Corey Hart's tune, *Sunglasses at Night*, booming at full volume.

Lynette cut the car engine when the song was over. She pointed at something outside the car windshield. "Hey look, that apartment, looks like a party, all the lights are on." Lynette climbed out of the car. "Come on."

After a quick return trip to Lynette's apartment to refill the Hardees soda cups with Chivas Regal, they stepped out into the night, laughing and staggering until they found themselves in front of an open apartment door.

"Hey Boys!" Marie yelled into the apartment.

"Whooooooooo! P-a-r-t-y!" hollered Lynette.

Boxes scattered the floor. "Who's moving?" They were too drunk to notice the open tail gate of truck out front where men stood loading and arranging boxes. They stepped in and found themselves in the kitchen. Marie totally stewed, grabbed hold of two loaves of bread. "I've got the bread," she yelled, bent over laughing.

"Where's the radio?" asked Lynette. "That's Sweet Home Alabama, we gotta turn that shit up." Lynette scanned the room. "Oh, there it is." Lynette twisted the knob to full volume.

Dancing with every move she had, she cha-cha'd over to Marie and grabbed a loaf of bread, climbed onto the kitchen table taking the dance home. Marie followed suit, giving up the Salsa steps all the way to the chair she climbed on. By now, both girls were gyrating, singing *Sweet Home Alabama* at the top of their lungs, swinging bread around like a hooker swings a pocketbook on the street corner. Two dark skinned young men burst in the room, sweating, and out of breath.

"L-o-o-ok, the Boys are here!" yelled Lynette.

"They are drunk, eh?" said the first man in the white t-shirt.

"How is it you see that?" asked the second man. He wore an FSU shirt. Both men, now laughing. The man in the white t-shirt spoke with a heavy accent.

"American woman crazy." He stood staring at the wild dancing. "What are you doing here?" he yelled over the music.

Marie and Lynette jumped from the table and chair, then made their way to the bedroom. The man in the FSU shirt caught Lynette slipping into a Gaza Jubba. "Put that down," he said.

Marie found a dark pleated kufi cap in an open suitcase and fitted it to her head. She paraded her way to the bathroom mirror to admire herself. The bathroom was empty except for a wooden crate on the floor.

"Check me out," said Marie. She stepped from the bathroom to see the man in the FSU shirt, staring back at her.

"You must go," he said. "We busy, moving out."

"Hey, it looks like you guys are moving," said Marie, now dropping the kufi back into the suitcase. She moved toward the living room and stood over the green vinyl sofa, where she picked up the Quran. "Man, can you read this stuff, wow! Lynette, look at this, I'll bet you can't read this." Lynette, who had been neatly folding the Gaza Jubba and putting it back into the suitcase, stumbled over.

"Let me see that," said Lynette. She grabbed the Quran from Marie, now flipping through the pages. "Nope, I can't read this." Lynette set it down on the green vinyl sofa. "Looks like you guys are moving," said Lynette.

"Yes, we are moving," said the man in the FSU shirt. "See, we are loading the van outside the door. "

"No more touching the Quran and no time for party tonight," said the man in the white t-shirt. He motioned his arms in an unsuccessful attempt to usher them toward the door. "You find another party. Ok."

Ritchie Valen's *La Bamba* on the radio set Marie in motion.

"A-a-a-a-rrib-a-a-a!" yelled Marie, now shaking her booty to the beat, and singing along.

"We'll leave as soon as this song is over," yelled Lynette over the music. She joined the dance, shaking what she had, while chanting with the melody.

"You need to go," said the man in the FSU shirt.

"They said they leave when the song's over," said the man in the white t-shirt. "Good song." A grin formed on his face. He reached for Marie's hand and began to dance.

The next morning, Lynette woke up with a hangover. Her mind was filled with nothing but negative thoughts, insecurity, fear, exhaustion, and anxiety. Marie had called Dillan a grease monkey. Why hasn't he introduced you to his family? She had asked. You deserve better, she had said. Is it because he isn't serious? Or because you're not good enough? Lynette had felt that blow before, and she wasn't going through that again. And what about that girl down in South Florida he used to fly down to see? And what about that time he stood you up? Marie had said. So, what if it was because he had got so drunk that he passed out in a bunch of ants, got sick and had a rash from the ant bites. He should have called. Why did he lie and say he had got into a bar room fight instead? Lynette heard herself speaking aloud, "Why the fuck do I need to be worrying about all this shit, anyway? I've got a Bachelor's degree to get. And it's my week off before summer semester starts, I should be relaxing." A fierce need for independence reared up inside Lynette. Then she sat down at the typewriter to write a letter.

* * *

After Marie set the timer, she washed her hands, and then began pacing. She looked at the timer. She sat, thumbing through the classified section of the newspaper. The sound of the timer mocked her. She spoke out loud to herself, "Waitress, no, I can't waitress, House cleaning, Well, I guess I could do that." She circled the ad with the pen. "Seafood Sales: $300 Sign on bonus. Training provided. All expenses paid. No experience necessary. Call 1-800-808-1357." She circled that one twice. She glanced at the refrigerator. She was famished. She could not remember ever having been so hungry. She rushed across the kitchen and stood now chomping on the last of the leftover pizza.

When the bell rang on the timer, she darted to the bathroom sink and looked at the stick in horror. The results were positive, the blue line was distinct, it was indicative of a test done correctly. The blue line seemed to stare at her from the stick, telling her what she already knew, but refused to want to know. Her period was late. She was guilty of skipping four birth control pills this month. And she knew what this meant.

On the bed now, her face in the pillow, she bawled. She couldn't think straight. Surely, the test was wrong. She would get another one. It would be negative this time and all would be set right. She wiped her tears and snotty nose on the sheets, and sat up, catatonically staring at the front door.

She went for a jog around Alumni Village. She ran until she was exhausted, sweaty and out of breath. A half hour later, back inside her apartment, she drank water from the spicket. Her mind, reeling with what ifs. Cash was running low and the hospital had not called her to work for weeks. The student loan money wasn't due in for another forty-five days. How would she pay her rent this month? Where would she get the money for an abortion?

A second test gave her the same result. "Dios Mío," she cried again. This time, sitting on the cold tile of the bathroom floor, she leaned against the hard wall, hating herself. *God, why didn't I take the damn pills when I was supposed to. I can't have this baby.* She remembered the classified ads and her telephone being turned on for the time being. She telephoned the first ad in the paper.

"I'm sorry we just hired someone." She telephoned the second ad.

"Yes, we are still hiring. We are meeting people in your area Thursday and Friday of this week," said the voice on the phone. "Which day would be good for you?"

"Thursday," said Marie.

"Morning or afternoon?"

"Morning," said Marie.

"Is nine o'clock alright?"

"Yes."

* * *

On Thursday, the curtains were closed in one of the private dining rooms at the Silver Slipper. Marie sat across from the man, who smelled of strong soap.

"So, tell me about yourself."

"I've worked mostly in the hospital, as a candy striper when I was a teenager, and then I worked as a cashier before I went to school for nursing. Now I work per diem at Tallahassee Memorial Hospital."

"Have you ever worked in sales?"

"No, but I did work at the hospital gift shop."

"No problem, our company offers a complete training package."

"Is there any reason you cannot travel this week?"

"No."

"Ok, because the training is in Hawaii, all expenses paid. Let's get you started on a questionnaire." Mr. Jones stood, opened the curtains, and led her to the ballroom through the hall of autographed photos. The room was full. People sat at tables covered in white linen flipping through stapled packets, pens in hands, heads down. Marie trailed Mr. Jones to the head table.

"This is Marie Martinez, and she is ready for a questionnaire."

"Hello," said Marie She reached out for a handshake, before accepting a packet and a pen. Then she joined the crowd at the tables. Marie answered pages of questions.

Would you rather sit quietly and read a book or go out on the town on a Saturday night?

If faced with arguing with a friend, do you choose to stay quiet or try to control the situation?

Do you consider yourself a leader or a follower?

Do you make love on a first date?

Do you consider your relationship with family good or bad?

Have you ever been convicted of a felony or a misdemeanor?

Do you like living alone?

Do you want to further your education?

What kind of learner are you?

Do you like yourself?

Do you consider yourself a happy person?

Are you satisfied with your life?

Given a choice, would you rather move to a new city or town every week or never be able to leave your place of birth?

List three things you like to do?

List three things you hate doing?

Are you sexually active?

Where were you born?

Do you consider your relationship with your parents: a) Strained b) Healthy c) Happy d) Non-existent

Do you have any pets?

If someone asked you to do something you didn't feel like doing, would you a) do it to please them, b) rebel, c) blow the person off, or d) do it just to keep the peace.

Do you consider yourself a person that goes with the flow or someone who swims against the tide?

The questions went on and on. An hour later, Marie was done and tired from all the reading. She hated all the reading. She stood to straighten her dress. There were still a few people with their heads bowed over the packets. Marie walked toward the man sitting at a long table. He wore a paisley tie and was smiling.

"All set?" he asked.

"Yes." Marie tried to look away from a scar over his left eye.

"Great," he said. "Training this year for sales staff will be held in Hawaii. How do you feel about traveling for a couple of weeks?"

"I love the idea," said Marie.

"Ok, we'll be breaking for lunch now, and then we'll let you know if you made it to the final round of interviews."

"Hawaii, wow," said Marie. Her round brown eyes widened. She watched the man scribbling something on a small green form. "I'll work harder than everyone here."

"Here's a voucher for lunch in the dining room. Be back here at one o'clock. Good luck."

After a chicken dinner, Marie sat under the chandeliers with other eager candidates, laughing about the personality test, and picturing luaus and first-class accommodations on Waikiki Beach. At one o'clock, she filed into the ballroom with the rest of the herd.

* * *

Dillan was devastated when he read the letter from Lynette. His strong grip on the handlebars of the roaring Kawasaki underneath him gave him something to hold onto. Falling apart was not an option. Not for a Marine. The wind blowing on him, replaced the wind that had been knocked from him on the first read through. White Snake's tune *Here I Go Again* blared from the radio. He leaned into the turn and parked the bike at the end of the runway. He watched a few planes taking off, and felt his youthful determination rising. He knew what he had to do. Thirty minutes later, he entered the airport lounge through the restaurant door with one mission on his mind.

Lynette stood at the cocktail waitress station, cleaning a pile of ash trays, when she saw the hurt and confusion on Dillan's face. He was on the verge of explosion. "Can I talk to you?"

"Let's talk about this later." Lynette spoke softly not wanting the two patrons at a nearby table to hear.

"You mean to tell me that after everything we've been through, you are ending it this way. Doesn't our time together mean anything?" Dillan held the letter in his hand.

Sam burst in from the restaurant carrying a case of pretzels. "Oh, my God, What's the matter? You two love birds having a little tiff?" He set the box on the table at the end of the bar and leaned his elbow on the box. His hand under his chin, his eyes were on Lynette.

"There is nothing to talk about," said Lynette. "Especially while I'm working."

"I love you, Lynette," said Dillan.

"Aw, this is better than my soap opera." Sam adjusted the paper cap on his head.

Dillan, scowling now, turned to face Sam. "Will you." He lifted his hand, index finger pointing at the doorway. "Out."

"Ok, ok, well, if things don't work out, you know where to find me if you decide to come to the other side." Sam winked and disappeared into the cafeteria dining room.

"I'll talk to you later," said Lynette.

"What time is your shift over?"

"Tomorrow, I need some time to think."

"Why don't you come to my place in the morning."

"Ok, what time?"

"Nine o'clock."

"I'll see you at nine o'clock then." Dillan's face softened. His steps were lighter on the walk back to his Kawasaki.

* * *

Lynette glanced up from the cash register at Sam bobbing and weaving through the cafeteria doorway. "Is the coast clear?" asked Sam.

Lynette's response was a nod with raised brows. Sam sat down at a bar stool.

"So, what was that all about?"

"Oh, I wrote him a dear john letter."

"Really." he popped his tongue. "I know just what you need. You need a night out."

"Maybe you're right, I'll pick you up at eight."

Sam scribbled his address on a napkin.

* * *

The night club crowd was sparse. It was dark, the music was loud and disco lights flashed about. "How old are you, Sam?" asked Lynette. She spoke loudly over the music.

"Eighteen, he said," Then he took a sip of his fourth tequila sunrise. "Well, almost."

"Are you from Tallahassee?"

"No, I moved here last year, after dropping out of high school. My dad kicked me out when he found out I was gay."

"Oh, man, that sucks!"

"Yah, well, I'm glad I'm gone. He's an asshole anyway. Come on, let's dance."

They tore up the floor to Donna Summers, *I will survive.* Shaking, gyrating, jerking and twirling, and spinning. Mostly forgetting what ailed them for a few minutes, the medicine of laughter a booster of healing for them both.

"That was so fun," said Sam.

"Wo-o-o-o." Lynette howled. She chasséd to the edge of the dance floor, then threw a couple of high fan kicks in relevé. "I need more margarita. Let's sit this one out."

Back at the table now, Sam was taking the cherry off the plastic sword. "So, do you think you and Dillan will get back together?"

"I don't know, I told him I'd talk to him tomorrow." Lynette licked the salt from the rim of her glass. "What about you, those guys I met, that were walking out the door, when I picked you up, is one of them your boyfriend?"

"Yah, Marty is."

"Kind of old for you, no? Marty looked comfy with that other guy, what's up with that?"

"Well, he took me in when I had nowhere to go." Sam spoke with resignation and acceptance.

"You have your whole life ahead of you, Sam."

Sam sucked on his straw until all that remained was the ice. "Come, on let's dance again, I love this song."

"It's a good one. Let's go," said Lynette. She sprung from her seat to the sound of the Temptations song, *Ain't too Proud to Beg*, then curtsied in Sam's direction.

On the dance floor now, laughing, and pretending to be John Travolta, Sam reached for Lynette's hands. They broke into a drunken jitterbug that dominated the dance floor. In triple step style, with lots of underarm turns, and inside turns, they ended with a rock step in a cuddle position. Clapping, winded and sweaty, Sam threw his fist in the air, hooting with joy.

"Where'd you learn to dance like that?" asked Lynette.

Sam spoke through deep breaths. "My mom, before she died." His eyes drooped and he dropped his head forward. "I think I'm not feeling very good."

"Well, let's get outta here," said Lynette.

Once inside the car, Sam reclined his seat. "Everything's starting to spin."

"Uh, oh," said Lynette. "Hang in there. We don't have much further to go."

He leaned on Lynette, as she walked him upstairs to his apartment. Once inside, he stumbled to the bathroom. From the kitchen Lynette could hear the heaving. She soaked a dish towel in cold water and folded it neatly. And when the heaving subsided, she tapped on the door, and opened it. Sam sat on the floor. His arms slumped over the open toilet.

"Here," said Lynette. She wiped his tanned face with the wet towel. "Come on, get yourself to bed."

"I'm sorry," said Sam. "We were having such a good time." His words barely audible, he leaned on Lynette as she walked him to the bedroom.

"Go lie down," said Lynette. "I'm gonna find you a bowl or something in case you lose your cookies again." Sam dropped himself onto the bed.

When she returned with a large bowl and a glass of water, Sam lay on his back, legs akimbo. Lynette set the glass on the bedside table, and the bowl on the bed. "Use this, in case you get sick again."

"I'm sorry," said Sam.

"We all drink too much sometimes. Trust me, I've spent nights on the bathroom floor, myself." Lynette sat down on the edge of the bed and turned to her purse. She found a bottle of Tylenol. "So, when's your roommate coming home?" she asked.

"I don't know," said Sam. "He's probably out partying."

Lynette removed the lid from the pill bottle.

"Take these when your stomach tells you you're done barfing." She set two tablets on the bedside table next to the glass of water.

Sam sat up. "You know, I have a strange desire to kiss you, right now. You're beautiful." Sam's expression was a mixture of confusion and candor.

Lynette scooted close. A wave of tenderness welled up inside her. She wrapped her arms around him. Sam returned the hug. Lynette pulled back, dropped her arms to her lap, and looked at his boyishly handsome face. She was a sucker for a stray. And she knew when kindness was in order. She used her finger to brush a lock of hair from his brow. "You're beautiful too, Sam." She kissed his forehead. "I'll be back in a second."

When she returned with a fresh cold wet washcloth sitting on a plate, Sam lay on the bed propped up on pillows. "Thank you," he said. "I feel better just getting all that tequila out of me."

"I bet," said Lynette. She pressed the cold compress on his forehead. "I'm gonna go home now. You should feel better by tomorrow afternoon." Lynette scooped up her purse from the foot of the bed. "I'll let myself out." With her hand on the doorknob, she looked back at him, waving back at her. "One more thing. While you're nursing that hangover, think about how you can get your ass back to school and get your GED."

"Ok," he said.

"Just find your way back to Sam." Lynette waved and closed the door.

* * *

When the front door swung open, the air was wrong in the apartment. Lynette flipped on the lights and stood scanning the room. With the Margarita buzz wearing off, her brain processing was sluggish. In the bathroom, she noticed a black coating on the fixtures. She swiped her fingers in it, rubbing them together on her thumb. In the living room her focus met something piled on the floor on each side of the front door. Her line of sight trailed up the brick wall from there. Where were the sconces? Where they once hung, only the screws remained. They must have caught fire. She had forgotten to blow out the candles. She walked around the room, inspecting the curtains, the furniture, and the door. She couldn't believe how lucky she was that nothing else had burned, and Tashi was back with her mom. Consumed with disgust for herself, she swept up the ashy remains into the dustpan, then fled the scene.

It was after three in the morning when Lynette pulled her car into Bayhead Mobile Home Park. On Horizon Court, the Clubhouse and the pool were dark and quiet. All the lights were off at Dillan's place, when she knocked on his back door.

"Lynette, what's going on?" Dillan stood tanned and barefoot in the doorway, sleepy eyed, in nothing but a pair of dungarees.

"Well, we said we would talk in the morning, so."

"Well, come in."

Lynette followed Dillan into his bedroom. He sat on the edge of the bed and Lynette joined him. They sat side by side, thighs touching.

"I'm glad you're here," said Dillan. "About the letter, I never meant to make you not feel good enough to meet my parents. I would love for you to meet them."

"You would." Lynette was trying not to break.

"Yes, I told them about you. And, I'm bringing the boat back at the end of the summer, anyways, you could come with me."

"Really," Lynette's eyes lit up.

"It's just, it's hard for them to travel," said Dillan. He spoke in a solemn tone. "My dad has Parkinson's Disease."

"Oh," Lynette broke. Her voice was thick. The truth brought with it, clarity and understanding. "What about that girl in South Florida that makes the tuna casseroles?"

Dillan shook his head. "I don't see her anymore." His voice was appealing. "I want to show you something." He reached for a book on the nightstand. In his strong muscular hands, the book looked like a miniature version. Lynette watched his large fingers turning to a marked page, and she glimpsed the name, Paulo Coelho. Dillan began to read. "'The eyes are the mirror of the soul and reflect everything that seems to be hidden; and like a mirror, they also reflect the person looking into them.'" Dillan's glassy almond eyes shot from the book straight at Lynette. Returning his gaze, she felt an innate visceral shift forward, and a tiny twinkle of the future.

* * *

The tops of the trees swayed, branches lashed about, the wind stirred a warning. Marie stood outside of her apartment, her brown hair blowing in her face, her suitcase in hand. She was pregnant for sure. Would she keep the baby? Was the father a priest? Or Ron?

Weren't both possibilities equally a horror? She was unmarried, divorced twice. Keep it or not, she needed money. With money she could get the creditors to stop calling and pay for an abortion. Walking down to the parking lot, her mind poured out all her mistakes. They were flowing all over her like lava from a volcano. Her last marriages had been a disaster. She remembered the sadness she had felt for having hurt her small step-son with the divorce. She had grown fond of him. Why was she thinking about this today? Now tossing her suitcase in the trunk of her Chevy, she saw Kerry approaching. *Dios Mío,* she thought.

"I know I owe you some money," said Kerry. She was thumbing through her wallet. "Here's twenty." The wind caught the bill, and Marie watched it whip underneath the car. Kerry got down on all fours. Her arm reaching underneath.

Marie bent to see Kerry drag it across the blacktop. "Thanks," said Marie, "I just got a bonus check, and I'm getting another one as soon as I finish training. In a couple weeks, I'll be back to start my new job. So, if you need to keep the twenty that'll be ok." Marie closed the trunk. "I know you need it."

"Thanks," said Kerry. She was putting the bill in her wallet. "Girl, I see that priest coming and going from your place a lot. You're asking for trouble. Word around campus is that guy's a player. Should be thrown out the parish. He's giving the church a bad name."

"Well, he is a man, you know, and he hasn't been ordained yet." Marie took a deep breath. Her eyes darted back and forth.

"Hey, when you coming back?"

"Two weeks." Marie stood unlocking the car door.

"What are you gonna be doing, anyway?"

"Selling seafood."

"Where you training?

"Hawaii," said Marie, now sitting in the driver's seat.

"Woah, Hawaii, ask 'em if they're still hiring."

"I will, maybe I can train you when I get back." Marie's hand pushed the door open against the wind.

"Now that'd be something. I gotta go, I'm going to church for the homily." Kerry wrapped her sweater tight around her and waved. "See you when you get back."

"Say a prayer for me." Marie closed her car door and watched as Kerry climbed into her rusty Ford Pinto and backed out of the parking space. With her fists, Marie beat on the steering wheel and sobbed. Would she be able to get an abortion in Hawaii? She could feel the waist band on her skirt growing snug. Her breasts felt different, enlarged, and sore.

Now at the Tallahassee Municipal Airport, done with the ticket counter, her bag checked, Marie hoped Lynette was working. Would a drink be ok? She'd be getting an abortion, so what did it matter? If only the bonus money was enough to pay for it. Well, once she got the second bonus, which was supposed to be double the first, she should have enough. Down the concourse she walked. When she opened the lounge door, she heard the juke box playing, *I've got friends in lower places,* CNN was on the television. Marie's eyes searched the room. Only two customers. Where was the bartender?

Marie took her seat at the end of the bar, near the fruit tray, where all the locals sat, looking out at the tarmac at the airplanes. She wondered if the Piedmont plane she saw was her flight to Atlanta. Through the restaurant doorway, in walked Lynette dressed in a blue jumpsuit with the bodice open in an oval, not low enough to see cleavage, but the outfit certainly showed all her curves. Her long sandy hair training down her back like a horse's mane. Her big gold hoop earrings flashing in the sunlight that shined through the window behind the bar. She was carrying the cash drawer. After sliding it into the register and shutting the drawer, she turned and noticed Marie.

"Hey, Marie. What are you doing here so early?" Lynette grabbed a napkin and laid it down in front of her, and before she had a chance to answer, she asked. "Want some coffee?"

"No, I'd like a Bloody Mary," said Marie. *Wouldn't the tomato juice be good for the baby? The vodka will be good for me,* thought Marie.

"Alright, coming up." With her left hand, Lynette reached into the ice bin with a highball glass, while her right hand reached at the shelf for a can of tomato juice. She set both on the rubber mat, grabbed the shot glass, measured out the well vodka, and then ripping the lid off the can of juice, poured its contents into the vodka, while grabbing a lime from the fruit tray and topping off the drink with a straw. Her drink mixing looked like a bartender ballet.

"So, tell me what you're doing here so early?"

"I'm flying out for training for a new job in seafood sales. I need you to check on Henrique, my bird."

"What? I don't know anything about birds." Lynette chewed on the inside of her cheek.

"Seafood sales? Huh?"

"Use the key in the plant outside my door. Just put in fresh water and food." Marie took a sip from her glass. "I'm going to Hawaii for a couple of weeks to train and then I'll be back to work the Tallahassee area."

"Oh, how'd you get that job?" Lynette was wiping down the beer cooler.

"Found it in the paper," said Marie, sipping her drink. "I passed the interview and test, and they handed me a plane ticket and a sign on bonus."

"Wow, that's incredible. Where are you staying when you get there?"

Marie read from her ticket, "DFS, Hawaii Daniel K. Inouye International Airport."

"I don't mean the airport. I mean the hotel, or the training center."

"Don't know, they're meeting me at the airport."

"Oh, sounds weird. My mom would say that it sounds too good to be true. Where'd you meet these people?"

"Big interviews at the Silver Slipper Ballroom."

"Did you fill out a W-4?"

"I don't know, they said I would be a contract employee. I signed a contract. And I'll be back after the training."

"What did it say?"

"What did what say?"

"The contract."

"Well, they didn't give me much time, and I just need this money. The hospital hasn't been calling me lately."

"Ooooo Lord, I've been grateful to be your friend now that I finally found one. And I don't want to lose you. Maybe you should stay and read the contract before you leave and take a flight out another day. It all just seems too fast." Lynette walked to the other end of the bar to a man with an empty glass. "Can I get you another beer?"

"No, you can cash me out," Lynette took his ten-dollar bill, then turned to the cash register. "Keep the change," he said. Lynette turned back.

"Thank you, sir, have a good trip." She scooped up his empty glass and turned to Marie. "My mom went to Hawaii when I was a little girl. She never forgot it." Lynette was sliding on yellow latex gloves. "She went to some wind tunnel or something. I remember seeing the pictures." Lynette began pumping glasses on scrub brushes in a sink full of soapy water. "I stayed with my grandmother." An interruption came from the voice over the intercom speaker.

"Piedmont Flight one twenty-two to Atlanta is now boarding at gate three."

"That's me," said Marie. She reached into her purse.

"It's on the house." Lynette tore off her gloves. She walked in front of the bar and stood next to Marie. "I can't believe you're going to Hawaii." She reached her arms out for hug. "Remember, if you can't be good," said Lynette.

"Be careful," said Marie. They were both laughing now and walking toward the door through the path marked with tables and chairs.

"Call me when you get there. And remember everyone wants to bone you."

"I'll remember."

"You remember to check in on Henrique," said Marie.

"I will, every other day."

"Thanks."

"I wish I could go with you. "

"Me too."

Lynette watched Marie head out the glass doors into the airport terminal. Was it her paranoia or was something off? What should she do about it? She knew it really wasn't her business. If Marie needed something, she'd call. The music had stopped, and the silence didn't suit Lynette's mood. She stepped to the juke box, dropped in a quarter, pressed A-four, and *Deep River Woman* by Lionel Richie filled the room. Smiling to herself, she remembered how Dillan had put his coin on this tune so many times before.

Chapter 11

Feeling jet lagged, Marie stood at baggage claim, watching the carousal for her suitcase and the crowd for someone holding a sign with Seafood Express International Inc. on it. She spied the sign, before the suitcase. Zigzagging her way through the sea of people, she reached the man wearing a blue airplane patterned Hawaiian shirt. "Hi, I'm Marie Martinez."

"Aloha, Marie," The man tucked his sign under his arm, then lifted a purple flower lei from his neck over his head. His skin was dark.

"I am Alika." He dressed her neck in the lei, and kissed her on the cheek, "Keu a ka u'i."

"Aloha, thank you," said Marie. She looked toward the baggage carousel. "Oh, my suitcase."

"Come, I will get that for you. Then I will take you to your ride."

It felt refreshing to be in the tropical air. Alika opened the van door for her, and Marie climbed in, taking a seat in the rear beside a woman, who also wore a flower lei around her neck.

"Hi, I mean, Aloha, I'm Marie."

"I'm Kathy, Aloha." Kathy's skin was fair with freckles.

For a while they rode in silence. Marie felt the breeze that blew in from the open windows on Rodgers Boulevard and Aolele Street on route to Interstate H1. The way was lined with towering palm trees against a backdrop of clear blue sky.

"Is this your first time to our Island?" asked Alika.

"Yes, I'm so excited," said Marie. "I love the ocean."

"I've never seen it," said Kathy. "In Wisconsin, we have no seashore."

"Waikiki Beach is one like no other. But we are an island surrounded by beautiful beaches."

"Oh, I can't wait to see them," said Kathy.

A Planned Parenthood Billboard caught Marie's attention. *Exit 22 off IH1E, 839 S Beretania Street.* Her attempt to memorize the eight hundred number failed, but with the time allowed from being stalled in traffic, she opted to write it in her planner.

"Alika, how far are we from the hotel?" asked Marie. She studied the exit signs and the six lanes of traffic. "I need to use the restroom."

"Not far now, fifteen minutes."

"I have to go too," said Kathy. "And I am so tired."

Fifteen minutes later, the van came to a halt on Seaside Avenue. Alika pointed outside the window. "Your building is in the rear of this building. Follow the signs that say Seabreeze Hostel." Alika transferred the bags from the trunk to the sidewalk. Marie saw Kathy offering Alika some tip money, so she figured she better throw in something.

"Oh, I almost forgot," said Marie. "Here."

"Mahalo," said Alika.

"Mahalo," said Marie. "Does that mean thank you?"

"Yes," said Alika. "You sound like a real native."

"One more thing," said Marie, "How far are we from the beach?"

"You are very close." Alika pointed West. "A couple of blocks that way to Waikiki Beach." He bowed, waved, then climbed back into the van and drove off.

The girls crossed the street, passed the first shabby building, and followed the arrows on the wooden driftwood signs painted with Hawaiian flowers and the words, Seabreeze Hostel until they stood in front of the door marked office. Marie tried the door.

"There's a bell," said Kathy, now pressing it.

"Press it again," said Marie. She spoke impatiently. The door opened, and a man stood looking out.

"Aloha," he said.

"We're with the Seafood Express International Sales company training program," said Marie.

"Yes, follow me." The girls trailed the man through a communal kitchen and sitting area. The clerk positioned himself behind a long counter. "Do you have some identification?"

The girls opened their purses and stood opening wallets. A Tabby was curled up and asleep on the counter.

"Cute cat," said Marie.

"Yes," said the clerk. "This is Kaipo."

The girls lay their photo identification on the counter for the man to see.

"Yes, Kathy and Marie, I have you right here." He gestured to a paper taped to the counter. "No food, drink, alcohol, or guests are permitted in the dorm rooms. Curfew is one o'clock in the morning. After that, the building and courtyard will be locked. You may use the kitchen until ten at night. There are refrigerators in the courtyard, to store your food."

"Excuse me," said Marie. "Where is the bathroom?"

"There is one in the courtyard around the corner, and upstairs, there is another at the end of the hall, across from the shower room." At the doorway behind the counter, the man parted chains of tiny seashells revealing a board full of keys. "Here's keys to your room upstairs, the first dorm on the left. Room Two."

Through the courtyard area surrounded by a concrete wall, and up the concrete stairs, they lugged their bags. The door of Room Two was open. Inside in a U position, were three sets of metal bunk beds covered in white sheets. Near the slatted cranked open window, stood a humming fan. The three bottom bunks were claimed. And there were women on them.

"Hi, I'm Marie, and this is Kathy."

"Hi, I'm Mei Li, and this is JoJo."

"Hey, I'm Stacey." Her plaited hair combined with her smooth ebony skin made her look twelve.

"Can I put my suitcase under your bunk?" asked Kathy.

"Yes," Stacey stood up, banged her head on the top bunk. "Ouch."

"You ok?" asked Mei Li. Her red lipstick was prominent on her small round face.

"Ok," Stacey stood rubbing her head.

"You can take this top bunk," said JoJo. She was looking at Marie with her thumb up, and her forearm jerking upward. Marie noticed the Italian horn dangling from a chain around her neck.

"Oh good," Marie drop kicked her suitcase under the lower bunk.

"There's lockers behind the door over there, if yous want one."

"Ok," said Marie. "I'm going to the bathroom first."

"I'll join you," said Kathy.

At the end of the balcony, they entered the door marked Toilet and Shower. There were three showers, three stalls, two sinks, and one broken mirror. Marie, inside her stall, after relieving herself, saw there was no toilet paper. "Kathy, any TP in your stall?"

Kathy answered with a hand full of TP reaching under the stall wall. At the sink, they shared a gooey bar of soap. "No hot water and no paper towels. We're not at the Ritz Carlton," said Marie. Kathy stood laughing and wiping her hands on the back of her black skirt.

"That's for sure."

After stepping out of the bathroom, they saw their bunk mates standing outside their room door, at the railing. They were looking at the courtyard below. Kathy and Marie joined them.

"You back," said Mei Li, now smiling with red lips in Kathy's direction. "We shop and cook downstairs last night. Maybe you cook with us, today."

"Ok," said Kathy.

"We met Cheri, the trainer," said JoJo.

"Uh huh, Cheri the trainer, she got a private room downstairs," said Stacey. "I seen it when I walked down to get a soda from the machine."

"She brought coffee at six o'clock this morning. She told us we should be expecting you and one other chick today," said JoJo. She pinched the clasp of her gold chain to move it to the back of her neck. "She said once all six of us was here, we'd be shipping out for training."

"Oh," said Kathy.

"Did yous see that rock 'round her neck," asked JoJo. "must be a four-caret diamond."

"She wear designer shoes," said Mei Li.

"Mmm hmm," said Stacey. "She gots that Gucci bag going on too."

"Girl, I hope I can make that kinda money with this Seafood Express, when I get back home," said Marie, "Who has done any sales before?"

"I sell at K-mart," said Mei Li, "but I want to attend University when I save enough money from selling seafood."

"I've been selling used cars in Janesville," said Kathy. "Janesville's an hour or so southwest of Milwaukee."

"My sales experience was at a hospital gift shop," said Marie. "I was a cashier."

"I sold subs in the Bronx," said JoJo. "What about you Stacey?"

"Aw, I ain't saying."

"Come on, why not? We all just told our stories. said JoJo. Who we gonna tell?"

"I gots a little girl back home in Jacksonville, and I just want to do right by her and make enough money to get us a place of our own."

"Who has your baby now?"

"She stays with my momma 'til I get back. I just hope Momma stays clean while she's got my little girl." Stacey reached in her pocket for something. "See here, this my baby Selena, she three." Her face beamed with pride.

Kathy held the picture now. "Oh, she's adorable." She passed the picture to Marie.

"She drinks, your momma?" asked Mei Li.

"No, worse," said Stacey, now shaking her head. "Crack."

Everyone fell silent. Marie looked at the picture of the sweet smiling girl. She thought about her baby, the baby she didn't want and would be ridding herself of. "I love her little yellow dress," said Marie, handing the photo back to Stacey.

"Hey since Cheri won't be around until the morning, let's see if we can walk down the beach," said JoJo.

"Alika said it was just a couple blocks from here," said Kathy. "I'll lock up the room."

Minutes later, the girls walked in a pack down Kalakaua Avenue past the International Market Place. The bustling street was full of shops, pubs, and restaurants with a flowing sea of buses, cars, bicycles, and people. Their first stop was at the ABC store.

"Thank God for the bonus check money," said Marie, now holding a bottle of Coconut wine in one hand, and a salad in the other.

"That's for sure," said Kathy. A beach towel of the Hawaiian Islands hanging off her shoulder, she held a sandwich and a bottle. "I got pineapple wine. It'll go good with yours." She giggled. "Let's hurry, the rest of the girls are at the cashier already."

"I'm coming," said Marie. She followed behind.

"I can't wait to see the ocean," said Kathy. The girls took their place in line.

A short walk later, they found themselves at the Duke Paoa Kahanamoku Statue, looking out at the water and waves of the Pacific Ocean. The five of them stepped off the sidewalk onto the golden sand full of tiny volcanic rocks, and seashells. A few steps from the shore, Marie lay her brown shopping bag on the sand, to take off her shoes. Kathy followed suit. The other girls leapt ahead and now stood with their feet in the water. Kathy ran to catch up. Marie sat eating her salad. Planned parenthood was only a few miles away, and she could certainly afford the abortion with the next bonus check. She was five weeks along tops. If she didn't have the abortion in Honolulu, she would have it when she returned to Tallahassee.

* * *

Father Juan couldn't get Marie off his mind. Was it lust or more than that? He had fooled around with girls before, but he couldn't hold it together this time. Marie was different. She got to him. He didn't mean to get himself attached to this one. What about the commitment to the church? Should he even be a Catholic priest? Would he be excommunicated before he set foot in major seminary? His meeting with Monsignor had revealed that rumors were flying around about his flaunted galivanting with college girls. True or not, Monsignor had said, it didn't matter, the rumors alone compelled him to question his commitment.

Father Juan believed God had called him his senior year of high school. Days ago, he had completed his undergraduate studies in Religion at FSU. Now he held his major seminary acceptance letter in his hand. He prayed and prayed. Why now couldn't he hear God? One thing was for certain: this life of duplicity would no longer do.

He bargained with himself. Once he was out of town, he could commit full heartedly to seminary school, but first he needed to see Marie one more time.

He walked swiftly south of campus, past Doak Campbell Stadium onto Lake Bradford Road. When he reached Alumni Village at the end of Levy Avenue, he had been walking almost an hour. Sweaty and hot, he stood in front of Marie's two-story brick building at the bottom of the stairs wiping his brow with the back of his hand. Feeling like his heart would burst, he saw Kerry coming down the stairs toward him. "Hello Kerry," he said.

"If you are looking for Marie, she's gone," said Kerry. "She flew out this morning."

"What? I just spoke to her at church yesterday."

"Well, she went to Hawaii for some job training."

"Training, training for what?"

"Some sales job, seafood I think."

His head exploded. He read something about this on the campus newsletter, something about a scam, and Asian prostitution. "No," he said, "It can't be."

"It can't be what?"

"A scam, did she say anything about where she was staying?"

"No, I don't think so, she said her bartender friend would be lookin' in on that bird of hers. Is she in some kinda trouble?"

"I'm not sure, but I'm going to find out."

"Well, you tell her to git back here." Kerry climbed into her rusty Pinto.

Father Juan didn't know if what he felt was love for Marie or love for God. In God's name, he didn't know, if he was motivated by Satan or Jesus, but he knew he had to reach her. He remembered the key Marie kept in the plant outside the door.

Now inside the apartment, he stood at the sink guzzling a glass of water. "Hola Henrique, where is your mami?" The smell of Marie's sweet perfume was everywhere. He looked through papers on the kitchen table, hoping to find some clue where she was. He sat on the green vinyl sofa, groping through her books and folders on the coffee table. Now in the bedroom, the newspaper caught his eye. The red ink on the classified page might be the answer he needed. After reading the Seafood Sales ad, he sat on the bed, and dialed the telephone.

"You have reached a number that has been disconnected or is no longer in service. Hang up and try your call again." He did dial again, then reached the same recording. What would he do now? He considered telling Monsignor. Then decided it would be better to handle it himself. Should he ask for sabbatical to atone for his sins? And if it was granted, should he fly out to Hawaii to get her? Maybe her flight had not landed yet. After calling a cab to take him to the rectory, he tore out of the apartment, carrying the classified page.

Back in his room at the rectory, Father Juan stood reading the article in the FSU Flambeau:

Hawaii has been identified as a major hub of human trafficking, a form of modern slavery. Victims can be young girls and women who are forced into prostitution, immigrant farmers and U.S. students lured to Hawaii with false promises by job recruiters, and domestic servants and laborers from other countries as well as our own local community. They could be someone you know. The most recent to hit college campuses is the seafood sales scam. Recruiters post help wanted ads in local classifieds and offer training programs in Hawaii.

"Oh, God," Father Juan, knelt to pray, asking for forgiveness, asking for help. How would he be able to find her? When his prayers had ended, he headed straight for Monsignor's office. Once inside, he sat in a chair across from Monsignor, now behind his desk.

"I need a sabbatical," said Father Juan. "To find some time to atone for my sins."

"I think that is wise. I cannot have you floundering anymore. You must be fully committed to your promises to uphold tenants of the faith and live piously before entering major seminary, let alone the diocese."

"I understand, Monsignor Murray."

"I can give you a three-day leave."

"I am most grateful. Thank you, Monsignor Murray," said Father Juan. "I must go now. My grief and guilt and temptation are too much. I must separate myself, the sooner the better. I think it best that I leave tonight. I am ridden with the need for solitude."

"Very well then. Do as you must, but be back for Thursday night homily," said Monsignor Murray. "And May God Bless You."

"Yes Monsignor, I will." Father Juan looked back over his shoulder before stepping out the door, "May God Bless you, Monsignor Murray."

* * *

Lynette looked up from the sink and saw Father Juan sitting at the bar right in front of her. His face was twisted with grief, his eyes were full of worry. "Are you alright, Father?"

"No, not really. I heard that Marie left for Hawaii this morning."

"Yah, I was just getting here when she left on a Piedmont flight around nine this morning. Can I get you something to drink?"

"Orange juice, please. Did you try to stop her?"

"I did, but she was so excited, going on about all the money she was gonna make to help her get out of debt and pay for tuition. I told her it sounded too good to be true, and she just argued that the worst thing that would happen is she wouldn't like it, the trip was free and she had never been to Hawaii." Lynette set the glass of orange juice on the bar. Father Juan turned to his backpack.

"Look at this." His hand was trembling. "I'm going out there to get her."

Lynette accepted the Flambeau news article he passed to her hand. She stood reading it in horror. "I knew something wasn't right. Did you call the police?"

"No, but maybe you should? Meanwhile, I'll go out and see if I can find her."

"But, how will you know where to go?"

"I don't know, but I have faith that I will figure it out. I'll call you when I get there and leave you a phone number, in case she checks in with you."

"Ok, I told her to call me when she got there." Lynette took a deep breath. "I'm working a double, so as soon as I get home, I'll check my answering machine." Lynette wrote her phone number on a napkin, then handed it to Juan.

"I know that these scams can end bad. If I don't reach her, we may never see her again."

"Yah, my grandmother and mom always tell me they don't want me to end up on a slow boat to China, now I know what they mean."

It was the wee hours of the morning. The ringing phone woke Lynette from a dead sleep. She stumbled to the phone. Marie was on the other line. "Hey, girlfriend, Hawaii is beautiful, wish you were here. I just had some pineapple wine, some coconut wine, went swimming and I'm meeting my trainer in the morning. Thought I'd call to rub it in."

Lynette's heart was beating fast. "Where are you staying?"

"At some place in Honolulu, It's a Hostel, Seabreeze Hostel."

"A what?" The call was interrupted by the operator.

"To continue this call, please deposit, three dollars and twenty-five cents." Lynette waited to hear Marie's voice again.

"A Hostel, that just means we're dorming it like college girls."

"Got an address?"

"Seaside Ave. Gotta go, I'm at a pay phone, and outta quarters."

"Marie, Marie, don't hang up, Marie." Lynette heard the click of the line disconnecting the call. "Aw fuck." She had a location name and a street name, something she could tell the police, and Father Juan, when he called to check in. Lynette realized she hadn't told Dillan about Marie's situation in Hawaii. She dialed the phone.

"Hey, Dillan. It's Lynette."

"I know who it is."

"Something awful has happened to Marie. She has been recruited into some sort of prostitution scam. She's in Hawaii, and Father Juan went to find her. Marie just called and well, at least I got a street name."

"What? When did all this happen? Did you call the police?"

"Today, but I didn't tell them about the address yet?"

"Well, hang up and call them now. I'm coming over."

After the call to the police, Lynette's head was spinning. The gravity of it all seemed to hit at once. She couldn't believe that her only college friend, was caught up in such a mess. She stood at the sink filling the tea pot. She expected Father Juan would call sometime in the afternoon. After turning on the stove, she paced the floor, then flipped the switch to the porch light. What should she do while she waited? After plucking a tea bag from the box, she carefully unwound the string to read the quote on the tag, *Never mistake temptation for opportunity.* She looked heavenward and spoke aloud, "I hear ya." After dropping the bag in the cup, she found the hamper was full, and stood sorting laundry, when the tea kettle whistled. She returned to her laundry piles with her cup of tea. When her cup was empty, Dillan knocked at the door.

"Hey," he set a canvas bag on the floor. Then reached out to give Lynette a hug and a kiss.

"So, did you call the police?"

"Yah, they're supposed to be in touch with the Honolulu police too."

"So where is Marie now?"

"Some Hostel. Have you ever heard of those?"

"They're like a commune aren't they?"

"The police said it was like a boarding house. Marie called it a dorm."

"So, what did she say on the phone?"

"She sounded clueless that she was in any danger. She's only been there a few hours anyway. The good thing is that she said her new boss wouldn't be seeing her until the morning. Father Juan is supposed to call when he gets there."

"I brought stuff to tap your phone line if she calls in again." He bent over his bag and showed her the recorder, the phone line, phone jacks and adapters, and a recorder control. After setting them all on the table, he immediately went to work.

"All you have to do is plug the phone line into the port on the recorder control and the cord from the control into the phone jack." Lynette watched him set the switch to record.

"Now, I plug the recorder cord in, the microphone cords in, and that's it."

Dillan looked at his watch. "We need someone to call us to test it out."

"Let me see if Warren's lights are on." Lynette stepped outside. Dillan stood at the open door watching as Lynette drew near her neighbor's window.

"They're on, I'm knocking." Lynette heard music coming from inside. The door swung open. Warren appeared wearing a pair of khaki shorts and a Rolling Stones t-shirt.

"Oh, my God, I was just thinking of you, girl. I love those pj's. Anyway, I'm making oatmeal raisin cookies for the Chem Society fundraiser, and I'm out of vanilla, do you have any?" Warren craned his neck outside the door, "Hey, Dillan!"

"Warren, will you call Lynette's phone to see if it's working?" asked Dillan.

"What's wrong with your phone?"

"Just call it," said Lynette. "Then come over for the vanilla."

"Alright, Alright." Warren shut his door.

Lynette and Dillan stood waiting for the phone to ring. After the first ring, Lynette answered. "Hello."

"Hello, you have that vanilla?" asked Warren.

"I'm checking now." Lynette opened the rusty metal cabinet door and peered in. "I've got garlic, cinnamon, onion powder, food coloring, and ah ha, vanilla." Lynette glanced over at Dillan, who stood with his thumb up. "We're in business."

"Great, I'm coming over."

"Ok, bye." Lynette held a small brown bottle. Dillan stood with the door open waiting for Warren, who rushed in, carrying a plate covered in aluminum foil.

"I brought you a few cookies," said Warren. "They're from the first batch."

"Something awful has happened to my friend, Marie." Dillan went over to the recorder to playback the phone conversation.

"What's going on?" asked Warren. They all stood listening to the recording of Lynette and Warren's conversation.

"All set," said Dillan.

"Marie may be caught up in some prostitution ring in Hawaii," said Lynette.

"Oh my God. This is like a bad nightmare," said Warren. "Are you sure?"

"It was in the FSU paper," said Lynette. "I gave the paper to the police last night."

"A priest is on the way to try to find her," said Dillan. He had been studying a black coating on the desk and was now rubbing his fingers together.

"A priest," said Warren.

"That's another story," said Lynette. "Dillan just tapped my phone in case Marie or the priest calls."

"Oh my God, this is surreal. Screw the cookies, I'm staying here." Warren sat down at the table. "Why couldn't your answering machine record the call?"

Dillan stood in the kitchen now, making a pot of coffee. "Because, it only records when you don't answer the phone, and cuts off when you answer it."

"I would love a cup of coffee," said Warren. "So, what are you gonna do now?"

"Well, we wait for the police, the priest, or Marie to call," said Lynette.

"Lynette, why is there soot all over everything?" asked Dillan, now rubbing his thumb on his forefinger. "Did you burn something?"

"Um, I, yah, my candles. I sort of left them burning and left the house."

"Those nice sconces you had on the wall?"

"Those were the ones," said Lynette.

"Man, Where's your vacuum?" asked Dillan.

"In the bedroom closet," said Lynette.

"Go get it and I'll vacuum this stuff up."

* * *

It was two in the afternoon when Father Juan called.

"Hello," said Lynette.

"Hey, it's Juan, I made it. I'm at the airport in Honolulu, any word?"

"I called the police and Marie's staying at a hostel, Seaside Avenue, It's called the Seabreeze. That's all I know. She was at a pay phone and hung up before I could warn her about anything. The cops have the address too, and I gave them the copy of the classified ad. They said they're gonna contact police in Honolulu."

Dillan stood by watching the recorder.

"Alright, I'll call you as soon as I find her."

"Godspeed, Juan."

* * *

At the Hawaii International Airport Juan climbed into the back seat of a taxi.

"Aloha, where to?"

"Seaside Avenue, the Seabreeze Hostel, please." Juan clutched his backpack in his lap.

The traffic was thick on Rodgers Boulevard and Aolele Street. The air was light, and the sun shone mocking him, lighting up the sins of the world. He was tired and felt sick from worry. Would he get there on time? Would she still be there? The cab stood in six lane traffic on Interstate H1.

"How far are we?"

"Not far, five miles or so, but the traffic slows us down. There must be an accident up ahead."

"Yes, I see."

"Is this your first time to the island?"

"Yes," said Juan, "I am trying to find someone, who may be in trouble."

"Oh, What kind of trouble?"

"A friend of mine applied for a job at Seafood Express International, and it may not be what she thinks it is."

"I have never heard of this company." The lines of cars began moving again. Juan opened his wallet and took out a twenty-dollar bill in anticipation.

"Our exit is next," said the driver. "It is number twenty-three, Punahou Street."

A short ride later, the cab pulled onto Seaside Avenue and stopped. The driver pointed out his window. "There, see the sign Seabreeze, it is behind this building."

"Yes, I see it," said Father Juan. He handed the driver his twenty. "Is this enough?"

"Yes, more than enough."

"Keep the change." Juan jerked open the car door and climbed outside.

"I hope you find your friend," the driver called out from the window.

The Seabreeze building was moldy green colored. Juan followed the signs leading to the office.

"Aloha," said the man at the counter.

"I'm looking for Marie Martinez. She would have checked in yesterday, with the Seafood Express Sales training folks."

"I'm afraid our resident list is confidential."

Juan thought fast, "I'm here on official church business, there has been a death in her family. I have come to meet with her about the funeral arrangements for her dearly beloved mother." He opened his bag to reveal his Cassock, Bible and rosary beads.

"Well, this isn't customary, but I think she is still here."

"Anna," A woman swishing a mop around looked up. "Go and fetch Marie from room two." She dropped the mop in a bucket and walked out the door.

"Father, you can wait in the courtyard," said the clerk.

Juan wanted to run down the hall and throw his arms around her. He prayed that she was there all the while knowing that he was unworthy and didn't deserve to have his prayers answered. He took a seat in in a lawn chair in the courtyard near the soda machine, and a potted plant. He watched the woman named Anna knocking on a door on the upstairs balcony. He saw the door opening. A redhaired girl peered out. He heard the murmur of voices. The door shut, and Anna walked to the stairs. Juan moved to meet Anna at the bottom landing.

"Sorry Father, Marie is not here."

"Ok, do you know where she would have gone?"

"Probably not far, she's walking. Her roommate says she went for coffee and lunch with the other girls."

"If she comes back, please tell her that Father Juan is here and that I am waiting in the courtyard." Juan handed her a twenty-dollar bill. "Also, it is important not to tell anyone else that I'm here. I don't want to cause any trouble for her with her new job. Marie will be full of grief about her mother's passing."

"Yes," said Anna.

Juan watched Anna return to the office, and he could see through the sliding door, she had picked up her mop again. Where was Marie? She was staying here, that was for sure. Juan hoped it wasn't too late to find her. He walked to the soda machine and put in some coins. A can of Pepsi appeared behind the plexiglass flap. He heard the screen door sliding. When he turned, he saw the man from the counter approaching.

"What's the matter, Father, she wasn't in?"

"No, out to lunch." Juan held the Pepsi in his hand. "May I wait for her here?"

"Yes." The man from the counter, returned to the office.

Juan returned to his seat in the lawn chair. He was removing the top from his Pepsi can, when he gazed at the entrance area into the courtyard. It was a miracle, there she was, walking straight toward him. Juan stood locking his eyes on Marie. He walked to meet her.

"Father Juan, I can't believe you're here." Marie's voice was thick with disbelief. She stood a proper distance from him, as she would were he her priest.

"I was in the neighborhood." Father Juan's eyes widened. "Can we take a little walk?"

"Well, I was about to get packed up, we will be headed for the docks in a couple hours. We're going out on one of the Seafood Express International fishing boats. Sort of a see the seafood when it's caught and meet the team behind the scenes sort of thing."

"Ok, a short walk, then." Father Juan picked up his backpack. They stepped out of the courtyard walking on Seaside Avenue toward Kuhio Avenue.

"Listen, I think you are in trouble," said Juan.

"What are you talking about?"

"Actually, I know you're in trouble." He spoke in an undertone.

Marie watched him reach into his jacket pocket. "Look," he said. He pushed the Flambeau news article in front of her.

"Your new job, and your boat ride is a front for a human trafficking scam."

"What's that?" Marie was unfamiliar with the term. She reached out and grasped the article in her hand and began reading. She shook her head and covered her mouth with her hand.

"No, it can't be," said Marie. Her voice was quavering. "I'm training for a sales position."

"Don't get on that boat. Get your things and let's head back to the airport." Juan was speaking softly and earnestly. "Now listen, I told the guy at the counter that you had a death in the family and that was why I was here, to advise you on funeral arrangements for your mother. A bereavement call. Act natural. Show no panic, say we are going to the church, or something or the funeral home.

"But the other girls, and Kathy?" asked Marie.

"Lynette has contacted the authorities in Tallahassee, and they're in touch with the Honolulu police. They're setting up some sting operation. The cops should be investigating the whole thing. Now come on, Let's get out of here. And head back to the airport."

"Are you sure? I mean, about all this?"

"Yes, I've never been more certain."

"But I have no return ticket."

"Don't worry. I have a credit card. We'll deal with that at the airport when we get there."

Marie searched Juan's face for a reason. "Why are you doing this?"

"I love you, Marie."

"We need to hurry before Cheri gets back. She's the boss lady."

"Go on," he said. His face turned toward the dingy building, where his eyes focused on the entrance to the courtyard, where Marie needed to enter to climb the stairs to retrieve her suitcase. "I'll call a cab at the pay phone, and then I'll be waiting at the bottom of the stairs."

"Ok," Marie took a deep breath. She could feel her palms sweating, and her mind spinning. *Try to act natural.* She walked down the dingy hallway to her room and used her key to open the door. The only one left in the room was Kathy and she was laying on her bunk trying to sleep off a hangover.

"What did you have for lunch?" asked Kathy. She held her forearm over her freckled face to shade her eyes from the sun shining in through the open door.

"You still can't hold anything down, huh?" said Marie. She stepped toward her bunk.

"Maybe I'll try some crackers," said Kathy.

"Sure." Marie slid her suitcase out from underneath the bed.

"Is Cheri downstairs yet?"

"No, probably not for another hour and a half." Marie tossed her sandals and some clothes in the suitcase. She didn't want to leave Kathy behind. "Kathy, pack your things and get out. That boat they're taking us on is not a real fishing trip. It's a one-way trip to being sold into prostitution. Get your stuff and come with me. My friend is here, and he is calling a cab right now. You can come to the airport with us."

"I don't have a ticket."

"It's ok, we have a credit card." Marie closed her suitcase. "And I still have fifty dollars of my bonus money, if you have any left, you can add it to mine and get yourself home."

"Oh God, are you sure?"

"Surer than ever. My friend, he's a priest, and would not have come all this way for nothing. He says the cops in the mainland are on this case, but they might not make it in time before that boat leaves the docks." Marie held a napkin and a pen in her hand.

"What are you writing?" asked Kathy.

"A note for the girls to run, and call the police, and that the job is a scam." Marie put the note on JoJo's bunk.

"Ok, then." Kathy stood up, loaded and zipped her suitcase, and within minutes the girls crept down the stairs. Marie saw a few men from the other dorm hanging out in the courtyard. She was grateful that they were so noisy. They would be the attention getters, not Marie and Kathy.

Father Juan was at the bottom of the stairs, and the three of them walked out to the street. They could see the cab heading toward them. Within minutes, the bags were loaded and three of them climbed into the back seat.

"Where you headed?" asked the driver.

"The airport," said Juan.

They sat in silence in the cab. The blue sky, palm tree lined highway, and tropical breeze were all disenchanting now. At the airport, Father Juan called the police from a pay phone, with updates. Marie called Lynette to tell her she was on her way home. Kathy called her boss at the car dealership, and he paid her way back to Wisconsin.

"Thank you both for saving my life," said Kathy. Marie hugged her and stuck a napkin in her hand. "What's this?"

"My address and phone number in Florida. Call me when you get home. And like my girlfriend always says, if you can't be good, be careful." Marie managed a smile from closed lips.

On the plane from Honolulu, Marie and Juan buckled in for the long flight to Los Angeles. Marie sat, staring out the airplane window. Juan reached for her hand, then broke the silence.

"Monsignor, told me I must be fully committed to my promises to uphold tenants of the Catholic faith and that I must live piously before entering major seminary."

"Oh?"

"He is aware of my flaunted gallivanting, as he put it."

"Uh huh, and what does that mean?"

"I want to redeem myself and re-commit to the church. I can't go on living this lie. I really care for you, but when I am ordained, I will be married to the church and I cannot break the sacred vow of faithfulness to it. I love you, Marie, but I love the church. I cannot have it both ways."

"Juan, how did you find me?"

"I had a little help from your bartender friend. And I sort of let myself in your apartment with the key in the plant after Kerry told me you had left. I couldn't leave you there, when I knew what those criminals were capable of. You are my Mary Magdalene. I couldn't let anything happen to you. I needed to know you were safe."

"You saved my life, No one could ask you for anything more."

Marie felt light-headed. What was he saying? Did he know? The cramps were getting stronger. Unbearable. She excused herself to go to the lavatory. She barely found the strength to close the door and latch it. When she slid down her shorts, and sat on the toilet, she saw the blood. She felt so much cramping. She wanted to cry, but she was grateful. She lifted the small cabinet door marked, Feminine Hygiene. She removed the Kotex and sat holding it in her hand for what seemed a long time. When she stood up, she saw the thick red clots in the toilet, and she knew that all was over. Two miracles in one day. Her eyes looked heavenward. *Gracias Dios.*

Chapter 12

When Lynette heard disembodied knocking, she threw off her bed covers, then sprung from bed to see who was at the door. To confirm what she had expected, she put her eye to the peephole. There was Marie, home safe. Hurriedly Lynette unlocked the knob, the dead bolt, and the chain.

"Lynette, it's Marie. I'm home."

"Girlfriend." Lynette swung the door wide. Four arms outstretched, friends embraced. "I'm glad you're safe."

"Me too, me too. Maybe I'll get you to that FSU football game after all," said Marie. "You were right, it was too good to be true."

"Yah, I'm just glad, Father Juan went to get you."

"Me too."

"Come in and sit down, want some tea?"

"Ok," said Marie.

Lynette stood at the cabinet, taking out mugs. "So, did you and Father Juan fly back together?"

"We did. He's home at the rectory. I just keep thinking about the girls that maybe didn't get away? I left them a note to leave the hostel. I hope they got it."

"Well, I wish the cops could have done more, all they kept telling me on this end, was that there was a sting operation in Honolulu, and how you hadn't been missing very long, and how you had called and were still safe. Other than contacting the authorities in Honolulu, there wasn't much they could do," said Lynette, now holding a box of tea in her hand. "I guess you'll just have to rely on faith."

"Dios Mío," said Marie, now sighing. She expected a longer than usual menstrual period with heavy cramping, and she was getting one. "I'm going to use the bathroom, and I'll be borrowing some of your pads."

"Help yourself."

The tea kettle whistled. Lynette stood at the stove pouring water into cups. Marie reappeared in the kitchen.

"I don't know what I'm going to do," said Marie. She sat down in the kitchen chair. "I'm broke."

Lynette set a mug on the table in front of her friend, and then stepped in front of the window, pushing the drapes open a crack to look outside. She held the hot mug in her hands feeling the warm steam rising on her face. "People are moving out of that apartment across the way." Marie stood and joined Lynette at the window.

"Those are two-bedroom apartments," said Marie.

"They look big, like a townhouse," said Lynette. "I wonder what the rent is there."

"I think it's between hundred seventy-five and two hundred a month." Marie lifted and dunked her tea bag.

"Hey, if we moved over there, and split the rent, we'd both be paying eighty something a month, and that's less than the hundred twenty-five I pay now and the hundred fifty you pay now," said Lynette. "I could cover you for the first month until you get on your feet. I'm making more money at the airport than I ever thought I would. The only thing is, I only have one more semester to go, before I do my internship in January. You'd have to move again, when I leave, unless you get another roommate."

Marie's eyes flooded with tears. "I don't care." Her voice was brittle. "Let's do it." Then she wailed like a suffering child. Lynette's forehead furrowed.

"Come on, let's sit down." Lynette led Marie to the to the green vinyl love seat. "You've been through hell, but you made it back. What you need is a lot of rest. I'm making you a grilled cheese, then I'm taking you home, so you can shower, go to bed, and sleep it off. I'm working today, but I'll stop by and check on you on my way home," said Lynette. Her eyes flickered with kindness. And from them, Marie found strength. "We still have five days before summer classes begin. And we get to use the new phone registration for classes, so no long line at the Civic Center." Then she glanced at the tag dangling from the thread hanging from her cup. And she read, *Friendship shares pain and tends wounds.*

* * *

Hours later, Marie's sleep was deep. It was filled with sky, clouds, ocean, and sun floating outside an airplane window. In her dream she had woken up on the plane. Father Juan was not in his seat. "Did the girls get out? Did they?" Marie mumbled. Her eyes blinked open to see Lynette standing over her.

"You were dreaming," said Lynette. She set a chocolate milkshake on the bedside table, next to a white bag. "How are you feeling?"

"Better." Marie rose from her bed, then headed to the bathroom.

"I brought you fish and chips from Captain Dee's and a some more Kotex."

"Thanks," Marie yelled from the bathroom. "What time is it?"

"After eleven," Lynette yelled back.

"At night?"

"Yup."

"Have you heard from Juan?"

Marie stepped into the room wearing a towel wrapped around her waist.

"No, I slept the whole time," said Marie. She stood now poking through her dresser drawer. "I probably won't hear from him. He told me on the plane, that he was going to major seminary school and planned to re-commit himself to the church."

"Huh, well, I hope he knows what he's doing," said Lynette. "I guess he really cares about you."

"How do you know?"

"I just do. A guy, priest or not, trying to cover his tracks or not, doesn't fly halfway around the world to save someone, unless there's a little medicine in them. Besides, like Shakespeare says, there's a little poison and medicine in all of us. No one is all one or the other. People are complex."

"You know there were other girls, some girl named Ivonne was one of them. I never should have got involved with him. He told me on the plane that he loved me, but he loved the church more. Well, like Einstein said, a person who never made a mistake never tried anything new."

"That's the spirit, girlfriend."

* * *

Dillan helped Lynette and Marie move into the Alumni Village townhouse. He and Marie took on the project of setting up house as if it were the only thing that mattered. He moved in his piano for sing-alongs. He cut and lay carpet in the living room. He handled all the heavy lifting. Marie did most of the cleaning, packing, and unpacking. Together they worked nonstop and tirelessly. On the morning of the move, Lynette left her old apartment to go to work for a double shift. After work, she came home to the new apartment, nearly all set up. Lynette couldn't believe that was over a month ago.

She sat now in the green vinyl chair next to an end table looking around at all the space. There was twice as much space as her old apartment. The bathroom and two bedrooms were upstairs. Marie insisted that Lynette have the bigger room, with the double bed and the desk, where Dillan had put her typewriter. Marie bought herself a futon to sleep on. Her schoolwork, she did at the kitchen table.

The living room had an eight-foot green vinyl sofa, which was arranged with its back against the sliding glass door, a coffee table in its front. On one end of the coffee table was a green vinyl chair positioned next to an end table, across the room facing the chair where Lynette sat, her back against the wall of the stairs, arms reach from the entrance to the kitchen. Sitting in it, Lynette also faced Dillan's piano, on which stood a beginner piano book, and sheet music composed by the band, Heart. Dillan brought the music over because he said the song suited Lynette's voice. The beginner book he brought, so Marie and Lynette could teach themselves to play piano. In the kitchen, there was three times as many cabinets, and counter space. From the round kitchen table, which held four chairs, there was a perfect view of Marie's ten-gallon fish aquarium. The bird cage stood next to the back door across from the stove.

Lynette recalled how Marie had surprised her the day she had brought home a second parakeet, a yellow one, so Henrique could have a friend. Lynette had named her Raquel. The first week they had Raquel, she found her way under the refrigerator. Dillan coaxed her out, yellow feathers flying, before the fan sucked her up. Lynette's reminiscing was now interrupted by a voice outside the front door, followed by the sound of a key jiggling in the knob. The door swung open and into the room stumbled Marie.

"Smells like popcorn, and what is that you are drinking, fresh coffee too?" Marie walked into the kitchen to drop her bag on the table. "Aw, this is great." She began pouring herself a coffee.

"Yup, I just popped some," said Lynette. "Brain food."

"Can I have some?" Marie was looking for something. "Where's the popcorn? did you eat it all already?"

"No, I'm pulling an all-nighter, so I made a grocery sack full," said Lynette, her barefoot, tapping the grease spotted brown bag. "Here, dig in."

Marie looked down at the bag, that she thought was trash, and sure enough there it was. An extra extra-large amount of popcorn. She sat down on the rug, her hand digging into sac. She shoveled a handful of popcorn into her mouth. "Aw, man this stuff is awesome. What did you put on it?"

"Ranch dressing powder, you know those little packs?"

"That's a good idea," said Marie. She stood up. "Well, I got to study too, so I'll hang out with you."

"How was the hospital?"

"Crazy busy, I'm glad I'm home," said Marie. "You know that apartment next door where that family with two little girls moved out? There's already a girl moving in and she has a boyfriend, who dove off the dock at Lake Talquin and broke his neck. He's paralyzed from the neck down. She said she's been at the hospital every day to see him. She thinks she's going to marry him like that."

"Aw, man, that's wicked sad," said Lynette.

"I couldn't do it," said Marie.

"Me neither," said Lynette.

"Did you see her new car?" asked Marie.

Lynette gave her the hairy eyeball. She was peering over a three-inch bound copy of Chaucer's works. Marie's incessant talking tonight was not going to cut it.

"Man, what are you studying?" Marie leaned over for a closer look at the book. "That is bigger than my Micro-Biology book."

"Chaucer. And I really need some quiet, this stuff is like another language, it's written in Middle English"

"Really. What's it about?"

"Well, right now I'm reading The Canterbury Tales. It's a bunch of stories of a bunch of people on a pilgrimage. They're leaving from somewhere outside of London and they're on their way to a shrine at a cathedral in Canterbury."

"Hmmm, we're all on a pilgrimage,' said Marie. "Some of us have a direction, some of us are along for the ride."

"Anyway," said Lynette. "I'm on the tale called *The Wife of Bath*, some woman who had five husbands. Lemme read some to you, 'He sought in ev'ry house and ev'ry place, Where as he hoped for to finde grace, To learne what thing women love the most: But he could not arrive in any coast, Where as he mighte find in this mattere, Two creatures according in fere. Some said that women loved best richess, Some said honour, and some said jolliness, Some rich array, and some said lust a-bed, And oft time to be widow and be wed.'"

While Lynette read, Marie had fetched her camera, and squatted on the floor, now holding it to her face. The heavy book was positioned so that only half Lynette's face could be seen through the lens. Lynette raised a brow and glared. Click went the camera. "Aw come on," said Lynette. "I look like shit."

"Lighten up, I'm just trying to have a little fun. This is your last semester. Don't you want some pictures of life at FSU?"

"Well, I'm not in the mood for fun, I have to be able to produce an essay long enough to fill two blue composition books for my final exam on this stuff. By memory."

"No multiple choice questions?"

"Literary professors don't believe in multiple choice, just writing and more writing," said Lynette. "Hell, when I finish this damn degree, I'm gonna be such a good writer, I'm gonna write a book about you and all the weird stuff you do." Then she threw a piece of popcorn at Marie, who laughed, then picked it up from the floor and ate it. Lynette shook her head.

"What? it landed on the rug."

"Right, that's cleaner than the tiles."

"Alright, listen I have to get this reading done. I thought you said you had to study too."

"Alright, don't get your panties in a wad, I'm going upstairs to change."

"Finally, some peace and quiet," said Lynette. Minutes later she heard the water running in the shower. She sat reading and taking notes and munching popcorn until she heard Marie's footsteps on the stairs. Lynette looked up from her notebook and saw that Marie was in the nude.

"Oh my God, will you put some clothes on." Marie pulled out a kitchen chair and sat bare assed bent over a laundry basket on the kitchen floor digging for something. "You're getting a snail trail all over everything," said Lynette. "I can't hack this. Don't you have a robe?"

"Clothes are uncomfortable, and my first husband said that my body was a playground, so I have more fun without a robe." said Marie. She was folding a uniform top. "I can't believe this is your last semester."

"I can, I'm so tired of working and going to school, I could just spit. My bones are aching from all these damned all-nighters." Lynette took a drink from her coffee. "Dillan wants me to go out on the boat tomorrow, but I have to get this studying done before I go. You want to go with us? It's the last boat ride before we take it back to Kansas."

"So, you're meeting Dillan's family." Marie was now sliding into a t-shirt. "When a guy wants his parents to meet you, it's serious."

Lynette watched as Marie opened the bird cage. "Hola, Henrique, y Raquel, mamá te extrañó hoy." Henrique hopped from his perch to the edge of his cage door and then fluttered out and landed on Marie's shoulder. Then Marie carefully closed the cage door. "Lynette, did you feed the fish?"

"No, but I'll do it now. I did give the birds fresh water, though."

Marie was sliding her hand into a latex glove. "Is that goldfish still alive?"

Lynette shook a small plastic container over the aquarium. "Nobody's floating at the top, so I guess so." Lynette turned from the aquarium to see Henrique sitting in the grip of a hand covered in a yellow latex glove. His little black and white head bobbing around, while Marie's left hand, held scissors that snipped at blue feathers on his wings.

"The airport manager and my friend Kim are coming on the boat too. It's gonna be a nice day." Lynette walked around the table to talk to the little yellow parakeet. "Hey Raquel, are you getting your wings clipped tonight too?"

"No feather cut for Raquel," said Marie. "I did her yesterday."

"So, what do you say, you wanna join us?"

"I would, but I got plans with Lamont." Marie set Henrique on the table. "We're studying at the law library and going to lunch." She took off her glove and spoke affectionately, "Chico bonito." Smiling she slid her index finger under his two pairs of front toes. Then she lifted him to her lips and kissed his little feathery head. She set him back in the cage. "Te Quiero Pretty boy," said Marie.

"Pretty boy," said Henrique.

"Look at the way that bird looks at you with lovin' eyes," said Lynette. "Anyway, we'll miss you on the boat." Lynette settled into her chair, now reading silently. Her finger rubbing the side of her face. "What's going on with you and Lamont anyway?"

"Nothing."

"You know what I think?"

"No, I don't."

"I think, you and Lamont are like Professor Higgins' and Eliza in *Pygmalion*, a play that became the movie, *My Fair Lady*."

"Oh," said Marie. "I'm definitely a fair lady."

"The problem with Higgins is that his life's passion is his work, not Eliza. Eliza is his side project. Kinda like, Lamont's passion is the law, and you're his side project. Not to mention, you're not in any frame of mind to be fetching anyone's slippers anytime soon."

"I thought Eliza and Higgins got married at the end of the movie," said Marie. She was standing at the sink washing her hands.

"That's Hollywood's ending, not the playwright's ending."

"How did the playwright end it?" Marie stood reaching into the kitchen cabinet.

"Not happily ever after," said Lynette. She opened her book, reading, her finger rubbing her face again. Marie used a bowl to scoop popcorn from Lynette's sac.

"Do you always pick your zits when you study?" asked Marie.

"Shut up. And mind your own book."

Marie carried her full bowl over to the vinyl chair across the room to the left of the piano "How do you read that Chaucer? I can't even read this." Marie looked over at a book on the end table next to a pack of cocoa bean cigarettes. She now sat tossing popcorn into her mouth.

"What are you reading?" Lynette sipped her coffee.

"A book for Spanish class," said Marie. She spoke through a mouth full. "You know something, I graduated from high school and never read a book before. I see you starting and finishing a book in twenty-four hours. I can't understand it."

"Let me see your book," said Lynette. She moved in front of Marie, who handed off a novel. Lynette turned the book over in her hand, read the front and back cover of Gabriel Garcia Marquez's *A Hundred Years of Solitude*. She flipped its pages and scanned chapter breaks. "You can't read this?"

"I haven't started," said Marie. "And I have an essay due next week."

"Well, if you ask me, you probably process all your information in Spanish, and translate it in your head before you can even begin to comprehend anything, let alone start memorizing shit, or writing about it. Maybe if you slow down and translate the words to Spanish."

Lynette handed back the book. Marie's round eyes widened. She thumbed through the pages.

"It's so long," said Marie.

"I can't believe you have never read a book, I like reading, actually," said Lynette. "You never read any Pipi Longstocking as a kid?"

Marie shook her head. "No, I sat in the back of my classes in high school braiding my friends' hair."

"No love stories as a teenager? Those were some of my favorites."

"I told you I have never read a whole book." Marie flipped open a pack of cigarettes.

"Well, you better start reading now. Sometimes it's the getting started that is the hard part. Besides, you may as well read, since you never sleep."

Lynette crossed the room to return to Chaucer. After she sat, she saw Marie lighting up a cigarette.

"What about when you were little," said Lynette. "Didn't your folks read to you?"

Marie looked like she was trying to recall a time, but could not, or as if that were the craziest question anyone had ever asked her. That's when Lynette realized Marie was serious, she couldn't read, at least not easily or without struggle. Lynette stood, crossed the room, and picked up Marie's book again.

"Let me read the first chapter to you," said Lynette. Marie tipped back her head and blew smoke from her mouth. Lynette began. "'Many years later, as he faced the firing squad, Colonel Aureliano Buendía was to remember that distant afternoon when his father took him to discover ice.'" Lynette paused. "Now, think about that first sentence in Spanish, then in English, and tell me what we read." And Lynette coached Marie like this through the first chapter, after which Marie began to read by herself. Lynette returned to Chaucer, and they read silently until the first light of the day showed itself on the curtains behind Marie's chair, and the sounds of birds chirping filled the apartment.

Now morning, Lynette lifted the cover from the bird cage. Raquel & Henrique were perched side by side. Four little eyes blinking. Bright yellow, and blue grey wings stretching. Henrique leapt to the bars of the cage using his beak to climb around. Raquel sat opening her beak in a yawn.

"Good morning, Raquel, Good morning Henrique, Time to wake up for us." Lynette looked over her shoulder. "Hey, Marie, can I let them free for a little while?"

"Ok," said Marie, joining Lynette in the kitchen. Lynette opened the cage door.

"Buenos Dios," said Marie.

"Buenos Dios," said Henrique. He climbed outside and perched himself on top of the cage to look out the window. Raquel clutched the cage bars now, her beak and toes making her way up to settle next to Henrique.

* * *

The day after the Kansas road trip, Lynette stood in her upstairs bedroom folding clothes and thinking about the long ride north west on Interstate twenty-two. With the windows rolled down and the wind blowing her hair, she had pleasured Dillan with fellatio. They had parked on a dirt road in Mississippi. The shade of the sweet gum tree danced over their bodies. And the music of purple finches and sparrows sang to the rhythm of their lovemaking. Their affection had been cut short by a disembodied foghorn of a voice. "This is private property." Lynette, laughed aloud now, thinking about how they had bolted stark naked back to the truck, dressing while the truck moved down the road.

At his parent's home in Tecumseh, they had slept in separate bedrooms. Lynette recalled the regret she felt on the first night, when she saw the contents of her suitcase, a bottle of wine, a pillow, and one pair of shorts. Still drunk when Dillan had picked her up for the trip at four in the morning, she had worn a hot pink dress and high heels for a road trip. No wonder Dillan's mother had insisted she try on and keep Dillan's cousin's clothes. The worst of it, was washing the one pair of underwear each night. Why she hadn't asked Dillan to bring her to a store to buy clothes she hadn't a clue. Embarrassment and shame, she figured, must have played a role.

To redeem herself, Lynette had worked hard helping with projects and chores around the house. Shoveling blacktop onto the driveway, was one such project. Lynette recalled how she stood in the back of the truck scooping asphalt and tossing it, so Dillan could disperse and smooth the tar with a rake. Then there was the construction of the wheelchair ramp, Dillan's labor of love for his father. Lynette had helped load and unload lumber and supplies for that job. There had been endless duties in the kitchen. Lynette washed dishes and watched Dillan's mom work tirelessly caregiving to his dad. She had cooked beautiful meals from scratch every day. Homemade biscuits, cornbread, pot roast, meatloaf, macaroni and cheese. Lynette had learned about Dillan's dad's life as a fighter pilot in World War II, his work as an engineer, and his time singing in a barbershop quartet. She had met his sister and her children. There had been church twice, once on Wednesday, and once on Sunday. She recalled standing with Dillan and his whole family in front of the pulpit as the preacher, spoke in tongues over Dillan's father, while the whole congregation prayed to heal him from Parkinson's Disease. There was a boating day on Lake Shawnee. And a day at the Potawatomi Indian Reservation, where Dillan had made two purchases, dangling turquoise earrings for Lynette, and a Potawatomi Dictionary for himself. The dictionary had been a highlight of the road trip home. While Dillan drove, Lynette read aloud from it, and they had a ball trying to pronounce all sorts of words. It was while reading the words beginning with the letter S, that one Potawatomi word shrouded itself in intimacy.

"What is the word for snake?" Dillan asked.

"Well, to name a few, you have, snake blow - *bébamodét,* snake green - *eskbegzet,* plain old snake - *genebek,* snake bull head – *shashagwése."*

"Shashagwése," said Dillan. His face formed a smokey smile. And that's when Dillan named his penis.

Lynette's daydream of Kansas ended there. She looked at the piles of folded shirts, shorts, jeans, underclothes, towels, dresses, skirts, jumpsuits, and linens still covering the bed. Negligees, panty hose, lace blouses, other provocative bartender garb and Marie's nurse uniforms were hanging dry from every knob in the two bedrooms upstairs. The shower rod served as another drip-dry location. A blanket that hadn't dried all the way draped the door. She wondered why she had waited so long to go to the laundromat. Adhering to a strict organizational laundry code: whites, darks, colors, delicates, uniforms, towels, and linens, Lynette and Marie had divided their dirty laundry, taking up ten washing machines that morning. She couldn't recall ever having had so much fun at the Alumni Village laundromat. Marie sure took the monotony out of chores.

A startling screech seized Lynette's attention to the scene outside her bedroom window. A car was swerving from the parking lot. It drove over the sidewalk, then down the grassy hill. Lynette's eyes gaping, she stood anticipating the crash into her apartment. She darted to the top of the stairs, just in time to watch. The loud bang shook the building. The sound of breaking glass, falling bricks, and scraping objects was the front end of the car driving smack through the sliding glass doors, plowing through the green vinyl sofa, which hit the green vinyl chair, which broke the leg on the piano, which ran into the fish tank, that flooded the kitchen. When the car stopped, Lynette realizing the stairs were undamaged, she climbed down and opened the front door looking on at the vehicle with its rear end sticking out of the living room. The driver climbed out of the car. She wore a hijab.

"Are you alright?" asked Lynette. She could see from the woman's eyes, she was frightened, but obviously standing and walking, and there was no blood. She did not speak to Lynette. Another woman climbed out of the passenger seat unhurt. Lynette called the police, then called Dillan. The Alumni Village maintenance crew came to the rescue. Dillan helped with the disaster clean up. The maintenance staff boarded up the hole and Dillan couldn't resist spray painting the plywood with the words, *No U Turn*. When Marie came home, she called the Tallahassee Democrat, hoping to get herself in the newspaper. She was terribly disappointed when the story was printed without anyone's name in it due to the University privacy policy.

Those poor women, thought Lynette. It had turned out that a mom was trying to teach her daughter to drive. Ironically, it was Vahid, who came to pick up the woman and her daughter from the scene. He did not speak to Lynette. She figured it was his fear of witchcraft, which caused her to feel that Karma was a bitch. And surprisingly, Dillan was not too upset about his piano. The damage was nominal as was the cost for repair. A good tuning and some carpentry by a local piano repair technician, and she would be as good as new. The fish may have died, but Lynette did not. She was grateful she had not been killed that day. For if she hadn't decided to do laundry that morning, she most certainly at that time of the afternoon, would have been sitting on the green vinyl sofa with its back against the sliding glass door watching the soap opera, and eating a grilled cheese sandwich. It was the clutching to routine that kept Lynette together, and on time. Today, however, she was lucky to be late for work at the airport lounge.

* * *

At the beginning of October, fumes of burnt sulfur filled their noses, their lungs, and clung to the drapes. In the kitchen, Lynette stood watching over Raquel and Henrique teetering on their perches inside the cage. They were gasping for air. Both the front and back doors to the apartment were open wide, smoke bellowing out. Dillan burst through the front door. Cradling an oxygen tank under his arm, he held a hose and a plastic garment bag in his hand. He went to work right away building a makeshift oxygen tent over the bird cage. Lynette prayed over the little birds' clinging to life.

"Come on you guys, just breath," said Dillan. "Well, hopefully this will help. I got the tanks from the airport."

"Thank you," said Lynette, now pacing the floor. "Oh my God, I fucken suck, I can't believe I did this again."

"I guess these are the eggs you left boiling on the stove," said Dillan. He lifted a charred pot and set it outside.

"I totally forgot to shut off the stove before I left to class. Do you think they'll make it?"

"I don't know." Dillan bent his face close to the cage peering through the plastic. "Henrique looks a little better, I think."

"Marie told me that he survived tumbling in the dryer once." Lynette scratched the back of her neck. "You know he was with her when her first husband beat her unconscious. She still believes that bird's the reason she survived."

"Well, he must be pretty strong, then."

"You know, he's ten years old. She's had him since her Cincé."

"Ten, huh."

Raquel dropped to the cage floor.

"Oh God," said Lynette.

Dillan lifted the plastic. He opened the cage door. He and Lynette looked down at the little yellow parakeet lying lifelessly.

"Is she still breathing?"

"I don't know." Dillan lifted her limp yellow body and laid her on a paper towel. He examined her closely.

"God bless you, Raquel, I'm so sorry. God forgive me," said Lynette. When Dillan solemnly pronounced her dead, Lynette covered her in paper towel. "Marie is going to hate me."

They watched and waited while Henrique continued his fight for life. With nothing more they could do to help him, Dillan wiped down the stove with a soapy sponge. In a kitchen chair Lynette sat, her head in her hands. She was wreaking with guilt. The sound of Marie's voice drove Lynette to look up. Marie's face grew more intense with horror, the nearer she got to the parakeet cage.

"Marie, I'm sorry," said Lynette. "I left eggs boiling on the stove."

"I brought the oxygen to help them breathe," said Dillan.

Marie was silent. She lifted the plastic and looked closely at Henrique, teetering and gasping.

"The smoke asphyxiated Raquel," said Lynette. "She didn't make it."

Marie's eyes stayed fixed on Henrique. She reached into the cage and lifted Henrique's fragile body to her face. "Can you give me that hose?"

"You want to blow the oxygen direct to his face?" asked Dillan.

Marie nodded, and Dillan passed her the end of the hose, which she held over Henrique's beak as he sat in the nest of her hand. They sat like that for a long while. Dillan and Lynette looking on, until

Henrique's head sunk lifeless. Marie put her mouth over his tiny beak, she blew tiny puffs of air into him and rubbed his tiny back. This went on for a good ten minutes.

"I think he's gone," said Dillan.

"Here." Lynette handed her a paper towel. "I wrapped Raquel already, and I'm gonna bury her." Lynette held a spoon in her hand and stepped outside to dig a grave.

Marie wrapped Henrique, leaving his head peeking out from the towel. When Lynette stood over the table reaching for Raquel's remains, Marie's glossy eyes bored a hole through Lynette. Then without word, Marie turned away, and took Henrique's remains upstairs.

"If only, the cage hadn't been so close to the stove," said Dillan. "The eggs exploded, you can see bits of shell and egg all over the place. And with the cage being so close, there was little chance they could survive the smoke inhalation." Dillan stood at the sink rinsing off a sponge.

"Yeah, if only," said Lynette. She was just outside the doorway, squatting over her grave site, when Dillan could see her praying and tossing the dirt over Raquel.

In silence, Lynette joined Dillan in the clean-up, before they both headed to the airport for work.

Something had snapped inside Marie that day. For two and a half weeks, she carried the dead bird around in a paper towel. The apartment was silent. No laughter, no all-night popcorn popping and coffee expresso study sessions. No acceptance of death. There was just a dark brokenness. And strain and intentional avoidance. On the rare occasion, Lynette did look at Marie, it was as if a dead person was staring back at her.

Lynette couldn't take the silence anymore. The week before Halloween in the morning, she cut orange construction paper to make a homemade card. She sketched a silhouette of a witch in front of a moon, and on the card in black marker, she wrote, *From one witch to another, Happy Halloween, please forgive this witch.* Then while Marie lay asleep on her futon, Lynette entered Marie's bedroom and quietly set the card along with candy corn, next to the dead bird in the paper towel.

Lynette returned to her room, where she waited patiently for Marie to wake up. And when she heard her stirring, a few minutes later, the silence broke.

"Girlfriend," called out Marie. Her voice silvery.

Lynette responded by craning her neck around the doorway to Marie's room.

"Can I come in?"

"Yes," said Marie.

Lynette sat down on the floor and looked at the morbid bird in paper and then turned to Marie. "I'm so sorry I killed your bird. I was a careless jerk."

"I loved him and I told him every day." Marie rolled over on her side and faced the morbid bird in paper. "And besides you, he's the only one who loved me unconditionally. We grew up together. I remember the day I got him, the first time he nibbled my ear lobe, when he first learned to say Hola. He was always there at night when I couldn't sleep and I was fighting demons." Marie turned to face Lynette. "And you know how I have trouble sleeping. He comforted me during both my marriages and divorces. He saved my life."

"And you gave him a good life. He knew you loved him," said Lynette. "I wish I could sprinkle fairy dust on him to make him come to life again," said Lynette.

"Me too." Forgiveness welling up, friendship replacing the hurt and the blame, from a deep self-isolation sealed with rings of trauma, like the rings in a tree trunk when it's cut open, Marie emerged, and her eyes were alive again. She sat up on the futon. "I know you didn't mean to kill him, but he's gone. I think if he took all my past hell with him, then maybe he freed me from it."

"Come with me," said Lynette. "Get your Bible."

Marie reached for Henrique in his paper towel wrap. She stood up and allowed Lynette to lead them downstairs. On the kitchen table, was a handkerchief in a small cardboard box, and a cup full of freshly picked dandelions, rosary beads, and a spoon. "Let me help you say goodbye," said Lynette, "It's time Henrique be laid to rest." Marie put the bird on the handkerchief in the box and covered him. Then she carried the box out to the stoop, where Lynette was digging. The stone that marked the grave of Raquel was nearby.

"Ok, you ready?" asked Lynette.

Marie laid the coffin in the hole. Lynette gathered the flowers and the rosary beads.

"Read something nice," said Lynette. Together they knelt over the bird cemetery. Marie held the Bible, flipping pages. Lynette clutched the rosary and began an Our Father prayer. Marie joined, and when they had finished with, "Forever and ever, Amen," Marie read from the Book of John: Chapter Eleven, Verse six. "'Jesus said, I am the resurrection, and the life. He that believeth in me, though he were dead, yet shall he live. And whosoever liveth and believeth in me shall never die. Believest thou this.'"

And then Lynette tossed the dirt over Henrique and Marie marked it with dandelions and a stone.

Chapter 13

The telephone rang. Marie, lying on her futon, rolled over and lifted the receiver to her ear. "Hello," she said, her eyes still closed.

"G'day, is Lynette at home?" said the voice on the other end.

"Who's this?" asked Marie.

"This is Travis, I'm calling from Sydney, Australia for Lynette Autry."

Lynette could hear the murmur of Marie's voice outside her bedroom. *Who the hell is calling at this hour?* Lynette lifted her head and her eye lids lifted in a squint to see the clock radio show ten past three in the morning. The hall light went on and cast light near the foot of Lynette's bed. Marie craned her neck into the room. "It's for you. Some guy named Travis."

"What. Holy shit," said Lynette. She tossed off her covers and now sat up in bed. "Tell him to hold on a minute."

"Ok," said Marie, turning back to her room. Lynette slid into her furry purple house coat with the Garfield pin and staggered downstairs to take the call.

"Hello, Travis, it's Lynette." She remembered the phone line upstairs was still open. "Marie you can hang up now."

"Lynette, how are you?"

"Just working and going to school." Lynette twirled the phone cord between her fingers. "This is my last semester before my internship starts in January. And I've got a big test tomorrow."

"My root, it's been such a long time since I've heard your voice." He spoke arousing in Lynette a sense of nostalgia. Lynette sighed. *Did he have to use the old pet name?* "I think about you a lot. I telephoned your mum. She said you were at FSU and that it would be ok to call. I started my own export business. I'm hoping to come to the states soon with the company. Maybe Christmas time."

Lynette looked at Dillan's piano, and she already felt like she was cheating on him. "Travis, listen, it's really late here as you know. But what really gets me, is that I would have never called your house at three in the morning Sydney time. It's just disrespectful. I've got a lot going on, I gotta go, Bye." Lynette hung the receiver on the wall mount in the kitchen. Then she paced the floor. "I think I need a cigarette." She reached for a pack laying on the end table. Then she saw Marie coming down the stairs.

"So, who's Travis?"

"My old boyfriend. We lived together for about eighteen months when I lived in Colorado. His family thought I wasn't good enough for him." Lynette realized she finally got past that not feeling good enough, thanks to Dillan. She was striking a match now.

"Who does he think he is anyway, calling this time a night," said Marie.

"I literally have built a new life for myself, I'm in my last semester at FSU. After my internship, I'll be graduating." Lynette rambled on. "New boyfriend, new friends and a new life. Travis thinks he can call out of the blue and just pick up again. What does he think, my life stopped when we broke up?"

Lynette was exploding, she knew by hanging up before Travis had a chance to say goodbye, this would probably be the last time she would hear from him. She wasn't the person he remembered. She sucked on the cigarette and continued pacing and ranting. Smoke rose around her head. "Damn right, it's disrespectful to call someone at three in the morning, even if there is a time difference. Like I told him. I would have never done that to him and his damn blue blood family full of Aussie convicts." She was blowing smoke from her mouth. "What a fucken bastard, calling and waking me up. I got that Classroom Management test today too. May as well stay up now and read. I won't be able to sleep. He's got me all worked up."

"If he was here," said Marie. "I'd do to him, what I did to my first husband."

"What's that?"

"Wait till he's passed out drunk and high and stick chewing gum in his hairy ass."

"No fucken way, you didn't."

Marie was laughing from the belly.

"Oh, I did. And when he woke up, he was hollering, 'Ma-a-arie-ee, my ass, Marie, Marie, help, my ass is stuck.'"

"Oh my God, that's fucken hysterical." Lynette was laughing from the belly now too.

"I'll put on some expresso," said Marie. "I can get some studying done with you."

"And for God sakes," said Lynette. "Will you put some clothes on." Lynette's eyes narrowed. "He used to sit there with this giant pint glass of milk. He'd put that Quick chocolate milk powder in it. I can still hear that spoon tapping the glass. He'd go through a gallon of milk every two days."

"Why'd you guys break up?" Marie stood wrapping herself in a blanket.

"He went home to Australia. he wanted to marry me, but his folks wouldn't let him. They wouldn't even let him work. They're wealthy, the country club sort. Shit, before I met him, he was dealing cocaine in San Francisco. His parents didn't even know him. Anyway, where was I?" Lynette sucked hard on her cigarette and spoke with smoke trailing from her mouth. "Oh, yah, the marriage planning. He snuck around at night and worked as a busboy. He mailed me a little gold ring." Lynette was waving the cigarette around. "I completed all the paperwork to sponsor him on a fiancée Visa to bring him to the states. We were gonna get married, but I just couldn't go through with it." She flicked a chunk of ash into the ashtray. "I thought, shit, what kind of shit would that be, where we started off with his family disowning him because he was with me. He would lose all his family money. They told him they would cut him off. And Travis, how was he supposed to live without money? He had said he wanted to work construction or something when he got here. Hah, he barely knew the difference between a flat head and Phillip screwdriver." Lynette stopped pacing and stood with a hand on her hip. "One time he decided he was going to fix the car, I say, Travis, you don't know how to fix the car, so he get's stoned, I come home from work, and he's got the whole car apart. And guess what, he couldn't get it back together."

"He really got to you," said Marie, "Didn't he?"

"Well, like Shakespeare said, "Better to have loved and lost than to have never loved at all."

"The expresso's ready." Marie was now pouring it into two glass coffee mugs.

"Oh good, I can feel it in my beaver," Lynette was laughing nervously now and snubbing out the cigarette. She watched as Marie took her cup to the chair on the opposite side of the room and sat down with her anatomy and physiology book and a highlighter.

Lynette stood in the kitchen adding cream and sugar to her expresso. The apartment was quiet. "Do you think I was too mean to him?" asked Lynette. She stood looking at Marie, who was now twirling her hair around her fingers.

"No." Marie returned her attention to her book. "You can call him and apologize if you want."

"No way." said Lynette lifting her coffee to her lips. She settled in her chair with its back against the stairs.

"Ok, then, forget about him."

Lynette sighed and picked up her binder and began studying her notes. For a long while, the room was quiet except for the turning of pages and sliding of highlighters. Lynette rubbed her temple with her finger.

"Stop picking your face," said Marie.

"Why? It helps me concentrate." Lynette stood up to stretch. "You got any more of that Guarana? I think I'll take one."

"It's on the kitchen table."

Lynette held a Guarana capsule in her hand. She popped it into her mouth. Then she swallowed it with a swig of cold expresso. She stepped to the window, opened the curtain to look out at the lawn. "Shit the sun's coming up, I better get rolling. Marie, I'm gonna have some oatmeal, you want some?"

"No, I'm on my whole grain diet." Marie stepped into the kitchen to see Lynette putting a half a pack of instant Quaker oats apple cinnamon back into the box. "Are you anorexic?"

"No," said Lynette. "Why?"

"You're only eating half a pack of that oatmeal."

"For your information I have one and half packs in my bowl, not only a half pack." Lynette stood at the sink filling the teapot with water. "You just mind your own business in the cabinets. I hope I don't have to start labeling my food," said Lynette. "Besides, what's up with all the ex-lax in the bathroom, are you constipated or bulimic?"

Marie changed the subject. "Do you think Dillan could look at my car. It's making a funny noise."

"I'll ask him. Hey, have you seen my multi-colored pen?"

"It's on your desk." Marie was now spooning left over grains into a bowl.

"I like it on the end table next to my chair, for when I study my notes. Will you stop cleaning my stuff. You organize shit and then I can't find it."

"Well, I'm just trying to help since you work so many hours."

"Well, I guess I'm just an ungrateful Honky Bitch," said Lynette, teasing.

"Damn Gringa," said Marie. "You know, sometimes it feels like I'll never graduate."

"You just have to stay the course," said Lynette. She opened the back door and stood, now, looking out at the trees and green grass. "Slow but sure. You know, the turtle won the race, not the rabbit."

"I'm worried about money," said Marie. "I'm not making enough cleaning houses."

"Just keep selling that Mary Kay," Lynette sat on the stoop looking at the bird cemetery. "You make your own hours, besides, you like the whole make-up thing."

"Oh, my hole my soul, I haven't sold any for two weeks."

"Make some flyers," said Lynette. The tea kettle whistled. "Time for my oatmeal, and then a shower. Man, are my bones aching."

"Oooooh Lord," said Marie. Lynette shut the door and shut off the stove.

* * *

It was Halloween night of 1987 when Lynette sat next to Marie, Dillan, and Paul in the bleachers midway up from the thirty-yard line at Doak Campbell stadium. The four of them joined in Seminole fanfare. The aroma of concession popcorn, hot dogs, sausage and fried chicken flavored the air. The baton twirling drum major in feathered headdress high stepped out ahead of the colony of Marching Chiefs, who took over the field. Gold colored flags rose, fell, and swirled. Musicians owned their spots in formation. Brass, woodwinds, drums, and voices lifted in song that filled the stadium with the Alma mater. The opponents in green from Tulane rushed onto the field taking their place on the visitor side lines. The marching band configured an aisle, through which the Seminole football team stampeded the field. The Fight song and War chant roared from the crowd and reached the city beyond the stadium. In a parted sea of garnet and gold, the white speckled Appaloosa horse with his rider, raising his flaming spear, charged the arena. Spectators raised their arms in the tomahawk chop. Renegade, the horse, reared, and Chief Osceola staked his flaming spear mid field, claiming Coach Bobby Bowden's turf.

When the national anthem played, Dillan stood like a Marine. He held his hat in his left hand. His right hand, he placed over his heart. Marie yelled, war wooped, and hooted through the whole game. And when Paul wasn't quiet, and eating, he was laughing. Lynette was glad that she finally made it to a game. And when it ended, the foursome sat watching all the people filing down the bleachers.

"Look at all these cups," said Dillan. He picked up one, turning it over in his hand. He studied the graphic of Chief Osceola on horseback on the sturdy thick plastic. Then he picked up another and didn't stop collecting them until he had a stack of twenty. Paul picked up a few. Lynette joined in for a collection that capped at ten. Most spectators had left the stadium. Marie sat and held a program book in her hand. She was looking over the team roster, and photos.

"This guy, number two." Marie put her finger on his picture. She spoke in a hoarse voice. "Deion Sanders, he was a machine out there."

"The cornerback?" asked Paul. He dropped down next to her. "If you ask me the whole team was a machine."

"Seventy-three to fourteen by the second quarter," said Dillan. "Tulane didn't have much of a chance."

Paul looked up at Dillan. "You got enough cups?" "Hey, I'm gonna wash these and use 'em. They'll make good party cups. And I can use some at the shop." Dillan sat down looking out at the stadium growing quiet. "Man, that was some halftime show."

"That was my favorite part of the game," said Lynette. She sat next to Dillan, thigh to thigh. "I was surprised it was Homecoming."

"Lynette and I were in marching band in high school," said Dillan. I played the tuba and you played trumpet, right?" Lynette nodded. "Did you hear the announcer say that half time music was written specifically for marching band?"

"What'd he call it?"

"The Boda Band Ballet," said Lynette. "I think."

"He said it was performed the first time in 1963." said Dillan. "It's probably in that program book, Marie's got."

Marie flipped through the pages. "Here it is." Marie read aloud. "Formation written by Robert Braunagel and music by John Boda, Professor of Composition in FSU school of Music. Dr John Boda, the leading composer of the twentieth century is now celebrating his fortieth year at FSU."

Lynette looked down at her gray sweatshirt with the Seminole head on the front. "Thanks for the souvenir, Marie."

"De Nada," said Marie. "That's your graduation gift."

"And thanks for motivating my ass to come to the game."

Marie lifted her hand in the Tomahawk chop. She chanted in a scratchy voice, "Awoooooh oh oh oh o o o o o o. One more time. 'You got to fight, fight, fight, for FSU! You got to scalp 'em Seminoles! You got to win, win, win, win, win this game, and roll on down and make those goals! For FSU is on the warpath now, And at the battle's end she's great! So fight, fight, fight, fight to victory! Our Seminoles from Florida State! F-L-O-R-I-D-A S-T-A-T-E, Florida State, Florida State, Florida State!'"

* * *

The day Lynette moved out of Alumni village was bittersweet. The Spanish mosh blew in a gentle wind on the limbs of the trees. Warren ran over to the truck to say goodbye. Dillan loaded the last of her boxes into his truck and her Toyota. Lynette was thrilled to be moving on.

Marie had already rented another one-bedroom apartment on the complex and was sitting alone in the dark, curtains drawn surrounded by boxes. She was full of grief, mourning losses, and bad decisions. Her friend was leaving, and she never expected that it would hit so hard. Then she heard a knock at the door.

"Do you have a dog in there?" said the familiar voice.

Marie smiled. Some weight lifted from her heavy heart. She slid the chain lock, unlatched the deadbolt, and opened the door. There stood Lynette with a bag and two cups of coffee from Hardee's.

"I stopped by to say goodbye. Dillan is going to gas up his truck and then I'll be headed for my mom's place. I can't stay long."

The two friends hugged. "Like the Bon Jovi song says, 'Never Say Goodbye.'" Marie's eyes swam with tears.

"Come on," said Lynette. "Let's have a little something to eat. Look, I got the new California Raisin Figurine." From the bag, she pulled a squinty faced purple trumpet player with blue sneakers and passed it to Marie, who smiled and turned it over in her hand. Lynette moved to the window to open the drapes. The sun lit up the room. Marie brought the drinks and the food to the table.

"I'm so grateful you're here," said Marie.

"You going home to your folks for Christmas?" asked Lynette.

"No, just New Years, I got a couple of shifts at the hospital."

"I'll miss you," said Marie.

"You too." Lynette bit into a raisin cinnamon biscuit.

"How am I gonna stay in this sour city without you?"

"I won't be far away. I got the internship in Panama City that I wanted, and when the high school's on spring break, I'll visit," said Lynette. She paused and wiped her face with a napkin. "Thanks for giving me memories of college outside the classrooms, books, and professors. Hey, we sure had fun last week decorating that Christmas tree at the picnic table." Lynette laughed and Marie joined.

"We did, didn't we," said Marie. "Thank you for everything, all your help and prayers. Thank you for being my friend. Hey, you know what? I'm thinking about changing my major to Spanish."

"Well, that's something. I'll be praying for that too. And that you have the strength and courage to finish strong. I'm almost there, myself. I just need to get through this internship and a little red tape."

"How can you be so confident?"

"Well, going to school and earning a degree is like picking ice on a glacier. Every day, I get up, grab my pick and hack at the ice. And one day, I know I'll look down and there won't be any picking left, and the glacier will be gone." Lynette tossed her food wrapper and empty cup in the empty bag. "I don't think about the end, just the picking."

"Oh." Marie held her coffee cup with both hands.

The sound of a horn was honking outside. "That must be Dillan, I gotta go." Lynette stood up, then met Marie in a hug.

"I'll see you later, Einstein."

"Nos vemos luego, Shakespeare."

* * *

Lynette and her supervising teacher hit it off at Hello. So much so, that Lynette was invited to live with her, her family, her ferrets, and dogs, Monday through Friday for the length of the internship. Lynette's new IBM convertible pc made writing her thirty-page internship report fast and easy. No more white-out, no more ribbons. In the classroom, Lynette's poise and presence proved to be above average. "You move and speak just like an English teacher. How did you get there so fast?" said the evaluating professor from FSU.

"I don't know," said Lynette. She was wearing loafers, a high neck blouse, and a suit jacket. Her hair was done up in a bun at the nape of her neck. She had sworn off the barmaid provocative look. "I'm just happy to be doing it," said Lynette.

Wearing his suit jacket, Dillan visited one Friday after school. His slightly Asian face got a reaction from a co-worker, "That's your boyfriend," she had said in a disparaging tone when Lynette returned after the weekend. Bigotry was written all over her forehead. Lynette never ceased to be taken aback with the southern hostility pertaining to race. Despite all the things she wanted to say during this encounter, she responded with a simple yes. Then watched the hairy eyebrow go up.

A week before graduation, Lynette got a craving of the paternal kind. She sent a letter to her father announcing her commencement ceremony. He responded by phone and agreed to rent a beach house at Alligator Point, where Lynette and he stayed together for a week. It was the first time she had woken up in the same house with him since she was six months old. When it came time to visit campus, pick up and sit for her graduation portrait, Lynette invited him to sit in with her. Not only did Lynette get to be under the same roof with her father for a week, for two days she got to be under it with her mother and him together. Lynette felt like the whole reunion was like a Phil Donahue episode.

They cooked steak and potatoes and green beans for dinner. They enjoyed a walk on the beach. At night, while Lynette and her mom lie in bed, Father knocked on the door, and when they called him to come in, they never expected to see him dance into the room wearing a towel around his waist and a towel around his head full of fruit. When he sang, *We Going Bananas* in a Caribbean accent and said, *Welcome to Aruba*, while attempting to Tumba, Lynette and her mom buckled over in sidesplitting laughter. And the three of them continued laughing for what seemed a very long time.

The merriment of the night gave way to the somberness of graduation day. At the Donald L. Tucker Civic Center, Lynette drifted in a sea of black caps and gowns and blue tassels with the School of Education, class of 1988. From her seat on the floor, she could see Dillan, and her mother and father waving down at her from the crowd. She returned the wave. Her smiling face beamed with pride. She looked to her left and to her right and thought it was odd that most of the people in her school were strangers to her. She was pleased when the long speeches came to an end and it was time for her college processional toward the stage. She heard The Pomp and Circumstance song playing behind the sound of her name being called. *I did it*, she thought to herself as she stepped across the stage to reach for her Bachelor of Science Degree. Her Classroom Management professor, who resembled her Father in appearance, mannerism, and Boston accent, shook her hand. "Do Well, Ms. Autry," he said. After throwing her cap in the air, and catching another, Lynette gathered in the line that trailed out into the sunny day, where Dillan waited in suit and maroon tie, with his thirty-five-millimeter Nikon preparing for a photo shoot.

Back at the beach house, Lynette gathered with her parents, Dillan, and friends from the airport for some celebrating. When all that was left were her parents and Dillan, the Chivas Regal turned things awry. Her father sobbed uncontrollably while hollering words of regret and contrition about his failures as a father and husband so many years before, to which Mother offered comfort and forgiveness.

Dillan and Lynette took to the sanctuary of the beach, wading far out on sandbars, where they collected sand dollars, under yellow beaked gulls flapping their wings. "Tomorrow," said Dillan. "After you bring your father to the airport, I would like to take you to Charles' and Mee-Yon's restaurant for dinner."

* * *

The awning outside the restaurant was green. Inside, there were chairs of red, and walls of green filled with symbols of Korean Longevity. One wall had a mural painting of pine trees with a bright yellow sun. Another, was rocks of black and white on a mountain in a back drop of blue sky and blue waters filled with turtles. Pujok hung above the front entrance. Mee-Yon greeted them and sat them at a table in the front by a window. There was a small vase of flowers next to the Guk-Gan-Jang on center of table. Mee-Yon brought them a bottle of wine.

"So glad you finally came to my restaurant. In my country, in Korea, we celebrate birthdays with miyeok guk and rice cakes. It's tradition."

"What's in it?" asked Lynette.

"Sea vegetable."

"Looks like seaweed"

"Yes, sea vegetables. Enjoy."

"As birthday food, Korean seaweed soup honors the birthday person's mother and the sacrifices she made. Koreans eat traditional soup to appreciate how their mothers had to recover and provide nutrients to their babies."

A man approached the table from behind Mee-Yon. "Happy Birthday, Dillan."

"Charles, sorry about the bankruptcy."

"Well, that's business for you. One minute you're flying on top and the next your belly up on bottom. Glory is short lived."

"Yeah, guess so."

"How long before Aero Associates closes up shop?"

"Not sure. Waiting for the attorneys to get back to me. Don't worry about that now. You still have a job until further notice. Besides the way things are going for you, you may have to re-locate and look for work elsewhere." Charles looked at Lynette and back at Dillan.

"Lynette's graduated from FSU last week."

"There, you see, life outside of the Tallahassee Regional Airport."

"So how was your trip last month?" asked Charles.

"We went to Des Moines, Iowa for my High School Reunion, Lynette got an award for being the most partying non-class member."

"I think it was that Bette Midler imitation I did on the DJ's mic," said Lynette. She looked at the gold chain around Dillan's neck. "Do you like it?"

"How's it look?" Dillan fondled the chain between his thumb and forefinger.

"Lynette surprised me with the chain inside a cake for my birthday." Dillan was leaning toward Mee-Yon, who was bending down for a closer look.

"Very nice," said Mee-Yon. Her face turned toward the door, where new customers were coming into the restaurant. "I be back with traditional, rice cakes. On the house."

It was a time of smiles and change. A time when Lynette was glad to say that this was her life. A time when instead of working full time and attending school full time at the same time, there would be just one job focus for Lynette, only on teaching. No more spreading herself so thin, that she couldn't keep up with everything. No more constant state of exhaustion. Things were moving forward just as planned. She was the first generation in her family to earn her Bachelor's degree.

* * *

A few weeks later, after another dinner, Lynette and Dillan were walking under the night sky. The planet Saturn shined significantly. All the clusters of stars effervesced. The constellations of Ursa Minor, Boötes, Libra and Lupus shimmered. The moon was a waning crescent. Soft cadence of calm waves from the Gulf of Mexico were rolling to shore. The white sand glowed beneath their bare feet. Laughter was coming from people nearby. Fireworks lit up the beach. Dillan stopped walking. He bent down and appeared to be picking up something.

"Look what I found?" His voice sounded as if it was a treasure.

"What?" Lynette turned her attention from a bottle rocket that had just fizzled out. Dillan was holding the palms of his hands cupping one over the other, cradling something inside. "What is it, a crab?" She looked closely to see what he was holding. Dillan waited while Lynette pinched the shiny object from his palms. Then he spoke thick with ease and devotion.

"So, you wanna get hitched?"

Lynette's response was to slide her finger into the diamond ring.

"Yes," she said, "I wanna get hitched." Her expression was a guarantee. Another round of fireworks set off and lit up the beach. Dillan and Lynette stood in a warm embrace.

"Hey Teacher, you ready to show your folks that ring?"

"Sure am."

Sealing the deal with a kiss, they walked hand in hand to the truck.

"Hey, you remember that old TV show, *Love American Style?*"

"Yah, I do."

"This feels like that."

AFTERWORD

And so is my tale of being an older than average undergraduate at Florida State University and a bartender at Tallahassee Regional Airport pre-September 11, pre-COVID-19 and pre-Individual Disability Education Act. It is my hope that if you are reading this page, you finished this book. And in doing so, you have gained an appreciation of the verdant nature of Florida's panhandle and the City of Tallahassee and its establishments, many of which have been shut down and demolished. And that you will realize underneath every political era lies an undertow of hidden agendas put into motion. That you will consider that Catholic priests need a term limit on celibacy. That college fraternity and sorority members should not mistake bonds established in sick secret humiliating initiation rituals centered around drugs and sex, and recordings of the same, for real friendship. That all living creatures need love and respect. That first-generation college women are complex. Trauma makes you weird inside. White privilege exists. Things aren't always as they seem. And that if you can't be good, you should be careful.

* * *

After writing this book, I am compelled to mention Massachusetts' Senator John Kerry's Iran Contra Cocaine and

Weapon smuggling Investigations of 1986, and Investigative Journalists, Robert Parry's and Brian Barger's Associated Press Release - *Nicaragua Drugs* on December 20, 1985. And the irony of it all during a time when the *War on Drugs* was a major political issue. Although shunned by the Reagan administration, Senator Kerry was vindicated after the release of his April 13, 1989 report on the Iran Cocaine and Weapon Smuggling matter. According to Robert Parry in an article on Salon.com Oct 25, 2004, Kerry's 1989 report "discovered that drug traffickers gave the Contras "'cash, weapons, planes, pilots, air supply services and other materials. Moreover, the U.S. State Department had paid some drug traffickers as part of a program to fly non-lethal assistance to the Contras.'" My experiences in Florida's capital city lend lightweight to the findings and information in the aforementioned, but weight nonetheless. Afterall, the matter was in the periphery of my experiences.

On another matter, I feel the need to declare that the seafood slave trade is real. According to the Center for American Progress in the report, *Seafood Slavery: Human Trafficking in the International Fishing Industry by* Trevor Sutton and Avery Siciliano, December 15, 2016, "The International Labor Organization estimates there are currently more than 20 million individuals being subjected to human trafficking and that forced labor generates $150 billion in illegal profits each year." Sutton and Siciliano go on further to say that "Reports in *The New York Times*, the Associated Press, and *The Guardian*, as well as publications by the Environmental Justice

Foundation and other nongovernmental organizations, provided accounts of migrants sold into slavery by unscrupulous labor brokers and human traffickers and forced to work in abysmal conditions without pay or under crushing debt loads. Many victims - some as young as 15 years old - described routine beatings and physical confinement with chains and manacles; others told stories of brutal maiming and even execution inflicted as punishment for attempted mutiny or escape."

According to FishWise (fishwise.org), a nonprofit marine conservation organization based in Santa Cruz, California, in a report, *Social responsibility in the Global Seafood Industry Background and Resources,* April 2018,

> "A six month Associated Press investigation into Hawaii's fishing fleet uncovered unfair labor practices and instances of human trafficking due to a legal loophole excluding certain fishing vessels from federal law. (Mendoza and Mason 2016) The recruiting processes and working conditions of some fishers and seafood industry employees are so egregious that these human and labor rights abuses have been referred to as modern slavery. Case studies from the last decade cite examples of fraudulent and deceptive recruiting, 18-20 hour workdays, homicide, sexual abuse, child labor, physical and mental abuse, abandonment, refusal of promised pay, health and safety violations and the removal or withholding of identifying documents ie; passports."

I'd like you to recognize Associated Press investigative journalists: Martha Mendoza, Robin McDowell, Esther Htusan and Margie Mason. Their work helped to free 2000 slaves from the seafood industry in 2016. Also, in 2016, President Barrack Obama appointed 11 trafficking survivors to the first-ever U.S. Advisory Council on Human Trafficking. Under President Donald Trump, the Interagency Task Force to Monitor and Combat Trafficking in Persons consists of 15 departments and agencies, which work to prosecute traffickers, and protect survivors. According to White House Fact sheet on October 11, 2018, the Department of Homeland Security initiated over 800 human trafficking cases, resulting in 1500 arrests, 530 convictions, and over 500 victims identified.

Furthermore, the Global Aquaculture Alliance, an international nonprofit association has developed standards for Best Aquaculture Practices certification, now being used to assure consumers that a seafood product is legal and sustainably harvested. And according to FishWise, Whole Foods and Wegmans use computer software that helps them source sustainably and legally caught seafood products. What can you do to help the cause?

To learn more about human trafficking, modern slave labor, and what can be done to fight against it, see below:

Associated Press Book, (2016) "Fishermen Slaves: Human trafficking and the seafood we eat."
https://www.ap.org/explore/seafood-from-slaves/index.html#main-section
https://www.ap.org/books/fishermen-slaves/index.html

FishWise (April 2018) Social Responsibility in the Global Seafood Industry Background and Resources Report
Available at: **https://fishwise.org/wp-content/uploads/2018/03/2018_Social-Responsibility-White-Paper_Final.pdf**

Mendoza, M., Mason, M. (2016) "Hawaiian seafood caught by foreign crews confined on boats" The Associated Press. Available at: **https://www.ap.org/explore/seafood-from-slaves/hawaiian-seafood-caught-foreign-crews-confined-boats.html**

Mason, M., McDowell, R., Mendoza, M., Htusan, E. (2015) "Global Supermarkets selling shrimp peeled by slaves." The Associated Press. Available at: **https://www.ap.org/explore/seafood-from-slaves/global-supermarkets-selling-shrimp-peeled-by-slaves.html**

United States Department of State OFFICE TO MONITOR AND COMBAT TRAFFICKING IN PERSONS (June 2016) Trafficking In Persons Report. Available at: **https://2009-2017.state.gov/documents/organization/258876.pdf**

The White House (October 2018) Fact Sheet – "President Donald J. Trump is Taking Action to End Human Trafficking" Available at: **https://www.whitehouse.gov/briefings-statements/president-donald-j-trump-taking-action-end-human-trafficking/**

And to learn how you can help victims of human trafficking, contact the following organizations:

Amirah House
https://www.amirahinc.org/
Main Office:
10 Tower Office Park, Suite 413, Woburn, MA 01801
info@amirahinc.org | 1-781-462-1758

Environmental Justice Foundation
https://act.ejfoundation.org/join-our-fight-oceans-and-human-rights
EJF, 1 Amwell Street
London, EC1R 1UL, UK
tel: +44 (0) 207 239 3310
info@ejfoundation.org

Freedom Network USA
https://freedomnetworkusa.org/
Email: info@freedomnetworkusa.org
Phone: (646) 504-9602
Mailing Address:
1300 L St NW, Suite 1020
Washington, DC 2005

Global Alliance Against Trafficking In Women GAATW
International Secretariat,
191/41, 6th Floor, Sivalai Condominium, Soi 33 Itsaraphap Road,
Bangkok-Yai,
Bangkok 10600, Thailand
Tel: +66 2 864 1427/8, Fax: +66 2 864 1637 gaatw@gaatw.org

STOP THE TRAFFIK
Registered in England & Wales No.6657145
Registered Charity No.1127321
Registered address:
1 Kennington Road, London, SE1 7QP, UK
Email: info@stopthetraffik.org Call: +44 (0) 207 921 4258

* * *

QUESTIONS OR COMMENTS?

Email the author at:

ofschoolandwomenauthor@gmail.com

CPSIA information can be obtained
at www.ICGtesting.com
Printed in the USA
BVHW082204280921
617680BV00001B/27